Networked David Lynch

Networked David Lynch

Critical Perspectives on Cinematic Transmediality

Edited by Marcel Hartwig, Andreas Rauscher and
Peter Niedermüller

EDINBURGH
University Press

Edinburgh University Press is one of the leading university presses in the UK. We publish academic books and journals in our selected subject areas across the humanities and social sciences, combining cutting-edge scholarship with high editorial and production values to produce academic works of lasting importance. For more information visit our website: edinburghuniversitypress.com

Edinburgh University Press Ltd
The Tun – Holyrood Road
12 (2f) Jackson's Entry
Edinburgh EH8 8PJ

Typeset in 11/13 Monotype Ehrhardt by
IDSUK (DataConnection) Ltd, and
printed and bound in Great Britain

A CIP record for this book is available from the British Library

ISBN 978 1 4744 9706 0 (hardback)
ISBN 978 1 4744 9708 4 (webready PDF)
ISBN 978 1 4744 9709 1 (epub)

Contents

Figures

Notes on Contributors

Chris Aarnes Bakkane is a freelance illustrator and academic with a BA and MA in film theory and criticism from the Norwegian University of Science and Technology, where he has also worked as an Assistant Lecturer in the field of film theory and film analysis. His MA thesis, *A Comparative Analysis of History On Screen: Depictions of The Battle of Stalingrad in Popular Culture* (2019) concerns how war is depicted on-screen and how it can shape the viewer's perception and cultural memory of warfare. He is the creator of the video essay 'In Dreams' (2017), which is an experimental approach to filmmaker David Lynch's dream-like narratives. He currently works as a video editor and producer for the Norwegian Labour and Welfare Administration.

Liz Greene is a Senior Visiting Research Fellow at the University of Reading. She is an editor of the journal *Music, Sound, and the Moving Image* and the co-edited book *The Palgrave Handbook of Sound Design and Music in Screen Media: Integrated Soundtracks* (2016). She publishes research in written and videographic forms. She is currently completing a feature-length social documentary film that stemmed from the research project *Brews and Brows: Shaping Stories from Eyebrows to Scousebrows* and is embarking on a new research project on *The Wizard of Oz* universe.

Marcel Hartwig is a lecturer in English and American Studies at the University of Siegen. At Chemnitz University of Technology, he completed his thesis on cultural representations of both September 11, 2001 and the attacks on Pearl Harbor as national traumata (published with transcript, 2011). He has contributed research papers to academic readers and international journals in the fields of media studies, television studies, literary criticism, gender studies and popular culture. Currently, he is finalising his post-doctoral project in the field of transatlantic studies, entitled *Transit Cultures: 18th Century Medical Discourses and Knowledge*

Media in the North American Colonies. He is also co-editor of *Media Economies: Perspectives on American Cultural Practices* (2014) and the *Rock Music Studies* special issue *American Rock Journalism* (2017).

Dan Hassler-Forest works as Assistant Professor of Media and Cultural Studies at Utrecht University. He has published books and articles on superhero movies, comics, transmedia storytelling, critical theory and *Twin Peaks*. He has recently completed two books on race and global media, focused on the creative work of performing artist Janelle Monáe.

Jannik Müller is a research assistant in media studies and media didactics at the University of Osnabrück, Germany. In his PhD thesis, he explores the hybridisation of photorealistic and cartoon aesthetics in contemporary computer-animated films. His other research focuses on the aesthetic and theory of visual effects in live-action films. His most recent article (2021) discusses the scientific accuracy of the black hole in *Interstellar* (2014). From 2018 to 2022, Jannik Müller worked in the department for media studies at the University of Siegen, Germany. He is a member of the DFG-funded research network *Animation and Contemporary Media Culture: Challenges and Potentials of Animation Studies in the Digital Era* (2020–23).

Peter Niedermüller is a researcher in musicology and digital humanities at the University of Mainz. He earned his PhD in 1999 with a dissertation on the madrigals by Carlo Gesualdo at the University of Würzburg. In 2011, he finished his habilitation on concert life in Vienna at the University of Mainz. Between 2011 and 2012 he was a visiting professor at the German Historical Institute in Rome. In 2019, he was appointed Professor in Mainz. His fields of research cover studies in musical interpretation (last publication *Klangkultur und musikalische Interpretation. Italienische Dirigenten im 20. Jahrhundert* [= *Analecta musicologica* 54], Kassel etc. 2018) and film music. He is a member of the Kiel Society for Film Music Research and a co-editor of the *Kieler Beiträge zur Filmmusikforschung*.

Mads Outzen is a PhD candidate in audiovisual media studies at the Norwegian University of Science and Technology (NTNU) and formerly a Fulbright Visiting Scholar at UC Berkeley. His doctoral dissertation is part of the interdisciplinary research project 'Face of Terror' and explores the ethical potential of facing terror with film, more specifically the potential for teaching and learning in audiovisually mediated encounters between survivors and spectators. Among other subjects of interest, his previous writing includes a thesis on structure and style in cinematic surrealism, as well as publications on the audiovisual essay and the facial close-up in documentary film. As well as his work as a researcher and a teacher, he also has considerable experience as both a film critic and film curator.

Andreas Rauscher (Dr. habil.) is a Visiting Professor for Media Culture Studies at the Albert-Ludwigs-Universität Freiburg im Breisgau. Formerly he held a position as Senior Lecturer at the department for media studies at the University of Siegen. He has also been a visiting professor of media studies at the Christian Albrechts-Universität Kiel and at the Johannes-Gutenberg-University Mainz. He is a journalist for several magazines on film and popular culture and a scientific curator for the German Film Museum in Frankfurt am Main (Exhibition *Film & Games: Interactions*. International catalogue available from Bertz Verlag, Berlin 2015). His research deals with film, game, comic and cultural studies, transmedia aesthetics and genre theory. Among his book publications as an author and co-editor are volumes on *The Simpsons*, superhero movies, comics and games, John Carpenter, *Star Wars*, the James Bond series and the Czechoslovakian Nová Vlna, as well as an introduction to game studies. In 2002, he received his PhD for a dissertation on the cultural and cinematic aspects of the *Star Trek* phenomenon and in 2011 he got his post-doctoral lecturing qualification (habilitation) from the Johannes-Gutenberg University Mainz for a study on *Ludic Fictions: Genre Concepts in Video Games* (2012).

Lioba Schlösser is a German film scholar. She currently lives in Leipzig and Berlin. Her PhD project focuses on androgynous characters in contemporary film. She works as lecturer and equal opportunities officer at XU Exponential University of Applied Sciences in Potsdam, Germany. Her research focuses on gender and queer studies, ritual and myth theory, as well as body theory. Moreover, she has published on body-political topics, genre theory and normativity discourses in film and streaming series. In addition to her academic work, she records film podcasts, writes DVD and Blu-ray collector's edition booklets, and publishes as a freelance journalist for German sub-culture and film magazines. Her latest publication is: 'Mythos und Wahrheit in Berlin 1977. *Suspiria (2018)* als politischer und sozialer Spiegel des Deutschen Herbstes.' *Berlin Visionen. Filmische Stadtbilder seit 1980*, edited by Stefan Jung and Marcus Stiglegger, Martin Schmitz Verlag, 2021, pp. 315–33.

Marcus Stiglegger is professor in film studies at universities in Germany and around the world (Austria, USA, Poland). In 1999 he published his doctoral thesis on the subject of politics and sexuality in cinema (*Sadiconazista*, 2nd ed.) and he has edited several books on film history and film aesthetics. His publications include books on the seduction theory of film (2006), western (2003), war films (2006), pop and cinema (2004), modern horror cinema (2010, 2018), David Cronenberg (2011), Dario Argento (2013), Akira Kurosawa (2014), Lucio Fulci (2019), genre theory (2020) and the film *Cruising* (2020). He regularly contributes to international conferences. His research interests are: body theory, transgressive philosophy and cinema, media mythology, performative aspects of cinema and the Holocaust in the narrative media. Stiglegger regularly produces supplemental material for international film releases on Blu-ray (for example, *Twin Peaks: Fire Walk with Me*).

Willem Strank is an independent researcher in film studies and musicology. He received his PhD from Kiel University, Germany with his thesis about *Twist Endings* in 2014. His main areas of research (with more than 50 publications) include film music, the representation of neoliberalism in media and the discourse of crisis in documentary forms. His second monograph, a single-volume book about global film history (*Handbuch Filmgeschichte*), was published in 2021.

Constantine Verevis is Associate Professor in Film and Screen Studies at Monash University, Melbourne. His publications include *Film Remakes* (Edinburgh University Press, 2006), *Second Takes: Critical Approaches to the Film Sequel* (2010), *Film Trilogies: New Critical Approaches* (2012), *Australian Film Theory and Criticism, Vol. I: Critical Positions* (2013), *US Independent Film After 1989: Possible Films* (Edinburgh University Press, 2015), *Transnational Television Remakes* (2016), *Transnational Film Remakes* (edited with Iain Robert Smith, Edinburgh University Press, 2017), *Flaming Creatures* (2020) and *Film Reboots* (2020). With Claire Perkins, he is founding co-editor of the series *Screen Serialities* published by Edinburgh University Press.

Bernd Zywietz is a media scholar and head of the political extremism department of jugendschutz.net, Germany's joint competence centre for the protection of minors on the Internet. He holds a PhD in Media Studies, worked as a lecturer in Film Studies and wrote and directed the short film *Lünsch* in 2004.

Introduction: Entering Lynchtown

Andreas Rauscher, Marcel Hartwig and Peter Niedermüller

During the 1980s and early 1990s, David Lynch redefined his status as cult auteur of midnight movies such as *Eraserhead* (1977) and of ambitious art-house productions like *The Elephant Man* (1980). Following the international success of *Blue Velvet* (1986) and *Wild at Heart* (1990), he was discussed as one of cinema's defining postmodernists, along with Peter Greenaway, Pedro Almodóvar, Lars von Trier, the French 'cinéma du look' and US independents from Jim Jarmusch to Quentin Tarantino. His references to artists like Francis Bacon and Edward Hopper as well as cult classics like *The Wizard of Oz* (1939) and rock ballads by Roy Orbison crossed the border between high art and pop art and closed the gap between the reflections of film scholars in academia and the coolness of everyday cultural knowledge. At the same time, he expanded the canvas of cinema by composing and producing music together with Angelo Badalamenti and Julee Cruise, from experimental industrial sounds to sublime pop, by staging performances like the *Industrial Symphony Vol. 1* (1990), and by entering art galleries with his sculptures, paintings, photography and designs.

Instead of directing commercials and video clips occasionally, the (net) work(ing) across media became one of the defining trademarks of Lynch's open-ended œuvre. In contrast to the autobiographical limitations and the distanced critical interventionist politics of traditional auteurism, 'Lynchtown' (Chion 1995) offered aesthetic abundance and multi-layered surfaces for participatory involvement. The TV series *Twin Peaks* (1990–2), created by David Lynch and Mark Frost, eventually introduced a new 'Golden Age of Television' (Thompson) for many critics and scholars. In hindsight, media scholar Henry Jenkins regarded the series to be, 'the cutting edge of what a decade later would be called transmedia entertainment' (Jenkins 2020: 33). Taking its cue from perspectives such as the above, Anne Jerslev, in her latest study *Blurred Boundaries* (2021: 3), takes a closer look at the overlap between Lynch's work as an artist and his work as a director by asking about 'the aesthetic, thematic and affective possibilities [his] artistic approach entails'. There she traces the continuities that exist between, for example, Lynch's fascination with textures and the 'spatial disorientation' (ibid.: 65) he creates in close-ups on what Chion calls 'microreliefs' (ibid.) across different media, also used in the opening of *Twin Peaks: Fire Walk with Me* (1992). The latter film, however, was not well received by either audiences or critics upon its release. This resulted in a significant reinvention of Lynch's artistic persona and style during the 1990s. Turning from the postmodern excesses and shiny lustre of pastiche towards 'interior mental landscapes' (Jerslev), Lynch dived into the rhizomatic abyss of 'psychogenic fugue[s]' (Lynch, in Pizzello 1997: 36) with *Lost Highway* (1997) accompanied by, among others, an industrial rock soundtrack curated by Trent Reznor. Taking inspirations from psychological neo-noir and supernatural mystery thrillers the film became one of the defining examples of what Thomas Elsaesser called 'the mind-game-movie' (Elsaesser 2021). It also reconfigured and expanded the semantic structure of the 'Lynch-Kit' introduced by French film historian and sound studies pioneer Michel Chion in 1995. Eventually this would set the stage for film philosophy by introducing contradicting cinematic ontologies and genre settings. The palimpsest that resulted from Lynch's own work on an abandoned television series became *Mulholland Drive* (2001), for which the director won his second Palme d'Or at the Cannes Film Festival. In 2016, this second part of his Los Angeles trilogy, which was completed with *Inland Empire* in 2006, was even voted the best film of the early twenty-first century by a jury of 177 film critics from thirty-six countries. Lynch's return to *Twin Peaks* for a third season in 2017, a reunion with co-creator Mark Frost and most of the original cast, received standing ovations at the Cannes Film Festival as well as high praise from the *Cahiers du Cinéma* in being voted the best film of the 2010s.

In this way, Lynch is now commonly referred to as one of the key 'auteurs' of (post-) modern American independent cinema, a darling child to subcultures as well as museum curators and festival connoisseurs, and one who is simultaneously understood as both a serious auteur and a postmodern entrepreneur. While the reception of Lynch very often resorts to multiple approaches (for example Lindsay Hallam on *Twin Peaks: Fire Walk with Me* (2018) and her interpretations in relation to the horror genre, to the series, to trauma films, and to the Lynchian œuvre), intertextual references (for example Michel Chion on *David Lynch* (1995) and the cross-references to film history), or transmedia world-building (for example Holly Rogers' reading of Lynch's use of sound as a cross-media trademark (2020)), his work merits an overall rereading as a transmedia network. Until recently, inter- and transmediality have not been the main themes of an edited collection on Lynch. Taking its cue from *Twin Peaks: The Return* as the paradox of Lynch's open-ended Gesamtkunstwerk, this volume seeks to draw together the cinema of David Lynch as a metatextual, intertextual, and transmedial network from an interdisciplinary perspective. Even though numerous books and studies on David Lynch's work were published during the heyday of poststructuralist approaches to cinema in the 1990s, with the exception of Anne Jerslev's latest book (2021), only specialised takes on singular theoretical perspectives or on certain aspects of his artistic œuvre have been undertaken in recent years. Building on research from experts in the field of David Lynch studies as well as novel perspectives from young academics, this collection gathers interdisciplinary international contributions from the fields of American studies, musicology and sound studies, film and media studies, cultural studies and gender studies. The critical exchange between different media and disciplines puts select views from the art life in dialogue with cult television, connects traditional musicology with sound studies, and reconsiders cinema through the lens of cinephilia as a cultural practice.

Music and visual art are key elements within what can be called Lynch's 'rhizomatic network', if viewed through the lens of Guattari and Deleuze's (1980) model of horizontally growing systems. In several ways he uses music, Lynch differs dramatically from other 'auteurs'. In the field of music, for example, this can be seen in the way Lynch distinguishes himself from directors such as Stanley Kubrick or Oliver Stone. For Kubrick, the use of 'classical music' and avant-garde works (especially by György Ligeti) became a trademark from *2001: A Space Odyssey* (1968) onwards and guaranteed the artistic integrity of a film. In Oliver Stone's *Natural Born Killers* (1994) the musical quotations from Giacomo Puccini and Alban Berg to Diamanda Galás and Trent Reznor are set pieces that are collaged to emphasise the artificial and manufactured nature of the film (as a kind of psychopathology of pop culture). The vast sound worlds of Lynch's films also feature musical references and quotations, but these are related to the semiotic fabric of his work in a variety of ways. By no means does the creative work of the 'soundman' Lynch find its limitations in the medium of film. It is also evident in a stage realisation such as *Industrial Symphony No. 1* or when he substituted for former Sex Pistols guitarist Steve Jones as a guest presenter on *Jonesy's Juke Box on Indie 103.1*. Therefore, Part I of this book, 'Approaching Intertexts', considers the perspectives of musicology and aesthetics further. In this part, the book moves from the general frames of previous scholarship to a more detailed discussion of intertexts in David Lynch's cinema.

In 'Approaching Intertexts', Peter Niedermüller illustrates the trans-media network of David Lynch by pointing to the corpus of the Western canon of 'E-Musik' ('serious music' as Adorno would put it (1962: 39)) and its use across Lynch's œuvre. His chapter takes film seriously as a transmitter of music and finds recurring standards in Lynch's work for topoi in his films that seem to be mitigated as a sonic screen onto which the visual imprints of Lynch's characters are projected. These discussions go beyond established inquiries about the relation between diegetic and non-diegetic music. By the same token, his chapter argues the ways that Lynch considers the reader's contextual knowledge about the music used in his films as essential intertexts for the topoi represented on the screen. Music, in this way, is not only an intermedial anchor, but also a prefigura-tion in which characters, situations and their relation to each other become a transmedia framing device for Lynch's films. A different intertextual point of reference informs Mads Outzen's chapter on the 'Changing Faces in the Cinema of Lynch'. His theoretical approach takes its cue from Aristotle's 'Metaphysics', Emmanuel Levinas's writings on faces and ethics as well as Gilles Deleuze's concept of affect to trace the tensions that result between aisthetic and aesthetic dimensions in Lynch's cinema. He would argue that the films affect a way of seeing faces and take into account physiognomy as a transmedia element in the corporeal sensation of pre-reflective film experiences in audiences.

In order to return to the sonic work in Lynch's œuvre, it has to be stressed that this soundman can neither be separated from Lynch the filmmaker nor from Lynch the visual artist (even if they have different significance and stress in the phases of their work). Lynch's camera never is completely rigid, yet many of the shots in his films are composed like paintings (often in a slight low-angle shot). Of note is also his collaboration with stage and prop designers. For example, even though *Dune* (1984) was not a commercial and critical success, this film is also a product of Lynch the sculptor. For Lynch, film is, therefore, not a limited genre of the visual arts (as it was for the former photographer Kubrick) but only a facet of an overall artistic endeavour. Thus, to return to the title of this introduction, there is no such thing as a 'Kubricktown', but rather a thin intertextual chain from movie to movie in Kubrick (for instance the 'matchcut' between the last shot of *2001*, and the first shot of *A Clockwork Orange*, 1971, cf. Kiefer 2006). Instead, a cooperative approach has to be taken into consid-eration as being informative about Lynch's artistic output. A case in point would be the franchise *Twin Peaks*. Part II, '*Twin Peaks* as Transmedia Network', revisits the TV series through the lens of collaborative struc-tures. The multi-layered work of the third season resists the comfortable practices of canonisation conveyed by the restorative commodities of the nostalgia industry. Here, *Twin Peaks: The Return* will be read as a network in itself, connecting motives and stages of the Lynchian œuvre.

As the corpus on Lynch has repeatedly shown, *Twin Peaks* as a cluster bookends the Golden Age of David Lynch as an 'auteur' on both the television and the cinematic screen. No discussion seems to be possible without finding intertextual references between Lynch's films and his and Mark Frost's TV series. Willem Strank's chapter looks at Lynch's body of work as a conceit by way of an extended metaphor on electricity. He would argue that the paradigmatic dimensions of electricity – such as circuity, charge, or voltage – preconfigure the symbolic allusions in Lynch's cinema. In this way, the medium Lynch uses to mitigate his narratives also preconditions the worlds his texts evoke. For example, the repeated use of discharges in the TV series is preframed by the media device's cathode-ray tubes. Strank aims to show the continuities between old media and old technologies, literal transmedia configurations in Lynch's creations from *The Grandmother* (1970) to *Twin Peaks: The Return*. While Strank argues about interlocking structures on an intradiegetic level, Constantine Verevis takes into consideration extradiegetic aspects to trace the role of the 'set' in Lynch's textual structures. As a result, he proposes a reading of Lynch's film worlds as an open w/hole. Consequently, his discussion of both *Fire Walk with Me* as a 'ruinous prequel' and the TV series take into consideration the intermedial reverberations between the corpus of *Twin Peaks* and shorts such as the 'Georgia Coffee ads' as well as *Premonitions Following an Evil Deed* (1995). A set of different aesthetic structures is recognised by Jannik Müller, whose focus is on visual effects. While categorising the visual effects used in *Twin Peaks: The Return*, transmedial references between Lynch's art world and his TV series become graspable. By the same token, Müller's discussions, in using Shilo McClean's taxonomy for visual effects, offer apt terminology and categories to reflect on the modern visual-effects-centred film industry and its intricate connections with highbrow cinematic productions. On a different note, Bernd Zywietz's auto-ethnographic study of *Twin Peaks: The Return* renders the TV series as a reified experience of nostalgia. Instead of applying a normative understanding of nostalgia, Zywietz traces this concept as a tool to reflect on the relationship between media, mediation, and meta-media. His close reading of the TV series highlights that the new instalment of the series is nostalgically encoding and re-coding itself and thus reifies an experience of David Lynch rather than what the series once stood for during the so-called Golden Age of Television. Dan Hassler-Forest tackles key transmedia forms of the *Twin Peaks* franchise. Thus, his chapter offers an application of various transmedia models to map out David Lynch's and Mark Frost's TV series as transmedia multitext and discusses its pioneering role in transmedia storytelling. In tracing the paratexts of *Twin Peaks*, Hassler-Forest discovers media-industrial practices applied in the series to bridge the gap between digital fandom and on-demand culture. Finally, the threads of Part II are woven together in Andreas Rauscher's treatise on the processes of world-making in the various multimodal framing devices to contextualize and raise interest in *Twin Peaks*. His knowledgeable excursion thus tracks the rich semiotic potentials in Lynch's body of work and the various genres that echo and resonate with the idea of 'acinema', a term coined by Jean-François Lyotard and applied to Lynch by Graham Jones and Ashley Woodward. In illustrating the aesthetic dimensions of strategies 'around' David Lynch's use of different media and their synergetic transmedia effects, Rauscher categorises the world-making approaches in the director's open-ended associative audiovisual network. He concludes that the configurations for experiencing and making sense of Lynch's œuvre allow for different, even contradicting points-of-entry and perspectives, from narrative exploration to aesthetic detours and film-philosophical reflections depending on the choice and combination of media.

The entropic implosion of the Twin Peaks cosmos initiated by *Fire Walk with Me* results in a fragile and thus configurable storyworld, haunted by its own cinematic transmediality. The resulting network that is *Twin Peaks* offers a new understanding of David Lynch as a collaborative artist whose cinematic worlds reverberate with real places, for example the topography of mid-century Los Angeles. This cue with regard to 'David Lynch's Transmedia Aesthetics' is taken up in Part III. The chapters in this section argue that transmedia storytelling, on the one hand, allows for a collective and participatory experience of film and other media. On the other hand, it also paves the way for the transposition of this experience to the liminal space between the artwork itself and its contexts. From such a perspective, Part III of this book deals with myths, media transpositions and genre intermediality. Marcus Stiglegger discusses the mythical topography of LA in *Lost Highway* (1997), *Mulholland Drive* (2001), and *Inland Empire* (2006). His paper illustrates how Lynch's topography is echoed in, or rather 'haunts' as Stiglegger suggests, contemporary perceptions of both Hollywood and the City of Angels. As his excursion to shooting locations of the above films shows, the myth of the 'real' LA often is intertwined with the experience and echoes of old Hollywood's genre mythologies about the city. Lynch reiterates these in the haunted images of his representations of these places – genre here is to be understood as a transmedia frame for the aesthetic choices in Lynch's work. A key archetype of old Hollywood's cinema would be the character of the femme fatale. In looking closely at this genre-defining trope in film noir and its interplay with cinematic representations of sexual desire, Lioba Schlösser's chapter discusses recurring images of women in David Lynch's cinema. She problematises a character template that favours a woman's hetero-sexual self-awareness over that of homoerotic desire. Marcel Hartwig assesses the multimodality of David Lynch-memes and the transposition of key aesthetics of Lynch's œuvre into new media contexts. Taking its cue from the "If David Lynch directed"-series on YouTube and other digital memes, his chapter looks at the ways new meanings and aesthet-ics are shaped in contexts that expand the Lynchian network to that of the memetic iconoclasm of social media platforms. In turn, these memes reshape the public commentary around Lynchian cinema and allow for a participatory public creation of David Lynch as a digital meme. Part III of the book thus illustrates the various ways in which the aesthetics of David Lynch shape and reconfigure transmedia contexts with regard to their media aesthetics. These transpositioned visual and sound cues impact the perception and understanding of objects and conditions in the physical world and offer new readings of David Lynch's open œuvre.

Such an openness invites reconfigurations and artistic reflections, which inform the final part of *Networked David Lynch*. Part IV, 'Video-graphic Criticism of David Lynch's Cinematic Work', provides an outlook on further critical investigations into the transmedia worlds surrounding the Lynchian œuvre and the format of the video essay as an innovative analytical as well as an associative tool. It collects two reports and reflec-tions on recent videographic criticism of David Lynch's cinematic work. Liz Greene produced five audiovisual essays on *The Elephant Man* (1980) and *Blue Velvet* (1987) that resulted from experiments in form. Her article explores how videographic criticism offers a broader opportunity for dis-seminating Lynch's rhythmic techniques as well as reframing the gaze. Her most recent videographic essay, *The Elephant Man's Sound, Tracked*, provides a greater backdrop to her discussion about how a film scholar's work can be drawn together in an audiovisual production that would allow for a greater dissemination of work on David Lynch by way of audio-visual analysis, archival work, and conducting interviews. Chris Aarnes Bakkane considers the thought and work process behind his video essay *In Dreams* (2017), applying associative experimental forms rather than a conventional analytical approach to the format. His text ties up this vol-ume's excursion into transmedia networks by offering the perspective of a graduate student, who improvises on preconfigured readings of Lynch as an auteur in creatively exploring Lynch's cinematic dreams in a videographic production of their own. His chapter illustrates choices and obstacles in working with copyrighted material and software and thus invites readers to follow suit and make creations of their own. As a result, this fourth and final part of the book discusses two possible routes for the application of the major insights of this book: that is an analytical, exploratory work illustrating David Lynch's œuvre as a transmedia network, or the experience of the networked Lynch as an impetus for a creative, participatory work of art of its own.

Bibliography

Adorno, Theodor W[iesengrund]. *Einleitung in die Musiksoziologie. Zwölf theoretische Vorlesungen.* Suhrkamp Verlag, 1962.

Chion, Michel. *David Lynch.* Translated by Robert Julian. BFI, 1995.

Deleuze, Gilles and Félix Guattari. *Mille plateaux. Capitalisme et schizophrénie.* Éditions de Minuit, 1980.

Elsaesser, Thomas. 'Actions Have Consequences: Logics of the Mind-Game Film in David Lynch's Los Angeles Trilogy'. *The Mind-Game Film: Distributed Agency, Time Travel, and Productive Pathology*, Warren Buckland, Dana Polan and Seung-hoon Jeong (eds). Routledge, 2021.

Hallam, Lindsay. *Twin Peaks: Fire Walk with Me.* Auteur, 2018.

Jenkins, Henry. 'Why *Twin Peaks*?' *Mysterium Twin Peaks. Zeichen – Welten – Referenzen*, Caroline Frank and Markus Schleich (eds). Springer, 2020, pp. 28–36.

Jerslev, Anne. *David Lynch – Mentale Landschaften.* 2nd edition, translated by Vera Ableitinger. Passagen Verlag, 2006.

Jerslev, Anne. *David Lynch: Blurred Boundaries.* Palgrave, 2021.

Kiefer, Bernd. '*A Clockwork Orange*'. *Reclams Filmklassiker*, Thomas Koebner (ed.), vol. 3. 5th edition. Reclam Verlag, 2006, p. 334.

Pizzello, Stephen. 'Highway to Hell'. *American Cinematographer*, vol. 36.3, 1997, pp. 34–42.

Rogers, Holly. 'The Audiovisual Eerie: Transmediating Thresholds in the Work of David Lynch'. *Transmedia Directors: Artistry, Industry and New Audiovisual Aesthetics*, Carol Vernallis, Holly Rogers and Lisa Perrott (eds). Bloomsbury, 2020, pp. 241–70.

Thompson, Robert. *Television's Second Golden Age: From* Hill Street Blues *to* ER. Syracuse University Press, 1997.

Filmography

2001: A Space Odyssey. Directed by Stanley Kubrick, performances by Keir Dullea and Douglas Rain, MGM, Warner Bros., 1968.

A Clockwork Orange. Directed by Stanley Kubrick, performances by Malcolm McDowell and Patrick Magee, Warner Bros., 1971.

Blue Velvet. Directed by David Lynch, performances by Kyle MacLachlan, Isabella Rosselini, Dennis Hopper, and Laura Dern, Dino De Laurentiis Entertainment Group, 1986.

Dune. Directed by David Lynch, performances by Kyle MacLachlan and Sean Young, Dino De Laurentiis Company, Estudios Churucusco Azteca, 1984.

Eraserhead. Directed by David Lynch, performances by Jack Nance and Charlotte Stewart, American Film Institute, Libra Films, 1977.

Industrial Symphony No. 1: The Dream of the Brokenhearted. Directed by David Lynch, performances by Laura Dern and Julee Cruise, Polygram, 1990.

Inland Empire. Directed by David Lynch, performances by Laura Dern and Grace Zabriskie, Studio Canal et al., 2006.

Lost Highway. Directed by David Lynch, performances by Bill Pullman and Patricia Arquette, CiBi 2000, Asymmetrical Productions and Lost Highway Productions LCC, 1997.

Mulholland Drive. Directed by David Lynch, performances by Naomi Watts and Laura Harring, Les Films Alain Sarde et al., 2001.

Natural Born Killers. Directed by Oliver Stone, performances by Woody Harrelson and Juliette Lewis, Warner Bros., 1994.

Premonitions Following an Evil Deed. Directed by David Lynch, performances by Jeff Alperi and Michele Carlyle, Fox Lorber, 1995.

The Elephant Man. Directed by David Lynch, performances by John Hurt and Anthony Hopkins, Brooksfilm, 1980.

The Grandmother. Directed by David Lynch, American Film Institute, 1970.

The Wizard of Oz. Directed by Victor Fleming, George Cukor and Mervyn LeRoy, performances by Judy Garland and Frank Morgan, Warner Bros. Pictures, 1939.

Twin Peaks. Directed by David Lynch et al., performances by Kyle MacLachlan and Mädchen Amick, Lynch/Frost Productions et al., 1990–1.

Twin Peaks: Fire Walk with Me. Directed by David Lynch, performances by Sheryl Lee and Ray Wise, CIBY Picture, 1992.

Twin Peaks: The Return [on DVD and Blu-ray *Twin Peaks: A Limited Event Series*]. Directed by David Lynch, performances by Sheryl Lee and Kyle MacLachlan, Showtime, 2017.

Wild at Heart. Directed by David Lynch, performances by Laura Dern and Nicolas Cage, PolyGram Filmed Entertainment and Propaganda Films, 1990.

Other Media and Sources Cited

'Jonesy's Juke Box.' *Indie 103.1*, Santa Monica, CA. 2004–9.

Greene, Liz (2020) *The Elephant Man's Sound, Tracked*, vimeo.com/413827977 (last accessed 2 May 2021).

Part I

Approaching Intertexts

Visits Paid to the 'Imaginary Museum of Musical Works': David Lynch and the Musical Canon

Peter Niedermüller

In her seminal book *The Imaginary Museum of Musical Works*, the philosopher Lydia Goehr argues that the musical work is not a timeless concept but a historical one that originated in Western Europe at the border between the Enlightenment, German Idealism and Romanticism. Beethoven thus becomes, as it were, the prototype of a composer who does not simply present music but rather musical works. Accordingly, this first chapter will focus on such works from the Western canon ('serious music' as one could put it, following Adorno (1962: 39)), as they were used in the films by David Lynch. The question of whether Lynch's activity as a sound designer and musician in return might have become canonical is beyond the scope of this paper.

For a long time, it was a mark of quality that film music was written specifically for each film. Stanley Kubrick's *2001: A Space Odyssey* as well as Dennis Hopper and Peter Fonda's *Easy Rider* famously deviated from this standard. There is an important difference between these two forms of film music. In the first traditional case, one experiences music as something new, when watching the film for the first time and the film itself stays the main mediator by which the music may be heard and experienced. In the second case the situation is often reversed; the viewer might already be familiar with the music in other contexts and thus will bring their personal connotations to the understanding of the audiovisual sensation (Cormick 2006: 19–30; see also Derrida 1990: 24–5).

In his use of music, Lynch may not be compared to Kubrick. Ever since *2001* Kubrick had almost exclusively been using Western art music in personally selected recordings as music for his films. This became a stylistic feature as well as an individual trademark (the only exception being *Full Metal Jacket*, where the pre-existing pop soundtrack represents the sonic world of the young soldiers in Vietnam). Even though Lynch chooses his sounds and music from a wider variety of sources, he also goes back to

Western art music again and again. Table 1.1 provides an overview on this use of music:

Table 1.1 Music from the Western canon in films by David Lynch

Films by Lynch	Musical work	Dramatic situation
The Elephant Man (1980)	Samuel Barber, Adagio for strings op. 11a (1938)	John Merrick's death
Blue Velvet (1986)	Dmitrij Šostakovič [Dmitri Shostakovich], Symphony no. 15 op. 141 (1971)	Opening titles
Wild at Heart (1990)	Richard Strauss, 'Im Abendrot' Tr 296 (1948)	Opening titles
—	—	Sailor Ripley and Lula Fortune at dusk
—	—	Lula 'losing' Sailor
—	—	Sailor's return to Lula
—	Krzysztof Penderecki, 'ΚΟΣΜΟΓΟΝΙΑ | Kosmogonia' (1970)	Phone call between Marietta Fortune and Johnnie Farragut
—	—	Murder of Farragut
—	—	Planned murder of Sailor
Twin Peaks: Fire Walk with Me (1992)	Luigi Cherubini, 'Agnus dei' from Requiem in C Minor (1817)	Laura Palmer's death
—	—	Closing titles
Inland Empire (2006)	Penderecki, 'Przebudzenie Jakuba' | 'Als Jakob erwachte' (1974)	Murder of Susan Blue
—	—	Nikki Grace's confusion
Twin Peaks: The Return (2017)	Beethoven, Piano Sonata in C sharp minor Op. 27 No. 2, slowed down to a quarter of the original speed	Woodsmen coming after the shooting of Evil-Cooper
—	Penderecki, 'Ofiarom Hiroszimy. Tren | Threnos. Den Opfern von Hiroschima' (1960)	Trinity Nuclear Test
—	—	After Bob comes to earth

A connection to death in these excerpts from the films seems obvious. There are five death scenes, one by suicide in *The Elephant Man*, and four more by murder (*Wild at Heart*, *Fire Walk with Me*, *Inland Empire* and *Twin Peaks: The Return*). Further on, there is another planned murder in

Wild at Heart and the ignition of the first nuclear explosion in human history with the Trinity test in *Twin Peaks: The Return*.

   This connection to death is also observed in the selected musical works: Samuel Barber's famous Adagio is an instrumental composition without a particular function, but it is often used for funerals (most famously at the funeral of John F. Kennedy). Luigi Cherubini's Requiem or Missa pro defunctis is a mass for the dead. The dedication to the victims of Hiroshima in 'Ofiarom Hiroszimy. Tren | Threnos. Den Opfern von Hiroschima' (Threnody. For the Victims of Hirohima)[1] by Krzysztof Penderecki speaks for itself. Richard Strauss's 'Im Abendrot' ('At Dusk') used in *Wild at Heart* alludes to death. Joseph von Eichendorff's poem (though only the instrumental introduction and no vocal part of the 'lied' is heard in Lynch's film) reflects the twilight years of an old couple finishing with the question: 'Is this death now?'[2] (Eichendorff 1856: 303). It would be too limited a view to conclude that Lynch only uses serious music for serious situations. There is a border between life and death, and by a shortcut we have arrived at a motif essential to Lynch's films. It is about the realm between the physical and the metaphysical. By way of his vision and his musical choices Lynch raises questions about the entanglements and limitations of these realms.

Realms and Layers in Lynch: Some Observations

As a rather simple example, one might think of *Blue Velvet*. Three times in the film Jeffrey Beaumont (Kyle MacLachlan) is shown wakening up. In one of the iconic scenes of the movie Frank Booth (Dennis Hopper) speaks the lyrics of Roy Orbison's song 'In Dreams' as a voice over to the recording to Beaumont: 'In dreams I walk with you, in dreams I talk to you'. If this quote is understood as a self-referential allusion, one is to discard the idea that there is a linear plot and one has to read *Blue Velvet* as a metadiegetic nesting of Jeffrey's dreams (see Niedermüller). Of course, this analysis leads directly to notorious discussions about *Lost Highway*, *Mulholland Drive* and *Inland Empire*, whether their narration should be accepted in their somehow 'chaotic structure' or whether one should not at least demarcate the levels of dream or deathbed experience and view them against a second level of action. In 1989, *Twin Peaks* confused television audiences by establishing the Black Lodge as a supernatural Other to the 'normal' plot of a TV series. By season three we come to understand that there is not a simple binary opposition between the city of Twin Peaks and the Black Lodge. Season 3 displays a 'universe [. . .] in which linear chronology and spatial succession have already been pulverized' (Cristina Álvarez López, quoted in Hainge 2020: 376).

There is also a binary opposition concerning music that does not work out in Lynch's filmic œuvre. A traditional principle in the analysis of film music is the distinction between diegetic and non-diegetic music. The distinction concerns whether the 'music [. . .] (apparently) issues from a source within the narrative' (Gorbman 1987: 22) of the film or is external to it. Though asking this question may be helpful in some instances, this distinction is not exactly precise. To make this clear, one need only ask whether one understands diegesis as a sequence of events (Souriau 1951: 233), as an arrangement of signs (Metz 1964: 64f) or as a universe in which the action takes place (Genette 1972: 238–40, see also Winters 2010: 225–7).

Even though the theoretical interpretations of diegesis are many and varied, the assumption of an extradiegetic realm of sound is equally debated. Robynn J. Stilwell asked, in 2007, whether there exists one closed 'off' space where all extradiegetic sounds take place. Does the off voice of a narrator plausibly come from the same place as non-diegetic film music does? Stilwell (2007: 196) used a spatial metaphor for this difference. The narrator is somehow more in front while the music is more behind. Ben Winters (2010: 242f) claimed that the concept of extradiegetic music is at odds with the filmic perception. Rather he accepts the presence of the music and argues that often the music can be understood as the acoustic counterpart of a bodily presence in the visual sensation. Or in the words of Steven Spielberg (quoted in Winters 2010: 224): 'Indiana Jones cannot exist without [his musical] theme. And, of course, the theme would be nothing without Indiana Jones.' Interestingly neither Stilwell nor Winters refer to David Lynch, though Lynch developed a vast repertoire of remarkable techniques that cannot be explained convincingly when conceptually contrasting the diegetic versus the non-diegetic realm.

For example, Jeffrey Beaumont's walk around Lumberton in *Blue Velvet* is accompanied by the audio of a local radio show. At the beginning of the sequence, a sign saying 'Welcome to Lumberton' with a pair of loudspeakers on both sides is shown, which might be the acoustic source in the 'diegesis'. Although Beaumont is moving away from the loudspeakers and his walk is interspersed with jumps, the volume of the radio stays the same and the broadcast is heard continuously without any interruptions. Of course, the radio show is important for the place of the sequence and its atmosphere; it is also highly plausible that it forms a part of the diegetic universe, but there is no good reason to assume that Beaumont can hear this radio show.

The music of Angelo Badalamenti is a particular signature of Lynch's films and an important atmospheric device. In many cases this Badalementi sound is strongly connected to places, especially in the first two seasons of *Twin Peaks*. Badalamenti's 'The Dance of the Dream Man' not only accompanies the Man from Another Place (Michael J. Anderson) but is also the signature sound of the Black Lodge. In a similar way, 'Audrey's Dance' flows through the corridors of both the Great Northern Hotel and the local high school. Badalamenti's soundtrack pleasantly invites audiences to memorise its themes and become acquainted with it. Also, his stylistically different music choices, especially in the use of pre-existing music, often have a shock aesthetic: For example, 'Heirate mich' ('Marry Me') by Rammstein is used in *Lost Highway* as if it penetrates the inner world of the film from the outside. The song starts when Pete Dayton (Balthazar Getty) directs his gaze to a projection of a porn movie starring Renee Madison/Alice Wakefield (Patricia Arquette) in Andy's (Michael Massee) living room. The point-of-view shot invites audiences to adopt Pete's gaze. In both its volume and its hard industrial style, Rammstein's rock song differs from Badalamenti's score that accompanied Pete's way to the house. Worth mentioning here are the German lyrics, which may be incomprehensible to and to some degree even aggressively attack the ears of an English-speaking audience. Even though it is perfectly clear that Badalamenti's and Rammstein's music act on different spheres at this point, it is also obvious that this difference cannot be described through the categories of the diegetic versus extradiegetic. Neither of the two can be considered diegetic. By the same token it is just as inappropriate to assume that they might come from the 'same' source somewhere in the non-diegetic off.

It is not only the sound of Badalementi's music that reappears from film to film, some musical gestures also repeat. This is true for the base line of 'Cool Cat' from *Wild at Heart*, which reappears in 'Audrey's Dance' in *Twin Peaks* and in 'Mr Eddy's Theme 2' in *Lost Highway* (the latter not written by Badalamenti). Also, a two-chord progression reminiscent of Dmitrij Šostakovič's symphony no. 15 (second movement, bar 11–12) should be mentioned at this point: Lynch listened to this symphony continuously while writing the screenplay for *Blue Velvet* (Rodley 2005: 135). This might be the reason why Badalementi used these chords (in transposition) as the closing motif for the main titles of *Blue Velvet*. Of course, these two chords are also the harmonic cell of 'Laura Palmer's Theme' in *Twin Peaks* and also formed some kind of jingle for Spelling Entertainment in season one (Niedermüller 2016: 322).

A device Lynch uses often but in very different ways in his films is lip-synching. In *Blue Velvet*, Ben (Dean Stockwell) perfectly lip-synchs to Roy Orbison's 'In Dreams' but it is clear that he is just posing for a tape in the cassette player with the recording on it. Booth's more aggressive lip-synching in the same movie to the same song has already been mentioned above. At the end of *Wild at Heart*, Sailor Ripley (Nicolas Cage) 'sings' 'Love me tender' for Lula Fortune (Laura Dern). The unreal effect is underlined in the squeaky technical audio editing of Lula's exclamation 'Sailor!'. In fact, one might think he is lip-synching to the recording by Elvis Presley, while it actually is a recording by the actor himself (as the end credits indicate). A different effect is achieved in *Twin Peaks* episode 2 of season 2 ('[Coma]'[3]), when James Hurley (James Marshall), Maddy Ferguson (Sheryl Lee) and Donna Hayward (Lara Flynn Boyle) make a home recording with James singing. Though the setting seems realistic, it is clear that the singing voice is not that of the actor Marshall, but a high and delicate 'Roy Orbison-like vocal timbre' of an unknown singer (Mazullo 503f). Finally, in the Club Silencio sequence of *Mulholland Drive*, Rebekah del Rio mimes so perfectly to 'Llorando' – her own cover version of Roy Orbison's 'Crying' – that it comes as a shocking moment when she collapses onto the stage, but her singing voice continues to play. Thus, lip-synching is an important device to transform the film persona into a musical persona, but it also can destroy the film's illusion; suggesting that film is just a technical artefact.

The above observations are grouped around three phenomena: the ontological status of music in film, the question of 'inside and outside', and the status between cliché and emphatic utterance. In the following, I will revisit select scenes from these three perspectives.

Case Studies

In *Wild at Heart*, Strauss's 'Im Abendrot' may be considered as one of the main musical themes. It is the music of the opening titles as well as of key sequences of the film. Another main musical element is 'Slaughterhouse' by the American thrash metal band Powermad. 'Slaughterhouse' as well as 'Im Abendrot' only appear as parts of their genuine instrumental sections in the movie. This might be a reason why scholars have neglected the lyrics of both pieces, though they are of course present for an audience familiar with the songs. 'Im Abendrot' tells of the twilight years of an old couple. Much of the poetic imagery in the lyrics is reminiscent of young Sailor and Lula, for example in line 1: 'Through hardship and joy [|] We have gone hand in hand'[4] (Eichendorff 1856: 303). Powermad's (1989) lyrics are the interior monologue of a criminal on death row. Such an imagery is addressed in Mike Miley's analysis (2014: 49–51) of rhythm and blues music as 'liminal territory' in *Wild at Heart*: Music here is not just an atmospheric device but represents the myths transported by the very genre itself, that of the bluesman at the crossroads. Such an interpretation fits perfectly with the lyrics presented here. Sailor's options are to follow the devilish Bobby Peru (Willem Dafoe) and end as a felon on the electric chair (of course only if he is not killed by Peru first) or to live life to its fullest together with Lula.

Yet it is not as simple an opposition that 'Powermad' stands for the wrong and Strauss's 'Lied' for the right choices. These two musical elements operate on different levels. Powermad's song stands for Sailor's body, his masculinity, but also his abysmal brutality. Sailor's murder of Bob Ray Lemon (Gregg Dandridge) is choreographed directly to Powermad's music. In this case, Annette Davison's (2004a: 178, 2004b: 124) assumption that such choreographies are an allusion to classical Hollywood musicals remains unconvincing. The gruesome fight between Sailor and Lemon is not staged as a 'tableau', rather it appears that the unchained camera can just follow the fast movements of the two. It gives the impression that the music is taking possession of Sailor's body (it also completely erases Glenn Miller's 'In the Mood' from the beginning of the sequence). In the cross-cuts between the sex and car scenes in the middle of the film, Sailor moves entirely to the rhythm of the music by Powermad (which here, however, is significantly used in a mash-up with older rock'n'roll-songs, such as Gene Vincent's 'Be-Bop-A-Lula').

A few scenes before Sailor and Lula come across the teenage victims of a fatal car accident at night and eventually find themselves stranded in Big Tuna, TX, Lula is taken aback by the horrific news from the radio. Sailor switches stations to a music channel that plays Powermad.[5] To this they then dance in the same strange kung fu style that was initially performed on the dancefloor of the Hurricane upon Sailor's release from prison. Suddenly, Strauss's prelude to 'Im Abenrot' kicks in and the camera moves backwards in a spectacular crane shot to capture the couple in the sun's twilight, caught in an intimate embrace. While Martha Nochimson's observation (1997: 48) that *Wild at Heart* is an anti-road movie generally rings true, this short segment stands in stark contrast with such a view as it celebrates the glory of being on the road. Here the soundtrack perfectly merges with the light palette and the narrative situation. Indeed, it appears as if the voice of Utopia is calling for Lula and Sailor, for Strauss's 'Lied' absorbs the song by Powermad, as Powermad absorbed Glenn Miller earlier in the film. Even more of Strauss's music appears throughout the film occasioned by Utopia's call, and her call is fulfilled at the end of the film: After Sailor rejects his decision to leave Lula and his four-year-old son Pace (Glenn Walker Harris Jr), he is reunited with them again to the music by Strauss, a scene that borders on literal kitsch.[6]

The use of 'Agnus dei' from the Requiem in C minor by Luigi Cherubini in *Fire Walk with Me* differs from the use of 'Im Abendrot' in *Wild at Heart*

in that it is not used as a 'leitmotif'. It only appears upon the murder of
Laura Palmer in the film and during the end credits. This can be ascribed to
a strategic use of music in *Fire Walk with Me* that not only alludes to music
from the television series but also uses new musical elements that deviate
from the series in terms of dramaturgy. Nevertheless, the semantic dimension of the Requiem in *Fire Walk with Me* is certainly comparable to that of
'Im Abendrot' in *Wild at Heart*. 'Agnus dei' is the last chant in the Roman
Catholic mass for the deceased, its full lyrics read:

> Lamb of God, that Thou bearest the guilt of the world, give rest upon Thee.
> Lamb of God, that Thou bearest the guilt of the world, give rest upon Thee.
> Lamb of God, that Thou bearest the guilt of the world, give eternal rest upon Thee.[7]

One should not mistake the use of the 'Agnus dei' for a simple (Christian)
plea for Laura Palmer (Sheryl Lee), though guardian angels do appear
in the film. Rather, it is a symbol that is very differently embedded in
the situation and works against the mythical framework of *Twin Peaks* as
it gradually unfolds in the television series and is expanded in the film.
The music of the 'Agnus dei' begins at the very moment Laura slips the
owl ring, which Mike/Philip Gerard (Al Strobel) had previously thrown
into the railway carriage, onto her finger. Until then, the sound of the
scene was characterised by uncanny, irregular drones. Bob's (Frank
Silva) outcry and exclamation 'No! Don't make me do this!', indicate
that his previous statement that he wanted to 'possess' Laura was meant
literally and not figuratively (in the way that Laura should be obsessed
by him). Since Laura is protected by the ring, this option is not available anymore. In revenge, Bob kills Laura through her father Leland
Palmer (Ray Wise), who continues to be obsessed by him. Laura finds
peace insofar as she is protected from Bob. But the place of this rest is
henceforth the Black Lodge, so there is no eternal rest in the Christian
sense. The music thus stands for a 'supernatural entity' (as Gordon Cole,
portrayed by David Lynch, says in *Twin Peaks: The Return*) or meta-
physical other.

Lynch's most emphatic use of classical music is surely the use of
Penderecki's 'Ofiarom Hiroszimy' in the eighth episode ('Gotta Light?')
of *Twin Peaks: The Return*. Lynch mentioned Penderecki earlier in connection with the possibilities an orchestra has compared to a synthesiser,
'an orchestra can play incredible abstractions and push music towards
sound [. . .] And my favorite guy is Penderecki who writes some really
avantgarde-things. The guy's a heavyweight' (Lynch, quoted in Rodley
2005: 240). These statements certainly also refer to 'Ofiarom Hiroszimy'
in particular. The piece develops its radical disturbing effect by way of

quarter-tone clusters. Although the players are sometimes given only approximate indications (for example at the beginning every instrument is to play as high as possible but the distances between the attacks of the different voices are clearly indicated), it has a high recognition value. This is due to the unusual sound effects achieved by variations in the sound bands of the clusters and unusual playing techniques; most listeners think they hear screams and sirens at the beginning, even though the score was set exclusively for fifty-two strings. 'Ofiarom Hiroszimy' also marked the beginning of Penderecki's international career after it was awarded the Tribune Internationale des Compositeurs by the UNESCO in 1961. By this time, it had also received its final title 'Ofiarom Hiroszimy'; at the premiere in Warsaw in 1961 it was simply announced with the prescribed performance duration '8'37''' (Thomas 2005: 165); incidentally this seems to be a very approximate value, the recording conducted by Penderecki himself (1994) lasts 9'55''. This is important because it makes clear that Penderecki wanted his work to be understood politically in that the extreme elements of the music resemble a human borderline experience, rather than a banal recreation of the Hiroshima bomb as a mere acoustic image. The same holds true for Lynch. He contextualises this music with the first atomic bomb test (code name Trinity, White Sands/NM, July 16, 1945). Further on, Penderecki's music begins precisely with the fireball. But from then on, the camera flies towards the mushroom cloud and dives into it. Inside the cloud the staccato of the visualisations clearly follows the soundscapes and sound fields of the music. Initially there are graspable representations of the nuclear fallout and events on the level of the atomic core, then images follow in an incomprehensible sequence to underline the monstrosity of the event itself. The second metrically clear section (concerning the form of the piece, see Gruhn 1971) of 'Ofiarom Hiroszimy' overlaps with the electrostatic effects at the petrol station before the 'woodsmen' appear. This is quite a clear indication that the 'woodsmen' stand in relation to the atomic bomb test. Likewise, the camera is immersed in the 'cosmic stream' that brings Bob to Earth. At this moment, a short acoustic reprise of 'Ofiarom Hiroszimy' is heard on the soundtrack and again images resembling those from within the mushroom cloud appear. Here, at the latest, the music underlines Lynch's understanding of the Trinity nuclear test as a catastrophe not regarding the extension of human civilisation or planet earth but rather as a watershed moment with cosmic implications.

Lynch's use of Penderecki's music is not limited to *Twin Peaks*. *Inland Empire* features Penderecki's 'Przebudzenie Jakuba' | 'Als Jakob erwachte' ('The Dream of Jacob' or 'The Awakening of Jacob'). The composition is based on a short passage from the Bible preceding Jacob's foundation of the settlement Bethel (Genesis 28, 16–17):

> Then Jacob awoke from his sleep and said, 'Truly the Lord is present in this place without my knowing it!' And trembling he said: 'How terrible this place is. Here is nothing but the house of God and the gate to heaven.'[8]

Even if the musical language of 'Przebudzenie Jakuba' is not as aggressive as that of 'Ofiarom Hiroszimy', the sonority of this orchestral piece emphasises above all Jacob's statement 'How terrible this place is' ('terribilis [. . .] est locus iste'). Accordingly, the divinity of the ostensibly inhospitable place could only be revealed to him in a dream. In *Inland Empire*, excerpts from the composition are used twice. The first excerpt begins when Susan Blue (Laura Dern) is stabbed in the stomach with a screwdriver by Doris Side (Julia Ormond). The music thus initially underlines the horror of the situation. When following the music closely in the editing and camera work of the film, the composition mainly reflects Blue's dwindling strength and her increasingly limited perception until she finally sinks to the ground among some homeless people on the Walk of Fame. Penderecki's music ends here. Blue dies shortly afterwards.

Then the director Kingsley Stewart (Jeremy Irons) shouts: 'And . . . and . . . print it!'. The homeless rise. The Walk of Fame was apparently just a backdrop from *On High in Blue Tomorrows*, a film within a film. Nikki Grace (Laura Dern), who was probably just playing Blue, also rises, thought as if in a trance. At this moment, Penderecki's music starts up again. Grace leaves the set distraught and uncertain. Apparently, she cannot understand the situation. For her, as for Jacob, the essence of the situation no longer emerges from mere appearance (or what is dream and what is reality). This might, on the one hand, support of the film in-between a film interpretation of *Inland Empire* (Grace awakes from her role and experiences the reality of the set confused). On the other hand, the allusion to Jacob might also emphatically discard such an interpretation, for the 'dream' has just shown the true state of the situation and thus renders the film set merely as Blue's deathbed experience.

Looking for the first film by David Lynch to feature Penderecki brings us back to *Wild at Heart*. The piece used here, 'ΚΟΣΜΟΓΟΝΙΑ', is a cantata on the creation of the cosmos, collaging texts from Genesis up to one by Jurij Gagarin, the Soviet cosmonaut. The piece appears three times in *Wild at Heart*, the first time (see also Davison, 2004a: 187–9 and 2004b: 129) at the end of a telephone conversation between Marietta Fortune (Diane Ladd) and her lover, the private detective Johnnie Farragut (Harry

Dean Stanton). In this sequence, it becomes clear how delusional traits increasingly overtake the nature of Fortune, the sociopath. She would like to save Farragut, but the decision to sacrifice him at Marcello Santos's (J. E. Freeman) insistence has already been made. She manages to put up a brave front on the telephone, but what Farragut cannot see is that she has hysterically painted both her entire face and palms with bright red lipstick (and that she vomits directly into the toilet after the phone call – still to the music by Penderecki). The second excerpt appears during the murder of Farragut, which is only shown in an elliptical form.[9] On the third appearance, the first situation repeats itself. Penderecki is heard while Sailor approaches the hut of Perdita Durango (Isabella Rossellini). In the following conversation, she will pretend that she knows nothing about 'a contract' on Sailor (meaning a contract killing).

The selected passages from 'ΚΟΣΜΟΓΟΝΙΑ' are aggressive and characterised by clusters. Seen in this light, it may seem almost too striking to understand this music with its incomprehensible network of merciless psychopathy, from Marietta to Santos to Mr Reindeer (William Morgan Sheppard). 'ΚΟΣΜΟΓΟΝΙΑ', however, differs from pieces like 'Ofiarom Hiroszimy' in that apart from its aggressive sounding passages it also features pleasing ones, since the Latin word 'sol' (sun) is musically composed with a 'clean' chord. Symbolically, the identification of the cluster passages with the chaos before creation is in some way inherent in Penderecki's composition, though Penderecki stated that this sun-chord would be the only passage in the piece where text and music would 'meet' (quoted in Thomas 182).

A (Very Short) Conclusion

Lynch always chooses the music he uses with great consideration. This applies to works of the Western canon as well as to other music. What can be demonstrated with the canonical works discussed here, however, is how much Lynch takes into account any contextual knowledge the spectator might have. To those unfamiliar with Penderecki, 'Ofiarom Hiroszimy' will nevertheless appear as the perfect acoustic backdrop for the Trinity test; those who identify the work will understand the reference to the dropping of the bomb on Hiroshima and the character of a threnody. Those unfamiliar with Strauss's 'Lied' will nevertheless hear a wonderful acoustic rendition of dusk in the prelude, but for those familiar with the 'Lied' as a whole and its lyrics, there is no semantic dissonance with the plot of the film. The initial problem that contextual knowledge of pre-existing music could also obscure an audience's perspective on a film, is always dispelled by Lynch.

Even if the viability of the categories of the diegetic and the non-diegetic has been called into considerable doubt, one must bear in mind that the pieces discussed here are deprived of an essential element of Lynch's films. In Lynch's work, there is always a stage and on it music is always performed in a meaningful way. One should think of the Roadhouse in *Twin Peaks* or Club Silencio in *Mulholland Drive*. Especially in *Twin Peaks: The Return*, Lynch virtually collects the summa of the music of his films and the musicians he worked with in the performances at the Roadhouse (see especially Rogers 253f). Yet neither Cherubini nor Penderecki are performed there. Certainly, this is not meant as a devaluation of this music. As a rule, music from the Western canon serves Lynch to provide access to the deeper 'mythical' essence of what is being shown. Strauss, for example, is a counter-design to the temptation of the devil at the crossroads, and 'Ofiarom Hiroszimy' points to the radically cosmic understanding of the mythology behind *Twin Peaks*. At the same time, however, this also reveals a traditionally romantic notion. Namely, that music, and especially music of high aesthetic quality, can signify something that cannot be signified otherwise.

Bibliography

Adorno, Theodor W[iesengrund]. *Einleitung in die Musiksoziologie. Zwölf theoretische Vorlesungen*. Suhrkamp Verlag, 1962.

Cormick, Mike. 'The Pleasures of Ambiguity: Using Classical Music in Film'. *Changing Tunes: The Use of Pre-existing Music in Film*, Phil Powrie and Robynn Stilwell (eds). Ashgate Publishing, 2006, pp. 19–30.

Davison, Annette. *Hollywood-Theory, Non-Hollywood Practice. Cinema Soundtracks in the 1980s and 1990s*. Ashgate Publishing, 2004a.

Davison, Annette. '"Up in flames": Love, Control and Collaboration in the Soundtrack to Wild at Heart'. *The Cinema of David Lynch. American Dreams, Nightmare Visions*, Erica Sheen and Annette Davison (eds). Wallflower Press, 2004b, pp. 119–35.

Derrida, Jacques. 'Signature Événement Contexte'. Limited Inc. Galilée, 1990, pp. 15–51.

Eichendorff, Joseph von. *Sämtliche Werke. Historisch-kritische Ausgabe*. Wilhelm Kosch (ed.). vol. I, Joseph Haddel, 1856.

Genette, Gérard. 'Discours du récit'. *Figures III*. Éditions du Seuil, 1972, pp. 67–282.

Gifford, Barry. *Wild at Heart: The Story of Sailor and Lula*. Grove Weidenfeld, 1990.

Gifford, Barry. 'Sailor's Holiday'. *Sailor & Lula: The Complete Novels*. Seven Stories Press, 2010a, pp. 251–324.

Gifford, Barry. 'Consuelo's Kiss'. *Ibidem*, 2010b, pp. 401–66.

Goehr, Lydia. *The Imaginary Museum of Musical Works: An Essay in the Philosophy of Music*. Oxford University Press, 1992.

Gorbman, Claudia. *Unheard Melodies. Narrative Film Music*. BFI Publishing and Indiana University Press, 1987.

Gruhn, Wilfried. 'Strukturen und Klangmodelle in Pendereckis 'threnos''. *Melos*, vol. 38, no. 10, 1971, pp. 409–11.

Hainge, Greg. '"When a Door is not a Door? Transmedia to the nth Degree in David Lynch's Multiverse"'. *Transmedia Directors. Artistry, Industry and New Audiovisual Aesthetics*, Carol Vernallis, Holly Rogers and Lisa Perrott (eds). Bloomsbury Academic, 2020, pp. 271–84.

Mazullo, Mark. 'Remembering Pop: David Lynch and the Sound of the 60's'. *American Music*, vol. 23, 2005, pp. 493–513.

Metz, Christian. 'Le cinéma: langue ou langage?' *Communications*, vol. 4, 1964, pp. 52–90.

Miley, Mike. '"David Lynch at the Crossroads: Deconstructing Rock, Reconstructing *Wild at Heart*'. *Music and the Moving Image*, vol. 7, no. 3, 2014, pp. 41–60.

Niedermüller, Peter. '"Jenseits von Hollywood: Musik und Zeichen in David Lynchs *Blue Velvet*'. *musica floreat! Jürgen Blume zum 70. Geburtstag*, Immanuel Ott and Birger Petersen (eds). Are Verlag, 2016, pp. 317–28.

Nochimson, Martha. *The Passion of David Lynch: Wild at Heart in Hollywood*. University of Texas Press, 1997.

Rodley, Chris (ed.). *Lynch on Lynch*. Revised edition. Faber and Faber, 2005.

Rogers, Holly. 'The Audiovisual Eerie: Transmediating Thresholds in the Work of David Lynch'. *Transmedia Directors. Artistry, Industry and New Audiovisual Aesthetics*, Carol Vernallis, Holly Rogers and Lisa Perrott (eds). Bloomsbury Academic, 2020, pp. 241–70.

Souriau, Étienne. 'La structure de l'univers filmique et le vocabulaire de la filmologie'. *Revue internationale de filmologie*, no. 7–8, 1951, pp. 231–40.

Stilwell, Robynn J. 'The Fantastical Gap between Diegetic and Nondiegetic'. *Beyond the Soundtrack: Representing Music in Cinema*, Daniel Goldmark et al. (eds). University of California Press, 2007, pp. 184–202.

Thomas, Adrian. *Polish Music since Szymanowski*. Cambridge University Press, 2005.

Winters, Ben. 'The Non-Diegetic Fallacy: Film, Music, and Narrative Space'. *Music & Letters*, vol. 91, 2010, pp. 224–44.

Filmography

Easy Rider. Directed by Dennis Hopper, performances by Peter Fonda and Dennis Hopper, Pando Company Inc. and Raybert Productions, 1969.

2001: A Space Odyssey. Directed by Stanley Kubrick, performances by Keir Dullea and Gary Lockwood, Metro-Goldwyn-Mayer, 1968.

Full Metal Jacket. Directed by Stanley Kubrick, performances by Matthew Modine and Adam Baldwin, Warner Bros., 1987.

The Elephant Man. Directed by David Lynch, with performances by John Hurt and Anthony Hopkins, Brooksfilms, 1980.

Wild at Heart. Directed by David Lynch, performances by Laura Dern and Nicolas Cage, PolyGram Filmed Entertainment and Propaganda Films, 1990.

Twin Peaks: Fire Walk with Me. Directed by David Lynch, performances by Sheryl Lee and Ray Wise, CIBY Picture, 1992.

Lost Highway. Directed by David Lynch, performances by Bill Pullman and Patricia Arquette, CiBi 2000, Asymmetrical Productions and Lost Highway Productions LCC, 1997.

Mulholland Drive. Directed by David Lynch, performances by Naomi Watts and Laura Harring, Les Films Alain Sarde et al., 2001.

Inland Empire. Directed by David Lynch, performances by Laura Dern and Grace Zabriskie, Studio Canal et al., 2006.

Twin Peaks. Directed by David Lynch et al., performances by Kyle MacLachlan and Mädchen Amick, Lynch/Frost Productions et al., 1990–1.

Twin Peaks: The Return [on DVD and Blu-ray *Twin Peaks: A Limited Event Series*]. Directed by David Lynch, performances by Sheryl Lee and Kyle MacLachlan, Showtime, 2017.

Other Media and Sources Cited

Powermad. *Absolute Power*. Warner Bros and WEA, 1989. CD.

Matrix 5. EMI Classics, 1994. CD.

Notes

1. Compositions by Penderecki mostly appeared in Poland and Germany at the same time. Thus, the German publications (Moeck in Celle and especially Schott in Mainz) bear a German translation of the original title (in the case of Schott's edition of 'ΚΟΣΜΟΓΟΝΙΑ' it is a transcription). In the case of 'Ofiarom Hiroszimy' Schott's German title page swaps the sequence of the dedication and the indication of the genre. In the same print of the score, the Polish dedication appears as headline above the score and 'tren' (meaning threnody, wailing song) in small print appears as an indication of genre over measure one.

2. In the German original: 'Ist dies nun der Tod?'

3. In the original American broadcast, the episodes of the first and second seasons of *Twin Peaks* bore no titles. The titles used later in the English-speaking realm are translations of the titles originally given to the German dubbed version.

4. In the German Original: 'Wir sind durch Not und Freude [|] Gegangen Hand in Hand'.

5. Davison (2004a: 179) interprets this strong musicality of Sailor's character very understandably as an indication that Lynch identifies himself with Sailor. This is also underlined by the fact that Sailor shows no further affinity

to music in the novel on which the screenplay is based. There is also no reference to Powermad (not to mention Strauss). Lula from time to time refers
to music there (Gifford, 1990: 36 or 51). But the most intense discussion on
music is led by minor characters in the novel (ibid. 138–40).

6. Also, here the film deviates from the novel. In the novel, Sailor meets Lula
and Pace after being released from prison and after some words simply walks
away (Gifford, 1990: 158f). He returns to Lula later in the second sequel to
the novel (Gifford, 2010a: 324), originally published one year after the film

7. In the Latin original: 'Agnus Dei, qui tollis peccata mundi, dona eis requiem.
Agnus Dei, qui tollis peccata mundi, dona eis requiem. Agnus Dei, qui tollis
peccata mundi, dona eis requiem sempiternam.'

8. In the Latin version according to the Vulgate: 'Evigilasset Iacob de somno
ait vere Dominus est in loco isto et ego nesciebam. Pavensque quam terribilis
inquit est locus iste non est hic aliud nisi domus Dei et porta caeli.'

9. This is another deviation from the novel. Farragut not only survives the pur-
suit of Sailor and Lula in the novel, but in its fourth sequel – also originally
published one year after the film – he, though old and ill himself, also survives
Santos with whom he became finally friends (Gifford, 2010b: 465f).

CHAPTER 2

Turn and Face the Strange:
Changing Faces in the Cinema of Lynch

Mads Outzen

'To me, mystery is like a magnet [. . .] It can become an obsession', David Lynch once said about his own work (Rodley 2005: 231).[1] To me, the mystery of the face seems to have a key role in this obsession, one that is central to both the expression and our experience of his cinema. In his first short film, the aptly titled animated painting *Six Figures Getting Sick* (1967), spectators are confronted with six strange faces that convulse, vomit and combust in repeat to the sound of sirens. Indeed, I would argue that this early experiment anticipates one of the most distinctive and disconcerting forces of Lynch's filmography: his manner of playing with and making strange the face.

Every face in *Eraserhead* is estranging, and similar tendencies seem to be a presence in differing ways and to varying degrees in all his later films. Deformities and otherworldly features return in *The Elephant Man* (1980) and *Dune* (1984), mysterious and monstrous attributes surface in *Blue Velvet* (1986) and *Wild at Heart* (1990), and even *The Straight Story* (1999) arguably has almost as many unfamiliar and unconventional facial close-ups as more straightforward ones. *Twin Peaks* (1990), *Twin Peaks: Fire Walk with Me* (1992), and perhaps especially *Twin Peaks: The Return* (2017), are seemingly haunted by surreal or supernatural appearances, while faces in *Lost Highway* (1997), *Mulholland Drive* (2001) and *Inland Empire* (2006) come to change as aesthetic ideas and narrative identities connect and collide with one another. As we face Lynch's films, it always seems like strange faces have found us.

When I speak of strangeness here and say that it makes sense to speak of a certain Lynchian 'faciality', what I mean is that these faces create new sensations that are other or otherwise than the way we ordinarily make sense of a face. Perhaps more precisely, my key proposition is that Lynch's 'face mystery' is fundamental to the 'feeling' of his films, and furthermore that it mediates how we as spectators may understand them. This chapter therefore explores both a special mode of intermediality, namely the relationship between the medium of film and the medium of the face, and a specific form of a visually representative network that addresses the interrelations between affects and ethics. In this sense, my approach starts from a particular idea of *aisthesis*, or that our sensuous encounters with cinematic faces open a sensibility in perception that comes before and goes beyond our logical comprehension. Even more concretely, following a more general look at the faces of Lynch, I then introduce some of Emmanuel Levinas's ideas about ethics and the face and Gilles Deleuze's ideas on affects and the face in film, before considering what a difference a face makes in the specific cases of *Lost Highway* and *Mulholland Drive*.

David Lynch at Face Value

'You have a very interesting face', Lynch said to the statuette in his hand at the end of his acceptance speech after receiving an Honorary Oscar in 2019, once again revealing his fascination with faces. Of course, many filmmakers love the face and the close-up, and cinema itself is in many ways an art of the face.[2] Yet Lynch stands out among most for his fascination with what faces can do as well as his facility for what can be done with them. There are many interesting faces in his films, and his films would not be as interesting if they were missing these many faces. Imagining any version of *Twin Peaks* without seeing a haunting close-up image of the face of Laura Palmer seems almost impossible, which to me is one good example of the importance of faces in Lynch's cinematic worlds. An affective description of his work of visual representation is beyond words like so many aspects of Lynch's cinema, these are expressions to be experienced.

At first sight, there are still prefacing things to say about the various facial arrangements within his films. There are overtly scary faces, such as the grotesque guises of the Mystery Man, the Bum and the manifestations of the Phantom, or psychotic but horrifyingly human-looking figures such as Frank Booth, Bobby Peru and the materializations of Killer Bob. These faces certainly affect us, they make us jump, squirm or just feel generally fearful or 'freaked out'. Others are eye-catchingly strange faces, like the creatively named Lady in the Radiator and the Man from Another Place, or the many other appearances of unusual figures in most of Lynch's films. Those faces clearly affect us too, but probably more than anything else just by moving us into states of feeling bewildered or 'weirded out'.

Stranger and perhaps even scarier, however, are what can be called the 'changing' faces of Lynch's films. These are those faces that, like the owls, are not what they seem. By this I specifically mean where a character deviates from what has been imaged or what we have imagined them to be, to become another or rather an 'other'. These are those curious cases where faces seem to be disrupted and disturbed by the way 'the repressed cease-lessly keeps returning in distorted and destructive form,' as Anne Jerslev has written so well ((1991: 27, my translation). Whether we consider the elusive dualities and even 'triplicities' in the *Twin Peaks* universe, or the equivocal physiognomies of Fred Madison/Pete Dayton, Betty Elms/ Diane Selwyn and Nikki Grace/Susan Blue, these are faces that at first are taken at face value. Thus, such a 'turn of face' potentially affects us in ways that have more lasting effects.

A central reason for this is that faces like these, unlike the owls, belong to focal characters who remain our focus within their cinematic worlds. To be sure, all the other faces that we encounter have crucial support-ing roles for both affective sensation and narrative sense, but it is first and foremost the faces of protagonists or prominent figures whose trans-formations may change what and even how we see. This is to say that faces play the lead and key part in the way Lynch's films instigate and, as Todd McGowan puts it, 'implicate the spectator in their very structure' to 'confront one with sequences that reveal one's own investment in what one sees', something that 'alters the cinematic viewing situation itself' (McGowan 2007: 2). In the most basic sense, my argument is that what is strangest and maybe also scariest about these changing faces are not the facial changes themselves, but that they may change our very way of see-ing faces as well as watching the films.

Whereas there are many thematic readings that deal with these 'Janus-faced' elements primarily as part of some more or less superfi-cial puzzle-box mystery, postmodern irony or performative absurdity, to me this multifaceted, or even multifaced, facial carousel seems far more subversive yet sincere. Of course, there are several theoretical perspec-tives, among them Jerslev on the uncanny and surreal and McGowan on fantasy and desire, that partially relate to my position.[3] However, I want to offer another framework, which is alternative yet not antagonistic. Indeed, my interest here is not only in the cognitive work of interpreta-tion, but also more in the workings of corporeal sensation that precedes and perhaps also precludes it. This also means that I attend to another form of analysis, abstract rather than academic, to try to evoke the film encounter itself.

In his so-called 'Lynch-Kit', Michel Chion asserts that the 'ear and hearing are at the core of Lynch's cinema' (Chion 2006: 159). Although I would concur that this is the case, I will here contend that there is a case for the face and seeing to form another core, one that beckons us to explore well beyond either being motifs or metaphors.

Beyond the Face of It

There is something about the face. As the most important site for our interpersonal relationships with other people, even our key component for social contact and communication, the face is fundamental as a medium. By the same token the face confronts us as a conundrum, that is as something always more than meets the eye, something that can never be fully grasped at once. Whatever the case may be, or whomever it may concern, faces do something to us – our bodies and our minds. In the following pages, this something will be further explored through two apposite philosophical approaches to the doing and being of the face.

What the face is and does, according to Emmanuel Levinas, is essentially ethical. 'Ethics' here specifically refers to an interminable relation between the self and a sense of responsibility. It is a node in an irreducible structure of intersubjectivity that exists between human beings and that is emanant from 'the face'. When facing a face, we encounter a face in its sensible appearance, yet at the same time also a face that sense-ably signifies from beyond, from a 'who', the absolute alterity of another, or 'the other'. This Levinasian face, if you will, manifests in tensions between the concrete and the abstract, visible and invisible, phenomenal and transcendental; it is there and not there, through which 'the idea of infinity, the infinitely more contained in the less, is concretely produced in the form of a relation with the face' (1979: 195–200). For Levinas, the face reveals its meaning as it repeals and resists our possession and power, to open up a new dimension before us – an ethical dimension.

Hence, in this essential sense: every face has an ethics. Encountering the face is an event as estranging as it is familiar. Ordinarily, according to Levinas, we receive the world only with reference to ourselves, represent others as a reflection of ourselves, and reduce them to themes, objects or roles in relation to ourselves. Through our own ego-logical processes of identification and interpretation, that is our habitual gaze upon the face, we assimilate and appropriate otherness to sameness. What this means is that we see others as other selves, whether viewed as similar or different from ourselves, and therefore do not really see others as other (Levinas 1979: 121–7). While the face finds us, disturbs us and demands something from us, this epiphany of the face necessitates a welcome for its teaching to be realised. In short, the ethics of the face is a potential.

Such a potential may be conceived of as a problem of perception, position or even posture, given that, here in the specific sense of Levinas, 'ethics is an optics' (1979: 23). Specifically, we may see this as two ways of seeing. The one is seeing what we 'want' to see, turning 'from' the face and thus making the other the same, or 'into' ourselves. The other is seeing that we 'cannot' see, turning 'towards' the face and thus taking the other as other, or 'upon' ourselves. How we see, wherein seeing also is feeling, is therefore how the expression of the face, without needing any face as such, possibly turns or transforms into a 'true experience of the *new*' (ibid.: 50). The being of the face is precisely as a being, a being whose doing is to incite and invite us to a 'relation without relation' (ibid.: 80), that is an ethical relationship or encounter, one that is the foundation of another understanding.[4]

Meanwhile, as per Levinas, the face is not an image, as the immediate and imperative disturbance of a face cannot be fixed but is discovered by the face disrupting fixation. While Levinas mainly writes of mental and not mediated images, the key contention remains that any intermediary means of seeing is already set, whence sense and meaning are ready-made. An image of the face cannot be faced by us and thus face us (Levinas 1979: 262–3). However, informed by Levinas-inspired scholar Hagi Kenaan (2021: xv–xx), my view is that images can be 'facings' too, facing like faces do, and by their manner of facing have a power to 'shake the eye' as well as a potential to make or take us towards a way of seeing 'otherwise'. Ultimately, this is to say that the face of an image can also face and thus be faced by us, and that there is therefore much more to what the cinematic face can be and do.

What the face in film is and does, according to Gilles Deleuze, is basically affective. 'Affect' here concretely attends to intimate relations of affectivity, as intense events that act upon our sensibility, that exist between cinematic images and its spectators, and that are empowered by the close-up, that is 'the affection-image'. When facing a face in film, what we encounter is a film image in its material appearance, yet also a film image that materialises as a face, affects us as a face and confronts us as 'faceified' ('visagifiée', see Deleuze 1986: 89). This Deleuzian face is, so to speak, a complete facial expression and experience: 'there is no-close-up *of* the face, the face is in itself close-up, the close-up is by itself face and both are affect, affection-image' (88, emphasis in original). According to Deleuze, the face in film generates certain affective qualities or powers. Thus, from images come movements of affect that are mobilised through moments of affection for spectators.

To use another turn of phrase: any face has its affects, but cinematic faces both magnify and modify their effects, that is the power of the face to move us. For Deleuze, in paraphrase of both Béla Balázs and Jean Epstein, the close-up abstracts the face from space and time, and extracts its expression to reveal its being – 'the feeling-thing' (Epstein, quoted in Deleuze 1986: 96). Face and affect, in this sense, form a set of expression and expressed, which remain separate entities while in a mutual relationship with each other. This set of 'face–affect', in that sense, manifests in and of itself. Such a doing furthermore displaces or disfigures the functions of a face as an individuating, socialising and communicating entity, and replaces or refigures its facing as the strange, unfamiliar and uncanny face of another, or the other (Deleuze 1986: 95–100). Yet, the face is not effaced to become nothingness. It is rather defaced as what we can see as a role or character of some different self to be refaced as who we can feel as the self of someone else – it mediates otherness.

Such a power may again be clearly conceptualised as an affective potential of how the poetics of a film can change our optics of a face, based in the idea that '*The affection-image is the close-up, and the close-up is the face*' (Deleuze 1986: 87, emphasis in original). Specifically, we may well take this to mean that cinematic faces are able to make us feel in ways that remake the very way we see a face. As we encounter a face on film, affection is realised in perception or, in other words, feeling becomes seeing (ibid.: 101–7). This is an affective event of sensing the possible otherness of others, and thus it is also an ethically coded experience. To be sure, Deleuze suggests that virtually all close-ups can do this, even those not actually composed of faces. Crucially, however, it is still the figure of the face that is seen as key to allowing for new understandings.[5]

There is something about the cinematic face. A key element for engagement and estrangement, the face in film is foundational both as medium and mystery. What the cinematic face does is bound up with both the affects and ethics of the space between the face of the image and the gaze of the spectator. In what follows, this relationship of face and gaze will be explored by way of the changing faces in the cinema of Lynch.

On a Dark Deranged Highway

After its atmospheric opening credits sequence, the first frames of *Lost Highway* present a close-up shot of a face. Surrounded by the darkness of the frame, and a droning ambient soundtrack, at first the man's face is illuminated only by the source light of a burning cigarette, before window blinds open to reveal its obscure expression. An intercom buzzes, and the man slowly walks over, presses the button to listen and hears the message 'Dick Laurent is dead'. He proceeds to walk over to the window to look out, as we hear what seems like the screeching of tyres and the sound of sirens, but he sees no one. The shot then shifts to the exterior, where we see the man in the window and then an establishing shot of the house, before it fades to black. As an introduction, one that later changes when we watch it unfold from a different point of view in the conclusion, this sequence is key to the film experience not only in the sense of narrative meaning but also in the sense of the affective meaning of the face.

Subsequently, as spectators we learn that this face belongs to jazz musician Fred Madison and that he lives in the house together with his wife Renee. The early scenes of them as a couple leave us with the idea that all is not well between the two. While this provides a point of entry to connect some exposition to the first and following facial expressions, these connections are tenuous and come with a sense that all is not what it seems. This feeling is soon reinforced when the couple discovers video tapes of their house, first filmed from outside and then from inside. More so, however, it is reiterated by images and voices about a dream, with Fred speaking over shots of himself looking around the house at night and Renee screaming as she is apparently attacked. These images fade only to show Fred as he wakes and looks over to see the face of a man superimposed over Renee's face.

The face of the unnamed man – who later appears as Mystery Man in the end credits – makes an unsettling return at a party scene. There this figure seems to be able to fade out everything and everyone around them and introduces himself to Fred, and to us, by asking: 'We've met before, haven't we?'. This line is the beginning of a strange conversation. Therein the man claims to be at Fred's house while being there with him, encouraging him to call home only to find out that the man is telling the truth. This line is also the start for our face-to-face gaze at a white-powdered, ghostly countenance, almost like a black hole and blank canvas at once. Affectively, with his pale and wrinkled skin, dark and intense eyes, menacing smile and maniacal laugh, what we face are sensations that resonate with an already intense and increasing sense that something is rotten along the road. Narratively, what is faced is also a catalyst for distinct changes in the diegesis itself and to our spectatorial relationship to its protagonist, as following this brief and impossible encounter it seems both Fred and his world disintegrate. While faces in the film are estranging from the first scene, this face turns us towards facing strange things.

First, this otherness forms as implicit impression. When we face Fred next, in moments of him looking around the house that are reminiscent of those of his earlier dream, the sensations emanating from his facial expressions dramatically change. Hearing a strange sound, he walks into the darkness and out of the frame. Fred's initial frightened face gradually fades into a menacing one as he walks back out of the darkness to what sounds like warped screams, changing the spectator's impression of Fred as someone in potential danger to someone who is potentially dangerous. Whereas it may not make any narrative sense, these affective sensations reverberate as Fred discovers a video tape documenting himself covered in blood right by Renee's dismembered body in their bedroom. Fred is arrested, found guilty of murder, and sentenced to death, all the while he pleads his case that he cannot remember anything.

Then, that otherness transforms to explicit expression. While in his cell, he has a vision of a cabin, where the Mystery Man resides and where time seems to work in reverse, before the lights flicker and a crackle of electricity brings us back to the highway of the opening sequence. What follows is a montage of fragmented and frantic close-up shots; Fred twisting and turning, haunted by horrifying memories of murder, and the face of another man – who we hear called to as Pete – standing and staring at some unseen event that engulfs him in blue light and thick smoke. For a moment, Fred and Pete's faces seem to face one another, in a movement where they face us in turn before they both fade away. In the next scene, we are taken into the cell and to a close-up not of Fred but Pete's face, fully different yet with similar cuts and bruises. Before our eyes and ears, it seems Fred has transformed into Pete and has been transfigured into a changed face – and we are transported into another place.

We soon learn that this face belongs to a young car mechanic named Pete Dayton who lives at home with his parents. In this other world, Pete was apparently involved in some unmentioned or unmentionable episode. He meets a violent gangster called Mr Eddy – who we later come to know as Dick Laurent – and his lover Alice, a blond mirror image of Fred's wife Renee. This new exposition reorients the world of the film, and the new expression that emerges from a changed face contributes to a sense of mystery and hidden meanings. This sense is crystallised through hallucinations in which Pete is beset by dreamlike and delirious images similar to those Fred had before. Pete, like Fred, pleads to his parents and the police that he cannot remember anything.

In Pete's space, no superimposed face comes to the surface, but faces still continue to impose themselves upon us. As troublesome doubles that both further and frustrate our understanding of the state of things, Renee's face is a copy of Alice's and Fred's face is continuously and curiously linked with Pete's. We as spectators may well make sense of the strangeness of this defacing and refacing of both characters and characteristics of the film – as the composition also changes[6] – in terms of trying to think it through. However, any such attempt to fixate these visual secrets through our habitual gaze is soon undone by an unaltered face, that of the Mystery Man. His distressing and disturbing presence forebodingly returns in a phone call, where he reintroduces himself to us, and to Pete, with words we have also heard before: 'We've met before, haven't we?'. This line starts another strange conversation. Herein, the man repeats the first sentences he previously spoke to Fred and then tells tales of death sentences in the 'Far East'. Hereto, the camera once more positions the audience to look into the unblinking eyes of an unearthly expression. Once again, this face provides a heightened sense that there is horror on this highway, while also prompting our new protagonist to disappear, once more turning us onwards to face stranger things.

Soon, Pete and Alice go to the house of Alice's friend Andy, who was also a friend of Renee, to rob him and then run away together. Here, Pete kills Andy by accident, finds a framed photograph of Alice and Renee together and sees a screened pornographic film starring both of them. A dazed Pete then seems to stumble through a doorway into another dimension. Suddenly, the setting turns into a hotel hallway and he walks in on Alice or Renee having sex with another man. As soon as he closes the door to the room, a close-up follows, in which we are to watch Pete's expression as he shakes and shivers all the while the shot is shrouded in blue flashes of light mimicking electricity. At this moment, Pete's face alters into one we feel we have seen before. Such strange sensations of déjà vu only continue as Pete and Alice drive out to the desert to the cabin in the vision shared by Fred and Pete and make love to the same siren song that Fred and Renee did before them, even doubling the expressions of their faces.

Thus, it is not all so sudden that Pete now transforms back into Fred, nor a surprise that the Mystery Man returns to tell him and us as spectators that Alice is Renee. We have aesthetically sensed and we have affectively realised this, but if we narratively begin to deduce or reduce such an understanding, faces again return to muddle our mastery over the mystery. Fred is chased by the Mystery Man's camera-gaze and arrives at Pete's dream-place, the 'Lost Highway Hotel', where he sees Renee cheating on him with Dick Laurent, after which he kidnaps and later kills him. How this happens, however, is that the Mystery Man returns and hands Fred a knife to slash his hostage's throat, then shoots him dead himself, only to vanish and leave the weapon in Fred's hand. The Mystery Man's face is once again a chilling sensuous climax as he pulls the actual trigger, which also acts like a final call or virtual trigger to turn inwards and face the strangest thing.

There exists a common tendency to analyse the above scenes by way of rationalised interpretations, closing the mysterious loopholes of the film through logic. It is tempting, for example, to make sense of the film in terms of psychoanalysis, doppelgangers and parallel worlds, or dream-frames and mind-games. While such approaches have their place, we may sooner learn to stop making sense and to let ourselves be lost in sensation following a kind of intuition. By confronting the film's changing faces, we may potentially come to understand that figuring out the mystery of the film is a senseless obsession, since the key is the very question, and that the true mystery is the insoluble mystery of the face as other. Thus, as strange as that may sound – indeed, to quote Fred instead, that 'that's fucking crazy, man' – faces are not only made strange, but themselves make strange, as faces that do not only change, but themselves change our way of seeing the face and the film itself.

This is precisely how the affective poetics of the face give way to an ethical optics. In the end, when the deranged face of Fred speaks those very words into the intercom which the seemingly depressed face of Fred hears in the beginning, before quickly running away and driving off to flee the arriving police to what is now also seen as the screeching of tyres and sound of sirens, the film does not come full circle. Rather, with a new point of view, the affective meaning of the face changes narrative meaning as well. Before the final credits roll, *Lost Highway* closes with a close-up shot of Fred's face, one that we can see and yet we cannot see, the face of an other. In *Lost Highway*, Lynch makes faces agents not for disclosure, but for disturbance, ceaselessly facing us with sensations that leave no leeway to look away, but that break the spell of our gaze and direct us to turn towards the film's strange change of face.

Like Dreams Drive You Mad

In *Mulholland Drive*, Lynch makes similar but different moves, lulling us into false sense-making security before pulling the rug – or rather the red curtain – out from under our gaze. During the opening minutes of the film, jazzy music and dancing shadows collide in a collage of people doing the jitterbug against a violet background. Suddenly, shining light fills the frame and a smiling girl is superimposed on the scene and steps into the foreground. Her close-up face dissolves into unfocused shots establishing the interior of a room alongside an elderly couple and the sound of clapping and whistling. Therein, the camera lurks around and tracks towards a bed, accompanied by unlocalisable low-frequency atmospheric noise. Eventually, the camera tilts down to reveal a red pillow and moves into it as the shot fades back to black.[7] Anyone who has watched and thought about the film would probably agree on the importance of this introduction to its story, but my consideration here is the face of the girl, since this is the girl that gives face to the film as an experience. This superimposed expression is the happiest one that we see, but it ultimately turns out to be the saddest one.

Following the film's opening sequence, we learn that this joyful countenance belongs to Betty Elms, a talented, enthusiastic small-town hopeful
who comes to Hollywood to follow her dream of stardom. When she arrives
at her aunt's apartment, Betty finds Rita, an amnesiac hiding there after
having survived a car accident, one that we are aware was an attempted
murder. In Rita, Betty finds herself the perfect mystery. Together the two
follow the fascinating white rabbit of Rita's identity, a journey into won-
derland in which they find a corpse and fall in love. On the face of it,
Betty, who from the outset is the focal character of the film, stays our
picture-perfect alter ego. She is who we 'know', or whose 'role' in this
world seems to be knowable, and who becomes our 'partner in crime' in
seeking its secrets. Yet, there lurks a clear and lingering sense that something is wrong with this picture or, as Louise Bonner says within the film
itself, that 'someone is in trouble', that 'something bad is happening'.

In *Mulholland Drive*, faces are the foundation of that feeling. From
the earliest scenes, we are faced with strange and scary faces: the wickedly
smiling old couple Betty meets at the airport, the horrific looking hobo
behind Winkie's, and the shady figures that seem involved with Rita's
failed assassination and the cowboy-led conspiratorial casting of Adam
Kesher's film. In contrast to the many unsettling faces of the film, Betty's
face is a 'safe haven'; a face that, so often emphasised through elegantly
composed close-ups, functions as an emotional source of confidence for
our engagement, and a face that supports our sense-making understanding of her as a subject and another self. This relationship is also precisely
why it is so effective, or rather affective, when her face changes, as it soon
turns into a site for encountering troubling doubling.

First, when Betty and Rita follow the lead of a woman's name and discover a rotting female body, their faces begin to blend. In a scene full of sus-
pense, the shock of the corpse ends with a silent shot of Rita running out
screaming, with Betty following suit, after which their facial images fold
into one another and continue to double each other in the following scenes.
At first sight, this mirroring of looks may seem both incidental and innoc-
uous. Yet, it simultaneously feels like a warning sign. Such a sense soon
shows itself to be significant as Rita starts to speak in her open-eyed sleep,
repeating sentences in Spanish and steadily saying the word 'silencio'.

Then, after she awakes, the stage is set for awakenings, when Rita takes
Betty – and us – to confront sensuous culmination in the mysterious 'Club
Silencio'. There a man, credited as the Magician, shouts from the prosce-
nium arch in front of a red curtain: '¡No hay banda! There is no band. Il
n'y a pas d'orchestre! This is all a tape recording.' He continues: '¡No hay
banda! And yet . . . We hear a band'. He introduces a clarinet, a trombone,

a trumpet, whose sounds do not line up with the images we see. 'It is . . . an illusion'. Suddenly, after the camera captures a quick glimpse of the puzzling face of a blue-haired lady on a balcony, the man summons thunder and lightning and disappears into smoke with a smile on his face, while blue light engulfs the theatre. What follows is an exceptional performance by Rebekah del Rio, in close-up, doing a Spanish-language a cappella version of Roy Orbison's 'Crying', with her body shockingly falling dead on the stage as the song goes on.

One of the most striking aspects of this scene is its faciality. In 'Club Silencio', close-ups of the faces of Betty and Rita continuously return to face us as spectators, and the affects that emerge from Betty's face effectively change how we see it. At first her face seems entirely spellbound, then soon terrified as she starts shaking, and in the end wounded as she starts crying excessively. As indecipherable as the changes in Betty's face seem, it allows us to understand intuitively what was wrong with the picture, and that we are looking at the face of someone who is in trouble, that is the one something bad is happening to, and that the two are in fact crying over her. Before we see the illusion break, we feel it instinctively. That is, ahead of being revealed narratively the broken illusion is already realised affectively. Beyond all these facial expressions, what faces us is the strangeness and the otherness of the gaze of the face.

This cinematic facing is a certain point of no return, where Betty's face turns from a 'window' to a 'doorway' into a new dimension. When the transformation then takes place, as Betty and Rita disappear, we are transported by way of a blue key box and through a mysterious cinematographic metamorphosis to another space. There, we enter a room we have been in and encounter a body we have seen before. Here, we face the similar yet different face of Betty.[8] We have grown accustomed to her face, but now it grows unknown. We have felt certain about her face, but now it feels unclear. We have seen ourselves in her face, but now we see otherwise. That is to say that her changed face opens up a changing gaze for us, or another optics, one accompanied by another poetics too as the aesthetic, even the face, of the film also changes alongside it.

The final sequence of the film reveals that this joyless countenance belongs to Diane Selwyn, a failed, disenchanted small-town hopeful who came to Hollywood to follow a dream of stardom. After she arrived in the big city, she found Camilla, an actress and a lover, and in Camilla she found herself a profound misery. Although through flashbacks and fantasies, we arguably fall down the rabbit hole of another story altogether, one of love and innocence lost, betrayal and jealousy, anger and shame, where Diane possibly commits murder by proxy and perhaps eventually suicide by psychosis. As Diane's delusion falls apart, so does our own illusion, that is as her imagination disintegrates so does our image of her; in this sense, what dies is really both her and our dreams.

Faces are fundamental to that understanding. In the subsequent scenes, we face familiar faces turned unfamiliar, encounter bodies unbounded as doubles, and are introduced to figured identities here unidentified. Headlined by doe-eyed and docile Rita returning as the dominant Camilla, most characters and roles we have encountered so far come back as both more and less scary or strange than they were before. Again, yet in another way, these faces and their affects, in the confusion they produce for us as spectators, also reiterate our relation to Diane. In her face, we now find 'no quarter'; a face that, repeatedly highlighted in heartbreakingly created close-ups, works as an affective source of estrangement that yet is also strangely a call to compassion, and a face that subverts our sense-making understanding of her as subject to ourselves, to instead see an other. This relation or troubled encounter is thus potentially one of responsibility.

This is to say that in the face of this otherness of expression, we as spectators are not only faced with a strangely changed face, nor do we only face the feeling that Betty may have been Diane's alter ego, her dreamed duplicate or her simulated self. Rather, we may realise that we made her ours, that we have seen what we wanted to see and seen her how we wanted her to be, and in this way that we could not and still cannot see. That is to say, if we face this otherness of experience, it is also to confront ourselves and change our way of facing itself. Now, as we are wont to do, we might begin making sense of the film's magnetising mysteries, finding missing and fitting misshapen pieces in a synthesis of signs and symbols – or a popular game of ashtrays and lamps, boxes and keys, and beds and pillows – fixing meaning after the fact. Before the face, meanwhile, already there are meaningful sensations felt by and only for themselves, which may turn our mind's eye towards seeing otherwise.

No matter how we make sense of the narrative mystery of the film, the affective mystery of the face still remains confined to the senses. On the surface, the climactic finale, from sounds of broken glass and a moment of madness that resounds from a broken heart and broken dreams, through delirious screams and demonic spectres, to a shot gone up in smoke, may once more confound our comprehension. In the face, however, there is ethical understanding. While ideas of fantasy and reality, alternate universes and dual identities, or streams of dreams from the realms of death may fade away, the expression of the face, of the other as other, endures to make us see that it is mystery in itself.

In the closing minutes of *Mulholland Drive*, a musical theme accompanies a montage of faces. Smiling bright in shining light, two-faced close-ups of Betty and Rita, Diane and Camilla, or all of the above, fade into frame, foregrounding different images of the city, shots that soon after dissolve onto the face of one alone. As image and music both fade out, the blue luminescence of the surreptitious club stage enters the scene, gradually fading away to face us with its red curtains, before the face of the blue-haired lady appears to whisper: 'silencio'. Like its introduction, anyone who has seen and speculated about the film would likely point to the significance of this conclusion to the story told, but once more my concern here is the face of this girl, since this is the girl facing us through the film. This 'superexposed' face in the end becomes the most imposing one, if we take upon ourselves the fate of the other.

Face Mystery in David Lynch

Lost Highway and *Mulholland Drive*, for all their similarities and differences in subject, structure and style, clearly echo each other as both being an 'about-face'. While the faster estranging highway of the former and the slower drive into strangeness of the latter deviate from one another in terms of the way we watch the films themselves, what figures at the core of the turn to the strange or the change of course in both is the face. There are many interesting faces in these films, yet the most interesting difference that the faces of their focal characters of Fred/Pete and Betty/Diane make is that they thoroughly confront our gazes as spectators. Their changing faces are disturbing first and foremost because they become disillusioning encounters.

My case is thus that Lynch puts to full use the force of the face as a medium and a mystery, or medium for mystery, and does so in a manner that potentially mediates our encounters with the films themselves. By way of what may well be called a certain means of aisthesis, these cinematic faces realise affects, in the sense of Deleuze, that lead us towards facing, in the sense of Levinas, the ethics of the face. In brief, what I have attempted to approach here is the possibility of a sensibility that is simultaneously prior to and past our reasoning, which is also precisely the reason it resists clear-cut articulation in words. However, it remains both present and resonant in Lynch's cinematic worlds. Thus, in lieu of any conclusion, this is rather an introduction to another and also possibly strange way of seeing Lynch's work, one that has explored a special mode of intermediality and a specific form of network, towards taking a closer look at otherness as an aesthetic, affective and ethical 'face-to-face' with film.

To me, face mystery is like a magnet in Lynch, as one that is essential to both the expression and our experience of his films and one that opens a potential for us to face the mystery of the other. While this faciality does take many forms, what these cinematic faces do is make us feel something that may also change our way of facing. That something is what this chapter has tried to trace: a making strange by way of changing faces that is also, in the end, a making 'see'. Seeing this something, as we turn and face the strange meaning of the face, is to be faced by, as Lynch says on a more general note, 'its mystery and the potential for a vast, infinite experience' (Cozzolino and Rockwell 2014: 40).[9]

Notes

1. To give the quote in full: 'To me, mystery is like a magnet. Whenever there is something that's unknown, it has a pull to it. If you were in a room and there was an open doorway, and stairs going down and the light just fell away, you'd be very tempted to go down there. When you only see a part, it's even stronger than seeing the whole. The whole might have a logic, but out of its context, the fragment takes on a tremendous value of abstraction. It can become an obsession' (Rodley 2005: 231).

2. Since the beginnings of film and the emergence of thinking about film, the face and the close-up have been at the core of cinema both as a medium and an art form. For some contemporary works that explore ideas about the facial close-up all the way from the earliest theory to the cinema of today see, for example, the excellent books from Steimatsky (2017) and Doane (2021).

3. Here the phrases referenced from Jerslev and McGowan in the previous two paragraphs are moved into a somewhat different context, while honouring original intentions. Both scholars have written much on Lynch, and the former also has a forthcoming book on his work anticipated this year, but for this text these words are those most appropriate to my own approach.

4. Otherwise, Levinas's ideas on ethics and the face are more comprehensive as well as complex. This is a simplified and shortened version intentionally limited to one of his major works, but still arguably builds on both another central one and key essays as well (see bibliography) as nearly all of his writings deal with the ethical meaning of the face and our responsibility for the other in one way or another.

5. Likewise, Deleuze's ideas on affects and the face in film also concern and connect with others in his earlier as well as later works, as well as reworks ones both from Balázs and Epstein (see bibliography). This is a sort of summary of some points that purposely stays within the outline of his specific writing on the close-up, the affection-image, or the cinematic face.

6. Like *Mulholland Drive*, it is not only the narrative that changes with the face but the aesthetic of the film. From different lighting and colouring in the

mise-en-scène to differing camera movements and cutting modes, the composition also goes through a certain metamorphosis, one that merits its own exploration and therefore is not elaborated more in this one.

7. As its antecedent, this is indeed not intended as any frame-by-frame description of how Lynch portrays faces in the film, nor a walkthrough of its shots, scenes and sequences, but instead aims to approach by approximation the way face encounters in the space between images and spectators possibly 'remakes' the very way we may make sense of it all.

8. Unlike *Lost Highway*, of course, where the changing face of our focal characters is an interchanging of actors, between Bill Pullman and Balthazar Getty, here one actress, Naomi Watts, is the face of both. Exploring what difference this makes is another interesting avenue, but one that is outside the scope of this short study.

9. To give the full quote: 'It's better not to know so much about what things mean or how they might be interpreted or you'll be too afraid to let things keep happening. . . Psychology destroys the mystery, this kind of magic quality. It can be reduced to certain neuroses and certain things, and since it is now named and defined, it's lost its mystery and the potential for a vast, infinite experience.' (Cozzolino and Rockwell 2014: 40).

Bibliography

Balázs, Béla. *Theory of the Film: Character and Growth of a New Art.* Translated by Edith Bone. Dennis Dobson Ltd, 1952.

Chion, Michel. *David Lynch*, 2nd edition, translated by Robert Julian. BFI, 2006.

Cozzolino, Robert and Alethea Rockwell. *David Lynch: The Unified Field.* Pennsylvania Academy of the Fine Arts, 2014.

Deleuze, Gilles. *Cinema 1: The Movement-Image.* Translated by Hugh Tomlinson and Barbara Habberjam, University of Minnesota Press, 1986.

Epstein, Jean. 'Bonjour Cinema and Other Writings'. Translated by Tom Milne, *Afterimage*, no. 10, 8–39, 1981.

Doane, Mary Ann. *Bigger than Life: The Close-up and Scale in the Cinema.* Duke University Press, 2021.

Jerslev, Anne. *David Lynch i vore øjne.* Frydenlund, 1991.

Jerslev, Anne. *David Lynch: Blurred Boundaries.* Springer, 2021.

Kenaan, Hagi. *The Ethics of Visuality: Levinas and the Contemporary Gaze.* Translated by Batya Stein. I. B. Tauris, 2021.

Levinas, Emmanuel. *Totality and Infinity: An Essay on Exteriority.* 2nd edition, translated by Alphonso Lingis. Martinus Nijhoff Publishers, 1979.

Levinas, Emmanuel. *Otherwise than Being: or, Beyond Essence.* Translated by Alphonso Lingis. Martinus Nijhoff Publishers, 1981.

Levinas, Emmanuel. *Collected Philosophical Papers.* Translated by Alphonso Lingis. Martinus Nijhoff Publishers, 1987.

McGowan, Todd. *The Impossible David Lynch.* Columbia University Press, 2007.

Rodley, Chris (ed.). *On Lynch*. 2nd edition. Faber and Faber, 2005.
Steimatsky, Noa. *The Face on Film*. Oxford University Press, 2017.

Filmography

Blue Velvet. Directed by David Lynch, performances by Kyle MacLachlan, Isabella Rosselini, Dennis Hopper, and Laura Dern, Dino De Laurentiis Entertainment Group, 1986.

Eraserhead. Directed by David Lynch, performances by Jack Nance and Charlotte Stewart, American Film Institute, Libra Films, 1977.

Dune. Directed by David Lynch, performances by Kyle MacLachlan and Sean Young, Dino De Laurentiis Company, Estudios Churucusco Azteca, 1984.

Inland Empire. Directed by David Lynch, performances by Laura Dern and Grace Zabriskie, Studio Canal et al., 2006.

Lost Highway. Directed by David Lynch, performances by Bill Pullman and Patricia Arquette, CiBi 2000, Asymmetrical Productions and Lost Highway Productions LCC, 1997.

Mulholland Drive. Directed by David Lynch, performances by Naomi Watts and Laura Harring, Les Films Alain Sarde et al., 2001.

The Elephant Man. Directed by David Lynch, performances by John Hurt and Anthony Hopkins, Brooksfilm, 1980.

The Straight Story. Directed by David Lynch, performances by Richard Farnsworth, Harry Dean Stanton, and Sissy Spacek, Asymmetrical Picture, Canal +, Channel Four Films, 1999.

Twin Peaks. Directed by David Lynch et al., performances by Kyle MacLachlan and Mädchen Amick, Lynch/Frost Productions et et al., 1990–1.

Twin Peaks: Fire Walk with Me. Directed by David Lynch, performances by Sheryl Lee and Ray Wise, CIBY Picture, 1992.

Twin Peaks: The Return [on DVD and BluRay *Twin Peaks: A Limited Event Series*]. Directed by David Lynch, performances by Sheryl Lee and Kyle MacLachlan, Showtime, 2017.

Wild at Heart. Directed by David Lynch, performances by Laura Dern and Nicolas Cage, PolyGram Filmed Entertainment and Propaganda Films, 1990.

Other Media and Sources Cited

David Lynch, *Six Men Getting Sick* (1967). Fibreglass, resin, acrylic and graphite with Masonite panel; projection, overall: 71 5/8 × 82 3/4 × 10 in.

Part II

Twin Peaks as Transmedia Network

Singing the Body Electric: Myth and Electricity as Both Sides of a Metaphorical Coin in *Twin Peaks: The Return*[1]

Willem Strank

Laura Palmer's ominous announcement at the end of the original two seasons of *Twin Peaks* (1990–1, Mark Frost and David Lynch) that she would see Agent Dale Cooper again in 25 years was eventually resolved both at the level of narration as well as in terms of distribution – the third season was broadcast approximately, but not quite, 25 years later. The third season, ostensibly called *Twin Peaks: The Return* for reasons of differentiation, follows on from the second season's cliffhanger and, while picking up on a number of narrative elements from the previous series, at times differs considerably in aesthetics. *Twin Peaks* was once famous for its bold innovations, paradigmatic of the 'second Golden Age of Television' (Thompson, see Dunleavy), and associated with postmodern television (Weinstock 9f.; Storey 198ff.). It provides for a vast area of research, too, as witnessed by the unusual number of anthologies devoted to this one series (see for example Sanna 2019, Weinstock and Spooner 2016, Frank and Schleich 2020). Neither *Twin Peaks* nor David Lynch's work in general have been particularly famous for their narrative achievements, however. Granted, the elliptic nature of many of their plotlines has resulted in a serious number of what I call 'fansplainations' online. Approaches towards Lynch and *Twin Peaks* from the camp of the humanities tend to emphasise their aesthetic and symbolic potential, and they do so with good reason. One particular metaphor that lends itself to self-referential lectures as well as attempts at explaining the myths at the heart of that small fictional border town we have all come to love and fear is that of electricity.

Electricity lends itself very well as a metaphor for the various media-related paths an artistic filmmaker may explore. Elements of circuitry, charge, voltage or power can easily be employed as metaphors, standing in for cyclical proceedings, possession, inner turmoil and supernatural abilities, to name but a few examples. Electricity harkens back to myth, too, as a natural phenomenon – the highest Greek authority when it came to their pantheon was always Zeus, wielder of lightning. And the most potent metaphor of them all, water as a (re)source and precondition of life, is reflected in the denomination of electric currents while actual currents may be exploited to harvest electricity. In modern times, electricity became one of the major forces of the Second Industrial Revolution, and all contemporary means of communication depend on it in one form or another. All the while, electricity surrounds us in our everyday life, it generates uncanny electromagnetic fields but remains invisible unless there is a sudden change in the balance of charge and voltage. That said, if electricity becomes visible, it emerges as a threatening source of energy – like a nasty little spark flying from a power outlet. If it becomes audible by means of resonance in power conversions, it turns into an uncanny humming sound reminiscent of trademark drones initially present in the sound design of David Lynch's work.

David Lynch's engagement with the television has linked him to the realm of electricity as a precondition for the small screen in at least two ways. With *Twin Peaks* he entered the area of cathode ray tubes (television sets) and that of electronic cameras constructed to channel and broadcast image and sound rather than immortalising them on film stock. While electricity has played a role in Lynch's idiosyncratic output since his early short films, it is *Twin Peaks: The Return* that inextricably links it to the mythical, the media and the hubris of man. The idea of this chapter is thus to undertake a reading of some of the iterations of electricity in the series that may give us an idea about how all these cables, connections and interfaces are connected with each other. The metaphor of electricity is thus concerned with the 'inside' – the inner workings of technology, the molecular causes for power and the mechanical preconditions for audiovisual mass-media to work. It is only in extreme situations that indications of electricity emerge at the surface – when a machine is overworked, when the voltage discharges. Discharge is a fairly common occurrence in *Twin Peaks: The Return* – objects (or people) begin to flicker, electric clouds are flung across the sky, objects are menacingly humming, hissing and crackling. Even the inner workings of people turn out to be charged by electricity at times: when Sarah Palmer literally takes off her face in front of an inquisitive stranger ('Part 14'), she reveals what looks like black and white projections from a television screen – visual imagery of a hand, a set of smiling teeth, uncannily dislocated inside her skull. When Diane is revealed as an artificial being, a 'tulpa', she finally implodes with a loud emission of electricity ('Part 16'). Like most of David Lynch's work, *Twin Peaks: The Return* does not put an end to the director's heightened interest in what lies beneath the surfaces of objects and people alike. It even juxtaposes the latter with the enigmatic realms of their 'outside'.

In his article about space and architecture in David Lynch's audiovisual work prior to 1998, Eckhard Pabst notes a fundamental opposition between civilised and pre- or anti-civilisational spaces: 'In its purest and most sublime form, the outside presents itself as black (or white) nothingness, that is, as a formless, indistinct state' (Pabst 1998: 25). In *Twin Peaks*, however, this shapeless outside turns into dynamically transformable states of permeability. Inconsistencies and inextricably confined external spaces, which often have paradoxical spatial structures, are otherwise built in similar ways as those described by Pabst as

> black [. . .] (or white [. . .]) nothing: [. . .] Not infrequent in David Lynch's films there are inputs or openings that lead straight to the bull's eye; and sometimes the camera penetrates or slides out of these areas to explore this disturbing neighborhood. (Ibid.: 26)

This is true in a social as well as in a spatial sense. During the first two seasons of *Twin Peaks*, Dale Cooper fuses (at least apparently) with the social system of the town of Twin Peaks, before he becomes part of the external, 'backstage' system of the Black Lodge. As a result, he overcomes the difference between the two systems, while his interdimensional trip culminates in a merger with a recurring demon called Bob. Season 3 largely removes the special status of the town Twin Peaks and strengthens the opposition between the space of the diegetic reality and the oppositional space of myth and electricity as represented by places like the lodges or the gas station. When Cooper fuses with Bob, he becomes a 'bipartisan' of both spatial systems of organisation – just like the mysterious entity 'Judy', the 'Giant', the man-turned-tree from Another Place, as well as the One-Armed Man. When the two spaces fall into disagreement, inexplicable things happen: People are sucked from one space to another, like Cooper who is sucked into a socket on his way back from the Black Lodge, or Bob who is sucked through a telephone wire. The world of electricity works as a connection, an interface that does not follow the rules of electricity we are accustomed to in our reality at all. Like opposing particles, the doppelgangers of Cooper trade places, and while even Dougie's family mistakes Cooper for Dougie, it takes a while for the dizzy Cooper to realise that he can only return to his former self by symbolically re-entering his electrical birth canal. He sticks a fork into the same kind of outlet he came from and, after he awakens from the resulting coma, he is finally able to act as himself again.

In all three seasons of *Twin Peaks*, the interfaces between the competing systems – the natural world of Twin Peaks, WA, and the virtual worlds of the lodges – are largely mediated by self-referential and reflective power outlets, which makes sense considering the rule of electricity as a profilmic necessity. The different settings of the TV series and their motifs suggest a doubling of the boundary between fiction and (extra-televisual) reality. In the first two seasons, these interfaces could be attributed to representations of stages (such as curtains, stage floors, props and duplications in the act of acting) – the dreams of Cooper, the Roadhouse, the Black Lodge. Since then, the miraculous phenomena, narrative interventions and projections of the Utopian observed by Pabst (20ff.) have transcended, though not left behind, the space of the stage, and are now manifesting themselves in new layers of the self-referential.

Interestingly, both spheres of the profilmic – electricity as a technological precondition as well as the framework of the stage, the costume and the act – are often interlinked. While the 'Roadhouse' often serves as a space of interference between the conventional and the supernatural, the 'Black Lodge' is like a backstage area for the mystical meta-play that most agents of Twin Peaks are largely unaware of (see Strank 2020a). In addition to the 'Black Lodge' and the 'Roadhouse', these types of profilmic motifs are repeatedly referred to on a smaller scale – Dougie's house is criss-crossed with curtains, bars and slats (see 'Part 3' and 'Part 4'). The tulpa 'Diane' enters the secret gathering of FBI agents Gordon, Albert and Tammy through a red curtain and is temporarily allowed access to the circle of 'Blue Rose' investigators ('Part 12'). These small details of the mise-en-scène emphasise Diane and Dougie's artificiality, which will be revealed towards the end of the season. These are but a few of the many examples, and furthermore, where there are curtains without stages and stages without curtains, there are also costumes without a frame: The three henchmen of the Mitchum Brothers, Candie, Mandie and Sandie, appear permanently out of place dressed up as 'cocktail waitresses', acknowledged by the hitwoman Chantal with the words 'looks like a fucking circus parade' ('Part 16').[2]

While the metaphor of electricity is connected to the framework of the stage through the idea of the profilmic, another self-referential element links it to technological means of communication. Even if *Twin Peaks: The Return* extensively reflects the technological progress of the 25 years between the respective chronological narrative situations, the telephone plays an essential role as an auditory medium of communication, just like in the first two seasons. Communication is largely unidirectional and sometimes marks the limits of knowledge to the outside. The calls from Margaret, the 'Log Lady', run through the entire season and replace the direct addressing of the viewer in the 'Log Lady Introductions' of the first two seasons. The Log Lady's information is always helpful but just as often enigmatic, reflecting many other means of (mis)communication in *Twin Peaks: The Return*: coordinates, signals, drawings. However, they continue to present Hawk with tasks that somehow advance the solution of the case and thus connect the Log Lady's 'outside' knowledge with the 'inside' problems of the town of Twin Peaks.[3] Similarly, Agent Cooper obtains information from his journeys through the 'outside'. At the same time, the telephone wire is another electrical connection, which is made abundantly clear when Cooper/Bob is sucked through one of these connections while visiting the mystical 'convenience store' and thus leaves the location again via its electrical inner workings ('Part 15'). Finally, when Agent Cooper picks up Carrie Page – instead of her doppelganger Laura Palmer – from her apartment in Odessa to bring her 'home', the phone in her living room keeps ringing but is no longer answered ('Part 18'): Who knows where (or when) they might have ended up instead if she had chosen to answer the phone?

At first glance, the series employs the telephone's modern iterations, for example the smartphone, in a similar way. Smartphone conversations are just as often enigmatic or elliptic. Some callers initially remain anonymous or at least nameless, such as Bob – even after having been contacted by him multiple times, Diane has not gotten around to saving his number ('Part 9'). As his 'tulpa', Diane mostly knows how to decipher Bob's cryptic messages anyway: the text message ': -) ALL' ('Part 16') triggers Diane to attempt an assassination of her supposed FBI colleagues. The asynchronous communication practice of text messages is chiefly associated with Bob, who leads his criminal empire largely through non-contractual, and therefore relatively 'anonymous' burner phones. It is the synchronicity that poses a problem to the population of Twin Peaks. For Jerry, who ventures far into the woods on drugs, the smartphone is the only remaining connection to the elusive 'inner world'. The situation becomes threatening when the pre-civilizational 'outside' cuts him off from it because he no longer has any reception ('Part 7'). In the Sheriff's Department, the always helpful Lucy does not understand the concept of the smartphone time and time again and gets a shock every time Sheriff Truman, who she had just spoken to on the phone, suddenly walks in the door ('how is this possible?', 'Part 4').[4] The showcase of modern technology is completed by a modern computer that has somehow found its way into the Sheriff's Department of Twin Peaks. It is used for investigative work in conjunction with the traditional police telephones. Scenes showing FBI agent Gordon Cole almost always frame him with mainframe computers almost as tall as a man. These are used to decipher the many competing codes in the series.[5]

While all these modern machines certainly need their share of power, the main sources of electricity in *Twin Peaks: The Return* are all connected to old media, and old technologies. Right at the beginning, Agent Cooper's and the viewer's focus is directed on the auditory instead of the visual. In the first episode, we can see the Giant sitting next to Cooper in the Black Lodge, advising him to 'listen to the sounds' ('Part 1'). Both turn to a gramophone, and slightly unpleasant scratching noises can be heard from its funnel, referring more to the playback device than to the possible medium of the record. Similarly, the 'arm' who has changed his shape in the past 25 years and now resembles an electrified version of the tree from David Lynch's early short film *The Grandmother* as well as his feature film debut *Eraserhead*,[6] introduces himself ('I am the arm') and then adds how it sounds ('and I sound like this—'). What follows are the noises of the premedial that come to the fore in *Twin Peaks: The Return*, noises of electricity instead of music. Of course, this is consistent with the permanent threat posed by the entity 'Judy', who communicates and acts by way of manipulating the very same sources of electricity, and thus controls the preconditional space of most playback devices. The earliest mentioning of communication media in the fabula can be found in a flashback to the year 1956. Eleven years after the atomic bomb test resulting from the 'Manhattan Project', semi-transparent, flickering entities (commonly called the 'Woodsmen') with the appearance of homeless men are forming (or being liberated) in the Nevada desert. One of them hijacks a radio station, kills all employees in the process, and interrupts the live broadcast for an announcement that they keep repeating steadily: 'This is the water and this is the well. Drink full and descend. The horse is the white in the eyes and dark within.' The strange message once again emphasises the aforementioned opposition of the 'inside' and the 'outside' (water/well; white/eyes; dark/within). Electricity is connected to this opposition in two ways: the difference between 'inside' and 'outside' may be understood as a cause for 'voltage', and electricity is an invisible force that is operating 'inside' of the apparatus of mass media (or simple suburban homes). By way of mass media distribution, it reaches many radio devices,[7] and exerts a potentially fatal effect on all those who listen.[8]

Dale Cooper's way out of the Black Lodge is more arduous than the initial farewell suggests, and leads him, via the detour of a New York glass structure, to another non-place: a fireplace room bounded to one side by an endless dark sea. In the room there is a woman with her eyes sewn shut, who can only communicate through breathing sounds and gestures. The roof of the construction whose interior can be understood as a fireplace room as well as a machine can be accessed via a ladder. On the outside, the 'room' proves to be a paradoxical construction – a closed vehicle in the vastness of outer space that does not correspond to the infinite ocean visible inside. This dreamlike discontinuity connects the space with the Black Lodge: while the Black Lodge only consists of interiors and knows no outside, the fireplace contraption is surrounded only by representations of the utmost 'outside'.

Eckhard Pabst (24, emphasis in the original) points out that in David Lynch's work 'the universe is now only *one* possible formal articulation of the contourless outside', which seems to account for *Twin Peaks: The Return* as well. Here, Cooper seems to have arrived outside of the 'outside' system. At the edge, Cooper would have the ideal observer's position to view the system from the 'outside', but from that position it only appears as a space: the Black Lodge, the black and white room, the fireplace room are transitional spaces, used by entities like Bob or 'Judy' to cross between the systems – they do not represent the external system, but the place of a possible fusion, a possible interface, which makes the 'outside' more intangible than before. It goes without saying that 'Judy' is acting through electricity: its space of action is in lines that are transitional spaces par excellence. Electricity is created only by voltage, it is measured only in the movement of electrons between the electromagnetic poles, as a dynamic difference. If 'Judy's' core property is that of electricity, then it is firmly located in the 'in between,' of which Dale Cooper finds the utmost possible – albeit potentially imaginary – outer façade as he explores the paradoxical structure of the fireplace room.

Dale Cooper's border crossing into the in-between space of the 'Black Lodge' has led to his merger with a resident of the outside system, namely the demon Bob. He was therein preceded by another FBI agent and frontier investigator in search of 'Judy': Philip Jeffries. Jeffries's journey ended with a permanent and thus final fusion: he merged with a machine ('Part 15'). His communication has become that of the machine: his 'writing' corresponds to the appearance of vaporous letters and the machine hums at regular intervals, as if representing Jeffries's breath. Gordon Cole is also convinced that Jeffries no longer exists 'in the normal sense' ('Part 17'); Jeffries knows more about 'Judy' than anyone else because in fact she has to work through him, since his existence now depends on her electricity. He is no longer visible as a human being, only his voice and his characteristic dialect have survived – again emphasising the ubiquitous focus on the auditive distribution of information, since Jeffries initially communicated only by telephone with both Cooper and Bob.

In addition to the typical television broadcasts that can be found in *Twin Peaks: The Return* there is the video podcast of 'Dr Amp' (formerly

Dr Jacoby) whose broadcast is a sort of amalgamation of conspiracy theory sermons and commercial television (intent on selling gold-painted
shovels). The self-given alias 'Dr Amp' refers to an amplifier – of messages by the use of mass media. Hence his show is referentially connected
(once again) to the auditive layer of the series as well as to the potential of
electricity, removing the biological limitations of the human voices by way
of amplification, or rather the mass medium of television. Dr Amp's red-
blue glasses add another, visual level of meaning when worn in front of the
camera: in addition to the conventional correlation with the colours of the
American flag, this refers to the anaglyph glasses, necessary for the decoding of red-blue 3D images. This underlines Dr Amp's distinction between
those with and without knowledge. While his viewers only see the glasses
as a two-dimensional image, Dr Amp is able to perceive the hidden layers
of the world in three dimensions.

Electricity in *Twin Peaks: The Return* not only fuels Judy, the Woodsmen and their mythical gas station. It is also necessary for the creation of
the artificial beings called 'tulpas'. The principle of doubling begins in
the paratext (with the name 'Twin' Peaks) and culminates in the final episode in which, incidentally, Carrie Page mentions that even the state that
Twin Peaks is located in has a homonymous counterpart in the District of
Columbia ('Part 18').

Doubling is another fundamental form of self-referentiality. As the
ancient story of Narcissus and Echo goes to show, the very idea of reflection is dependent on the (visual) surface and the (auditory) reverb. Both
aspects of the audiovisual have their own processes of reduplication.

In *Twin Peaks*, Bob can be understood as an agent of duplication or
possibly the axis of symmetry itself. Cooper looks in the mirror while possessed by Bob a number of times (starting in 'Part 4') which refers to the
cliffhanger at the end of the second season, and his fingerprints – the ultimate proof of the singularity of identity – show anomalies that have to do
with a mirror image ('Part 5'). The idea of the 'tulpas' explains, however,
exhaustively that doublings only occur on the level of signifiants and can
therefore cause a lot of confusion for the inhabitants of the storyworld as
well as the viewers[9] – however, the essence (the signifié) remains ultimately
unaffected. Cooper escapes Bob's obsession by doubling up himself. Bob
is able to inherit many, but not all, of his properties and thus controls a
Cooper shell instead of embodying the actual man: people who know him
well can still tell the difference the way they can identify a bad actor.

The narcissistic principle is thus elaborated on and counteracted in a
variety of ways, but the doubling aesthetics of the series also extend to the
level of sound: the lethargic Cooper who replaces Dougie gains spectacular

popularity in his social environment by only repeating the last words of the previous utterance, ironically presenting what the diegetic society considers the ideal conversational partner to be like.[10] However, as a result of his involuntary social practice of echoing other people's words, Cooper's own agenda is all but hidden away under the lethargic surface – he just repeats the lines like an actor would repeat their text.[11] If the echo is too perfect, however, it is interpreted as an act of mockery. The disfigured man jailed in Twin Peaks' Sheriff's Department also habitually echoes the utterances of his interlocutors (or the noises surrounding him, like those coming from the woman with the eyes sewn shut) but that is seen (or misread) as provocation. In other words: there appears to be an acceptance of the kind of self-referentiality that is taken to be a pleasant breach of the fourth wall, while the act of mockery may be rejected for cutting too deep. In the same vein, Lynch's[12] treatment of electricity may be regarded as nostalgic progress pessimism by some.

One of the main preconditions of audiovisual media is electricity – whether it is generated by friction or by voltage is ultimately irrelevant: anyone who wants to produce a television series will need electricity for a large part of the production apparatus. The Manhattan Project, set as the earliest point of the *Twin Peaks* storyworld, combines the destruction of elements that belong to the 'inside' or microcosm (nuclear fission) with the release of enormous amounts of energy or electricity. The 'outside' is therefore correlated with a superordinate principle at both the micro level and the macro level. Nuclear power and radioactive emissions are semiotically related to the FBI's 'blue roses', cases about inexplicable phenomena. Both are below our limits of perception and make themselves felt only as an index: the mushroom cloud is caused by nuclear fission, electricity is caused by the movement of electrons instigated by voltage. The interfaces are particularly noteworthy, as they fuse the two worlds and link them to the phenomenon of electricity, while at the same time (mass-produced) electricity is a metaphor for the post-industrialised world. Sockets, cigarette lighters and electricity pylons are interpreted by some as 'God', and as threats from an unknown 'underneath and beyond' by others. Nuclear power is also used to symbolise the potentially ultimate hubris of mankind in the narration of *Twin Peaks: The Return*. Its unforeseen consequences are visible in the link between the Manhattan Project experiments and the strange egg appearing some eleven years later harbouring some nasty unknown creature. Furthermore, the aftermath of actual atomic bombings on Hiroshima and Nagasaki is also present in the form of symbols: clocks frozen in time, shadows burnt into the concrete, spontaneous implosions of electrical appliances and broken windows.

The flickering homeless spirits known as the Woodsmen walk the line between this world and the beyond much like the irradiated 'hibakusha'. The demons are visibly affected by – maybe even charged with – electricity. This can be deduced from their flickering appearance – it is as if the radiation has become manifest and visible: forgotten victims, who return as dark memories and open up a new habitat to the mutations from another world. According to *Twin Peaks: The Return*, the birth of the atomic bomb seems to have torn the fabric of the world apart and ostensibly damaged the border either between the real and the unreal or between alternate universes. Moreover, all these segments of the 'syuzhet' are clothed in a self-reflexive materiality: photographs taken in 1945 or 1956 – in accordance with the status of the medium – are black and white and thus refer to their own mediality. When Andy is abducted to one of the Lodge interfaces, he is doomed to witness a short version of the pre-history: he can be seen in a black and white environment, but images of the 'Black Lodge' present themselves to him in colour, as if it was not only the medium of 1945 and 1956 that depicted the world in black and white but as if a black and white world was represented by and conserved in the material.

This corresponds to the fact that the memory of February 23, 1989 – the fictional starting date of the main plot (Cooper's arrival in Twin Peaks) – is later represented in black and white. Unlike the other archival footage from the second season, the mediality or materiality here is only a pretext for the concept of the 'past', which is set back to a time before the world has entered into the symbolic age of modernity. In other words: The medium 'is' the message, to echo Marshall McLuhan. Further, the medium expresses the history of itself in the form of an experimental film. In 1977, Bernhard Lindemann has already pointed out that every experimental film must be a metafilm because it marks its deviation from the norm through its deviation from the norm. *Twin Peaks* is a meta-series that narrativises such a self-reflexivity and transforms it into motivic circles that in turn refer to themselves. It perpetually operates at the interface between the system and the environment, permanently addressing the difference between fiction and reality, both intra- and extra-diegetically.

As the missing Jerry Horne watches Bob sacrifice his firstborn son Richard on the altar of electricity, his anger is directed at the medium that has enabled him to witness the scene rather than at Bob himself: 'Bad binoculars!' However the problem in *Twin Peaks: The Return* is not the medium itself, but rather its users. The third season picks up the aforementioned tension between 'outside' and 'inside' that the first two seasons have established and continues to focus on the progressive deconstruction of symbols of unification. At the beginning of each episode, Laura Palmer's image metonymically stands for a multitude of things: the concept of the home-coming queen as an expression of perfection and innocence, the symbolic preservation of an ideal moment, the case of Laura Palmer and the loss of innocence of the system 'Twin Peaks'. The latter was initiated by the initial process of investigation, that is the arrival of the FBI in the small border town. This image, however, is a grotesque reduction to one facet of a complex character, and while Laura can apparently finally be saved from Bob by going back into the past, the rescued Laura is not even by name identical to the person in the photograph. This principle of unreliable reduplication is at the heart of the entire series. Some examples: Albert donates a photograph to Gordon as a substitute for the real Mount Rushmore ('Part 4') and thus reduces the idea of the travel experience to absurdity.[13] Ike the Spike receives his orders of assassination in the form of photographs, but the subject's identity has to be questioned in a storyworld full of doppelgangers. Bushnell is not at all identical with his younger boxer-ego, with whom he adorns his office, and in the 'outside system' the fake inhabitants of the 'interior system' are reduced to identical golden spheres, that is the shape or the 'soul' of the tulpas. Hawk's map, ultimately, illustrates that images in the series are subjected to strategies of decoding and thus entangled in a system of visual misinformation and misguidance. When Sheriff Truman enquires after the striking black symbol on the edge of the map, Hawk tells him that he would prefer not to know its meaning. The symbol without a signified is the last instance of the deconstruction of meaning – time and space can only be constructed from the difference of images, and if the building blocks of these differences are no longer valid, time and space have lost their meaning. The woman with her eyes sewn shut (Naido) has already internalised what Cooper still has to learn: 'When you get there, you'll already be there.'

We have seen that electricity in *Twin Peaks: The Return* is used as a metaphor of self-reference. As such, it is capable of amplification (in the mass media) and the reduction of distances (through telephone wires or cellular networks). It is a global phenomenon in a post-industrialised age yet linked to inexplicable phenomena brought upon man by themselves, particularly through the release of the biggest possible amount of electrical power with the invention of the atomic bomb. By playing Zeus, man brought back the supernatural into the age of post-enlightenment. It is the fuel of mythical devices of the in-between (Judy), the blood of hybrid man-machines (Jeffries), and the source of energy for the creation of 'tulpas', artificial humans. The atomic bomb has brought about the infestation of the Palmer family and the constant threat of the Woodsmen. It has released demons and potentially torn open the very fabric of the world, challenging the once-sealed connections between alternate versions of time and space.

Notes

1. This article is closely related to two other articles about 'Twin Peaks', which mainly deal with the permeability of stages (Strank 2020a) and self-referentiality in *Twin Peaks: The Return* (Strank 2020b). There will naturally be some parallels between the three articles as their results stem from the same research.

2. The aesthetic proximity between *Twin Peaks: The Return* and *Inland Empire* (David Lynch, 2006) is at its closest here.

3. The 'log' also refers to a 'logbook' (interestingly, from a linguistic point of view, the origin and result of the same object: log book and thus comparable to the Japanese Kanji for 'hon', which can mean tree and book, but also origin) and thus suggests that 1990s *Twin Peaks* almost prophetically predicted the ubiquity of the 'weblog'.

4. The fact that according to Andy this happens 'over and over again' ('Part 4') corresponds to the fact that breaking this cyclical habit enables Lucy to confront Bob ('Part 17') – the same Bob who was first introduced with the words 'Bob Bob Bob again and again' ('Part 2').

5. In another instance of a playful interference of the inside and the outside, some codes are part of the diegesis while others – like the oft-recurring number 253 (25 years, 3 seasons?) – are clearly planted as exercises for the viewer.

6. Strikingly, in *Eraserhead* the tree is placed in front of the picture of a nuclear explosion.

7. A young girl introduced in an earlier scene falls asleep, allowing a creature hatched from an egg in the desert, which appears to be a mixture of bird (beak), mammal (hind legs), and insect (wings), orally to penetrate the girl's mouth and be swallowed. One possible theory is that this is Sarah Palmer.

8. The sense of hearing is generally powerful in *Twin Peaks: The Return*. Cole's hearing aid repeatedly refers reflexively to the process of listening, to the danger of being overheard and to the possible physical damage caused by auditory sensory impressions. The sound design of the season, which in contrast to the previous seasons uses much less music, follows its own logic, with most of the noises aiming at the representation of electricity.

9. See 'That is Agent Cooper!' – 'No, it's not.' ('Part 17'). Also, Dougie's wife Janey-E notices and mentions a lot of differences between Agent Cooper and her husband but proceeds to live with Cooper, effectively accepting him as Dougie based on his appearance ('Part 3').

10. This is a major similarity to the HBO series *John from Cincinatti* (David Milch, Kem Nunn, 2007), in which a protagonist who 'fell from the sky' in a similar manner habitually repeats the phrases of others and is subsequently stylized by some as an impenetrable figure of redemption.

11. This means that the 'comatose' Cooper is also in complete opposition to the highly proactive Cooper. Also, this is one of countless allegories of directorship in the series – for more about that see Strank 2020.

12. Although this chapter's approach is not meant to be concerned with the makers' biographies in any way, it may seem odd that, more often than not, it neglects to

mention Mark Frost – the reason is that electricity really appears to be Lynch's 'baby' – it is a motif in most of his work (and not so much in Frost's) and he has constantly mentioned it in interviews (most disconcertingly in Chris Rodley's *Lynch on Lynch*).

13. Quite possibly a gentle nod towards the famous photograph scene in Jean-Luc Godard's *Les Carabiniers* (1963).

Bibliography

Dunleavy, Trisha. *Complex Serial Drama and Multiplatform Television*. Routledge, 2017.

Frank, Caroline and Markus Schleich, eds. *Mysterium Twin Peaks. Zeichen – Welten – Referenzen*. Springer, 2020.

Lindemann, Bernhard. *Experimentalfilm als Metafilm*. Olms, 1977.

Pabst, Eckhard. '"He will look where we cannot." Raum und Architektur in den Filmen David Lynchs'. *'A Strange World'. Das Universum des David Lynch*, Eckhard Pabst (ed.). Ludwig, 1998, pp. 11–30.

Rodley, Chris. *Lynch on Lynch*. Revised Edition. Farrar, Straus and Giroux, 2005.

Sanna, Antonio (ed.). *Critical Essays on* Twin Peaks: The Return. Palgrave Macmillan, 2019.

Storey, John. *Cultural Theory and Popular Culture. An Introduction*. 5th edition. Pearson, 2008.

Strank, Willem. '"When you get there, you will already be there" – Selbstreferenz und -reflexivität in *Twin Peaks: The Return*'. *Mysterium* Twin Peaks. *Zeichen – Welten – Referenzen*, Caroline Frank and Markus Schleich (eds). Springer, 2020, pp. 321–44.

Strank, Willem. '"When you see me again, it won't be me" – Permeabilität und Dispermanenz am Beispiel der Bühnensequenzen in Mark Frosts und David Lynchs erster Iteration von *Twin Peaks* (1990/91)'. *Selbstreferenz in der Kunst*, Nicolas Buck and Jill Thielsen (eds). Ergon, 2020, pp. 355–72.

Thompson, Robert J. *Television's Second Golden Age. From* Hill Street Blues *to* ER. Syracuse University Press, 1997.

Weinstock, Jeffrey Andrew. '"It is Happening Again": New Reflections on *Twin Peaks*'. *Return to* Twin Peaks. *New Approaches to Materiality, Theory, and Genre on Television*, Jeffrey Andrew Weinstock and Catherine Spooner (eds). Palgrave Macmillan, 2016, pp. 1–28.

Weinstock, Jeffrey Andrew and Catherine Spooner, eds. *Return to* Twin Peaks. *New Approaches to Materiality, Theory, and Genre on Television*. Palgrave Macmillan, 2016.

Filmography

Eraserhead. Directed by David Lynch, performances by Jack Nance and Charlotte Stewart, American Film Institute, Libra Films, 1977.

John from Cincinatti. Created by David Milch and Kem Nunn, performances by Rebecca de Mornay and Greyson Fletcher, HBO, 2007.

Inland Empire. Directed by David Lynch, performances by Laura Dern and Grace Zabriskie, Studio Canal et al., 2006.

The Grandmother. Directed by David Lynch, American Film Institute, 1970.

Twin Peaks. Directed by David Lynch et al., performances by Kyle MacLachlan and Mädchen Amick, Lynch/Frost Productions et al., 1990–1.

Twin Peaks: The Return [on DVD and Blu-ray *Twin Peaks: A Limited Event Series*]. Directed by David Lynch, performances by Sheryl Lee and Kyle MacLachlan, Showtime, 2017.

CHAPTER 4

The W/hole David Lynch: *Twin Peaks: Fire Walk with Me*

Constantine Verevis

In 2007, David Lynch created a short film – *HollyShorts Greeting* – for his acceptance of the fourth HollyShorts Film Festival Visionary Award (2008). There is much to admire in this four-minute film, from a variation on the backwards talking from *Twin Peaks* (1990–1) through an impromptu shuffling dance by Lynch, and on to – in anticipation of *Twin Peaks: The Return* (2017) – a lineup of beguiling chorus cuties. Perhaps of most interest, though, is Lynch's instruction that we 'keep [our] eye on [the] donut, not on [the] hole'. This is, of course, a delicious conceit because Lynch has always been interested in holes – that is, in portals or openings – that take you somewhere unexpected, somewhere dark and beautiful. Moreover, as Gilles Deleuze reminds us in *Cinema 1: The Movement-Image*, we should never confuse wholes with parts, or sets. Deleuze writes: 'sets are closed, and everything which is closed is artificially closed. [. . .] But a whole is not closed, it is open, and it has no parts' (1986: 10).

This chapter appeals to the w/hole David Lynch – his open set of films and artworks – to argue that those who initially objected to *Twin Peaks: Fire Walk with Me* (1992) thought that the part (the prequel film) would close out the set (the first and second seasons of the television series) when in actuality it worked only to extend the mystery. As Lynch would have it:

> To me, a mystery is like a magnet. Whenever there is something that's unknown, it has a pull to it. . . . When you only see a part, it's even stronger than seeing the whole. The whole might have a logic, but out of its context, the fragment takes on a tremendous value of abstraction. (Rodley 2005: 231)

If *Twin Peaks: Fire Walk with Me* frustrated its initial audience – especially its *Twin Peaks* fan base – then this might be because the experience of (serial) repetition is displaced from a closed set or sequence of texts – the connection and continuation of a film prequel and television series – to an open w/hole. In a move away from a holistic (totalising) understanding of sequelisation, one that aligns direct intentionality with an industrial practice that fulfils the promise of another episode, this chapter argues that Lynch constructed his prequel, *Twin Peaks: Fire Walk with Me* (hereafter, *Fire Walk with Me*), through a systematic rewriting akin to that of a secret remake: the logic of a *ruinous prequel*.[1]

An Opening: Before *Fire Walk with Me*

Following the 'midnight cult success' of *Eraserhead* (1976), the 'fame and esteem' of *The Elephant Man* (1980), and the 'gargantuan disaster' of *Dune* (1984) (Atkinson 1997: 14–15), Lynch is said to have retreated for a year before re-emerging with a film – *Blue Velvet* (1986) – that would establish him as an international auteur and resonate across the cluster of projects that immediately followed: *Wild at Heart* (1990), *Industrial Symphony No. 1* (1990), *Twin Peaks* and *Fire Walk with Me*. Lynch's immediate predecessor to *Blue Velvet*, the monumental *Dune*, had proven difficult for many. Richard Corliss observed, with reference to the film's opening sequence, the 'animated lecture', and its closing line, 'for he is the Kwisatz Haderach!', that where most science fiction offered escape, 'a holiday from homework', *Dune* was 'as difficult as a final exam. You have to cram for it' (Corliss 1984: 53). *Blue Velvet* presented as another kind of problem, Barbara Creed writing that it 'threaten[ed] to make interpretation redundant, so openly [did] it flaunt its Freudian themes and narrative' (Creed 1988: 97). Transparent yet opaque, *Blue Velvet* presented as Lynch's most formally controlled film, one in which the Oedipal drama unfolded through an oscillation between, on the one hand, the failures of filiation, and on the other, the restorative order of affiliation, or contiguity (see Said 1983: 16–24). This was in turn rendered as an opposition between the repetitions of the Imaginary (nature, family, desire, darkness and the film's motif of the naked flame), and the Symbolic (culture, community, law, light and the institutionalised flame of the electric lamp). Psychoanalytic vocabulary aside, such symmetries accorded with Lynch's description of a portal between the forces of darkness and light: 'We live in a world of opposites, of extreme evil and violence opposed to goodness and peace. . . . In struggling to understand the reason, we learn about the balance and there's a mysterious door [a portal] right at balance point' (Rodley 2005: 23).

Blue Velvet laid bare the murderous impulses that inform the domestic milieus of both *Twin Peaks* and *Fire Walk with Me*. No one familiar with *Blue Velvet* had reason to be surprised that Leland Palmer (Ray Wise) was Laura's (Sheryl Lee) killer. It also marked the beginning of Lynch's musical collaborations with Angelo Badalamenti – the creation of a series of deep and pulsating, hypnotising compositions – which was especially intense in the period 1986 to 1993. Commenting on Isabella Rossellini's rendition of *Blue Velvet*'s title song, Philippa Hawker wrote 'only a sadist could make [Rossellini] sing, and only a confirmed masochist could sit through one of her sets at the Slow Club' (Hawker 1988: 7). In part an observation about Lynch's (then) bicoastal love affair with Rossellini, the comment identifies that Lynch's collaboration with Badalamenti was occasioned (at least partially) by an invitation for the composer to coach Rossellini through her (Dorothy Vallens') rendition of 'Blue Velvet'. Upon hearing Badalamenti's arrangement of her vocals – supported by a piano, lightly brushed drum kit, guitar, saxophone and upright bass – Lynch enlisted Badalamenti to write further music for *Blue Velvet*. This included not only the segue (at the Slow Club) from 'Blue Velvet' to the beautiful dark of 'Blue Star' (lyric fragments of which were later reprised for Julee Cruise's 'Into the Night' for the *Twin Peaks* soundtrack) but also 'Mysteries of Love', for which they shared credit as songwriter (Lynch) and composer (Badalamenti) (Norelli 2017: 21–30). Much more than ambient filler to paper over Lynch's fragmented narratives, the Lynch-Badalamenti collaborations actively contributed to the filmmaker's quest for a 'logic of sensation': a musical amplitude that underscored Lynch's *dis*figuration of the visible world (Deleuze 2003: 73).[2]

Inscribed in the lyrics of 'Blue Velvet' – 'like a flame burning brightly' – and aligned with a 'desire . . . very quickly reborn after the brief vertigo of its apparent extinction' (Metz 1982: 59)[3], the motif of the flame was carried over to Lynch's Palme d'Or winning *Wild at Heart*. The film's opening – a flame struck from a single match that erupts into a wall of billowing flames – was reworked across the narrative, in particular the fiery murder-death of Lula's father as witnessed by Sailor (Nicolas Cage) and later recounted by him to Lula (Laura Dern). More significantly, the flame functioned symbolically in the film's scenography of desire. As described by Slavoj Žižek, the raging fire is an '*opening in reality* [through which] the substance of the real breaks in': '*Wild at Heart*'s narrative fragments from old cinematic genres (film noir, soft-porn, musical comedy, etc.) [are] a patchwork designed to prevent us from "burning our fingers" too much on the real' (Žižek 59, emphasis added). Badalamenti's contribution to *Wild at Heart*, although more limited than that of *Blue Velvet*, nevertheless included another significant Lynch–Badalamenti composition, 'Up in Flames'. Performed for the film by blues singer Koko Taylor, the song was reprised by Cruise for *Industrial Symphony No. 1*, the contemporaneous theatre production that premiered at the Brooklyn Academy of Music in November 1989 (and was videotaped by Lynch for wider distribution).

Labelled 'a triple exposure dream' – 'A dream of the broken hearted. A dream about floating and falling and rising upwards' – *Industrial Symphony No. 1* featured Cruise suspended like an angel, her body (in anticipation of Laura Palmer's) dramatically falling into the void.

Lynch's post-*Blue Velvet* projects closely shadowed (and interlaced with) one another: the *Twin Peaks* pilot premiered in the USA on April 8, 1990, just a month ahead of the *Wild at Heart* premiere at Cannes Film Festival in May 1990 (see the timeline in Norelli 2017: 35–6). For *Twin Peaks*, the Lynch–Badalamenti relationship again proved essential, with the composer following Lynch's instructions first to write 'Laura Palmer's Theme' and its variation, 'Love Theme from *Twin Peaks*', both of which appeared on the album, *Soundtrack from Twin Peaks* (released in September 1990). Once the pilot was ready to move into production, Badalamenti provided further music, adapting the Lynch–Badalamenti composition 'Falling', previously recorded for Cruise's debut album *Floating into the Night* (released September 1989), for the signature '*Twin Peaks* Theme'. Michel Chion makes note not only of the unifying power of the '*Twin Peaks* Theme', but also of the way its coupling with a dramatic shot of the plummeting waters at Snoqualmie Falls enabled Lynch to conjugate the expression (and various meanings) of 'falling' across his lyrics and his films (Chion 2006: 111). Riding the wave of enthusiasm for *Twin Peaks*, Lynch next signed a three-film contract with the newly founded French production company CIBY 2000, proposing a *Twin Peaks* film – a cinematic prequel, *Fire Walk with Me* – set during the final days before Laura Palmer's murder, and thus seemingly catering to the curiosity of *Twin Peaks*' growing fan base. As Chion describes, Lynch offered a personal explanation for his desire to bring Laura Palmer back from the dead:

> At the end of the series, I felt kind of sad. I couldn't get myself to leave the world of *Twin Peaks*. I was in love with the character of Laura Palmer and her contradictions, radiant on the surface, dying inside. I wanted to see her live, move and talk. (Chion 2006: 134–5)

By the time Lynch commenced filming on *Fire Walk with Me* (around mid-1991), *Twin Peaks* had become a multimedia sensation and had already undergone various forms of remediation. The success of the first season had spawned a series of media artefacts and commercial spin-offs, the most visible of which included: *The Secret Diary of Laura Palmer* (Jennifer Lynch 1990); '*Diane . . .*' *The Twin Peaks Tapes of Agent Cooper* (audio cassette) and *The Autobiography of F.B.I. Special Agent Dale Cooper: My Life, My Tapes* (both, Scott Frost 1990); and *Welcome to Twin Peaks: Access Guide to the Town* (Mark Frost et al., 1991) (Nieland 2012: 83). In this way, *Twin*

Peaks exemplified what are now widely understood as 'electrical currents' in contemporary intermedial storytelling (Grossman and Scheibel 2020: 80), but at the time *Fire Walk with Me*'s remediation of the *Twin Peaks* television series mystified and frustrated its initial audiences, receiving an especially hostile reception in France and the USA. Chion reported that 'Lynch was accused of playing the spoiled auteur who thinks he can get away with anything, even with showing contempt for the public' (Chion 2006: 143). The problem was that *Fire Walk with Me* not only presented (internally) as a discontinuous prequel – a film with a dis-connection between its first and second panels – but also as a film of 'fragments' that conjured, but did not conjugate, the parts of the television series. Despite (or because of) Lynch's insistence that 'there couldn't be a fragment that doesn't relate to everything' (Spies 2010: 20), the film's intermedial storytelling blurred boundaries and resisted closure. This implied, as Julie Grossman and Will Scheibel have it, an ethics of world building that worked 'against objectification [and totalisation] in all of its forms, [and] in the identities of selves and texts' (Grossman and Scheibel 2020: 80). Although subsequently reassessed as Lynch's 'unsung masterwork' and adopted as a 'decoder ring' for *The Return* (Lynch and McKenna 2018: 311, 491), its initial audiences did not realise that *Fire Walk with Me* was first of all a 'text of bliss', not linear and imitative, but *diagrammatic*: plural (see Barthes 1975: 56).

Another Opening: *Fire Walk with Me*

Fire Walk with Me begins with an abstraction – the flickering static of television snow – which not only signals its remediation, its departure from television, but also its resistance to representation (imitation): a signal that is at once 'electrically present and semiotically absent' (Nieland 2012: 84). In this opening, the screen is a 'fragile membrane' with a multitude of currents – episodes of the two television seasons and everything these had accumulated – pressing upon it, the most arresting of which is 'a low-pitched, mournful melody . . . played by a muted trumpet, like a soft requiem for Laura' (Chion 2006: 142). For the film's soundtrack, Badalamenti returned to revise and expand upon the themes and mood of the music from the television series, creating – as is evident in 'Theme from *Twin Peaks: Fire Walk with Me*', which accompanies the opening credits – a sound that was darker, and more melancholic.[4] As Clare Norelli further elaborates in *Soundtrack from Twin Peaks*, Badalamenti begins the theme with a reworking – a mutation – of the 'Doom' motif from 'Laura Palmer's Theme' for *Twin Peaks*, heard now, prominently, at the beginning of the film on synthesised strings, laid over gentle snare drum brushwork. This motif is repeated four times at a very slow pace – drawing out the feeling of impending doom – until it makes way for a mournful, muted trumpet melody. As Norelli puts it, 'the instrument's dulled tone sounds resigned, pained, as if it [were] a stand-in for the voice of the tortured Laura Palmer herself' (Norelli 2017: 117).

Fire Walk with Me begins with an abstraction, but not with a blank surface. The film's first panel, the 'Teresa Banks' prologue, is invested entirely with all sorts of clichés – a world overrun by representations – from which the latter section will ultimately depart (see Deleuze 2003: 11). As Chion and others have noted, the 30-minute prologue – the investigation concerning Bob's first victim – takes elements that are immediately recognisable from the television series (most evidently, a body on the water, wrapped in plastic) but shows them 'slightly deformed by iteration' (Nieland 2012: 84). As Justus Nieland describes, the prologue inverts, and thus disfigures, the familiar tropes of the *Twin Peaks* series 'by positioning [these] singular icons against a series of types they both resemble and differ from': Teresa Banks (Pamela Gidley) is not the homecoming queen, Laura Palmer; FBI Special Agent Chester 'Chet' Desmond (Chris Isaak) is not Special Agent Dale Cooper (Kyle MacLachlan); Haps Diner is not the Double R Diner; the uncooperative Sheriff Cable (Gary Bullock) at Deer Meadow is not the affable Sheriff Harry S. Truman (Michael Ontkean) of Twin Peaks, and 'Carl Rodd's [Harry Dean Stanton] rank cup of "good morning America" [is] not the ever-"damn fine coffee" of Cooper's connoisseurship' (Nieland 2012: 87). *Fire Walk with Me*'s disfiguration of the series is nowhere, in the prologue, more evident than in the appearance of Agent Cole's 'mother's sister's girl', Lil (Kimberly Ann Cole), the 'animated stick figure' (Nochimson 1997: 178) who performs a series of exaggerated theatrical gestures for Agent Desmond and Agent Sam Stanley (Kiefer Sutherland) to interpret. Although these are decoded by Desmond, Nieland argues that the point of the segment is to 'set Laura's story in the register of melodrama', and circumvent the limits of representation: 'to bypass the ambiguities, insufficiencies, and misprisions of being in language altogether for truths spoken by corporeal gesture' (Nieland 2012: 86).

The end of *Fire Walk with Me*'s prologue is announced by the arrival of Special Agent Cooper, who goes to the Fat Trout trailer park to investigate clues of Desmond's own disappearance, confiding to Diane that FBI Deputy Director Gordon Cole's (David Lynch) unsolved 'Blue Rose' case has yet another victim to claim. The second panel begins ('One Year Later'), heralded by the '*Twin Peaks* Theme' and a shot of the Twin Peaks road sign at the entrance to the town. It is followed by a tracking shot of the resurrected Laura Palmer as she walks along a leafy suburban street, with schoolbooks clutched to her chest. These emblems of *Twin Peaks* might provide viewers with some reassurance, but the estrangement does not end – does not close here – but only goes deeper into the w/hole. In its second panel, *Fire Walk with Me* continues to make its argument for 'open borders' (Grossman and Scheibel 2020: 80), persistently redrawing the contours and circuits of the television series. This is in part effected by revising a 'foundational opposition' from *Blue Velvet*: that of light and darkness, as drawn out through the figures of the Madonna and the Whore. But rather than assign different characters (Sandy/Dorothy) to these positions, Lynch collapses, in the figure of Laura, the distinction between stabilising and threatening fantasies such that the fantasy object itself becomes a destabilising force, irreducible to either of the oppositions (McGowan 2007: 134). Laura is not one or the other, but rather 'an *opening* suspended in time', a figure in a world of 'polarising forces and shadow selves' that links one reality with another (Silva 18, emphasis added).

Essential to this destabilisation is the presentation of Laura as a subjectivity that is broken up, traversed by intensities and currents. In *Twin Peaks*, Grossman and Scheibel describe *Fire Walk with Me*'s deeply 'empathic and revelatory' depiction of Laura Palmer, a characterisation that registers 'the strength and power of a woman fighting (over decades and across time and space continuums) against both masculine forces and the stereotypes about women that . . . entrap her' (Grossman and Scheibel 2020: 8; see also Hallam 2018: 121). In *The Impossible David Lynch*, Todd McGowan similarly insists that the radical innovation of *Fire Walk with Me* is not that it animates the 'stilled image' of Laura, but rather that it subjectivises Laura, the hitherto virtual object of desire, from the television series. Significantly, McGowan argues that Laura is a fully realised subject insofar as the film exposes her fundamental emptiness, 'the hole inside her' (McGowan 2007: 131). In other words, Laura's subjectivity is an emptiness that remains irreducible to a fixed and stable self. Beneath the different identities she assumes, or has imposed upon her – daughter, homecoming queen, girlfriend, prostitute, drug user – is a void (w/hole) rather than a coherent (fixed or *set*) personality (McGowan 2007: 131–2). In turn, Nieland persuasively connects this to the film's generic framework, arguing that, in *Fire Walk with Me*, Lynch 'consistently frustrates the melodramatic convention that feminine virtue demands visibility, [or] ocular proof of personality's truth' (Nieland 2012: 89). Both Nieland and McGowan link this emptiness to 'falling' where – like the figure of Cruise in *Industrial Symphony No. 1*, placed upon aerial riggings from which she dramatically plummets – the limits of sensation (of sound and image) are broken. In *Fire Walk with Me* the connection between Laura's 'affective inscrutability and her spatial indeterminacy' (Nieland

2012: 90) is rendered in a conversation between Laura and Donna (Moira Kelly) in the Palmers' living room that reveals Laura's lack of anchoring and her awareness of it. Donna asks Laura, 'Do you think that if you were falling in space that you would slow down after a while or go faster and faster?' Laura responds, 'Faster and faster. For a long time you wouldn't feel anything. And then you'd *burst into fire*. Forever. And the angels wouldn't help you, because they've all gone away' (*Fire Walk with Me*, emphasis added).

The passing reference to (the motif of) 'fire' identifies one further 'contradiction' in *Fire Walk with Me*: namely (as Chion identifies), in contrast to previous works – *Blue Velvet* and *Wild at Heart* – 'the film does not totally fulfill [its] contract. [. . .] The beautiful title remains inert on the screen, and even on a symbolic level, the role of fire [. . .] is minimal' (Chion 2006: 144). There is, of course, the galvanising moment when Laura, visiting Harold Smith (Lenny Von Dohlen), expels the words 'fire . . . walk . . . with . . . me', and another, when outside the Roadhouse, Laura encounters the Log Lady (Catherine E. Coulson), who cautions her: 'when this kind of fire starts it is very hard to put out'. In the latter instance, the significance of the motif of fire pales, though, when compared to the inspired Lynch–Badalamenti collaboration on the *Fire Walk with Me* soundtrack – both musical compositions and sound design – that 'entirely renews' (Chion 2006: 142) the world of *Twin Peaks*. Laura's arrival at the Roadhouse (aka The Bang Bang Bar) is announced by Cruise's on-stage performance of 'Question in a Blue World', itself a kind of reprise of Dorothy Vallens' rendition of 'Blue Velvet'–'Blue Star'. More striking, though, is the following segment in which Laura and Donna make their way to The Power and the Glory, a seedy bar and meeting point for prostitutes and truckers over the border in Canada. In this remarkable sequence the sound track is mixed so that the pounding diegetic music – 'The Pink Room', written by Lynch and performed by Andy Amer, Dave Jaurequi, Don Falzone and Steven Hodges – entirely overwhelms the dialogue, so much so that it (somewhat wryly) necessitates the use of subtitles (Rodley 2006: 187–9). In retrospect, it can be seen how the astonishing soundtrack for *Fire Walk with Me* (released in August 1992) in many ways enabled *The Return*, most evidently in way the latter is structured around the Roadhouse performances – by the Chromatics, Au Revoir Simone, Sharon Van Etten and others – that punctuate most of its eighteen parts.

A Series of Openings: After *Fire Walk with Me*

The idea of a 'ruinous' prequel comes from Marie Martin's notion of the 'secret remake' – a cinematic rewriting in which a 'source film [is] remade by a second film, which [by] employing a logic of condensation, displacement and figuration, brings out its latent or suppressed [. . .] quality' (Martin 2015: 32) – and more particularly is suggested by Adrian Martin's concept of the 'ruinous sequel'. In the latter instance, Adrian Martin rails against the conservative idea that sequels have primarily to do with continuity and 'coherent, mappable fictional worlds', arguing instead that a film-world is an open whole: 'a vast assemblage of fragments, sensations, associations, [and] allusions' (Martin 2009: 49). In place of conservative ('holistic') sequel-talk, Martin advances the notion of a 'modernist sequel': 'not the mere continuation of an original film, but a pointed "taking up" of it, [in] some manner of commentary or critique' (2009: 49), or (following the work of Marie-Claire Ropars-Wuilleumier) conceptualising it as a *dispositif* of destruction', one which will 'create fault lines in the source texts', and proceed 'by duplicitous reflection and identity-destruction' (2009: 51). Understood in this way, the radical gesture of sequelisation in *Fire Walk with Me* is to rend further holes in its narrative fabric: not only to leave its questions unanswered, but also to exacerbate its secrets and 'enhance its corrosive mystery' (2009: 57). This contention around the fundamental discontinuity of cinema – the idea that 'any film is . . . a *swarm* of mutually interfering worlds' (2009: 50, emphasis added) – can be drawn out through the best-known example of Lynch's Ricky Boards, *Bee Board* (1986–7), the box of twenty mounted bees that Lynch gifted to Rossellini. *Bee Board* presents a series of bees pinned to an entomological board, each one of which is labelled with a name: 'Ronnie', 'Hank', 'Dougie', and so on. As described by Greg Hainge, the procedure at work here is 'simple': units taken to be identical and considered as part of a continuous but limited set are engaged with *differently* since each part of the swarm is individuated: 'the whole [or set] no longer overrides the individual elements' (Hainge 2015: 37).[5]

An understanding of the open w/hole – which is obliquely gestured to in the HollyShorts greeting – can be further advanced with reference to, and through the contrast between, two further short works by Lynch. The first is the closed set of the four sequential, 30-second duration *Twin Peaks* Georgia Coffee advertisements – 'Lost', 'Cherry Pie', 'The Mystery of the "G"', and 'Rescue' – that Lynch made for Japanese television in 1993. This 'mini-series' of commercials presents as a type of limited remaking and remediation, but one – unlike the vast circuits encountered in *Fire Walk with Me* – that is direct and linear. The advertisements introduce two new characters – Ken and Asami – but otherwise feature characters/actors from the television series – principally Special Agent Dale Cooper, supported by Deputy Hawk (Michael Horse), Lucy Moran (Kimmy Robertson), Deputy

Andy Brennan (Harry Goaz), Shelly Johnson (Mädchen Amick), and the Log Lady – and were shot on the sets of *Twin Peaks*, recreated at Raleigh Studios in Hollywood (Malkinson: np.).

The first *Twin Peaks* Georgia Coffee episode, 'Lost', begins at the Twin Peaks Sheriff's Department, where Cooper listens as Ken tells him about his missing girlfriend Asami, who sent him a postcard from Twin Peaks. Ken notes that when they searched her room, all they found was a photograph of Asami by her car, and a mounted deer head. Lucy and Andy bring in a pot of coffee and some cups, but Cooper and Ken pull out cans of Georgia Coffee. Cooper then points out a symbol, the emblem of Big Ed's Gas Farm, on the deer head. In the second instalment, 'Cherry Pie', Cooper and Ken arrive at the Gas Farm where they find Asami's car, a triangle of red snooker balls on its front passenger seat. A graphic match to a slice of cherry pie finds them at the Double R Diner where Cooper refuses Shelly's offer of coffee, taking out a can of Georgia. At the end, Shelly provides another clue, a red paper crane left with her by Asami. Episode 3, 'The Mystery of the "G"', finds Cooper and Ken back at the Sheriff's Department, where Cooper notices a letter 'G' on the crane. Lucy brings in some Georgia Coffee. Connecting pins on a map of Twin Peaks, Andy points out that they form the letter 'G'. Hawk in turn identifies that the location at the last pin is Glastonbury Grove, home of the Black Lodge. The final episode, 'The Rescue', takes Cooper, Ken, Andy and Hawk to the Ghostwood Forest at night. Cooper enters the Red Room of the Black Lodge where he finds and – accompanied by a dramatic flash of lightening-electricity – retrieves Asami to reunite her with Ken. The final scene shows Ken and Asami, along with Cooper, Hawk, Andy and the Log Lady taking a sip of Georgia Coffee.

The *Twin Peaks* Georgia Coffee advertisements are a marvel of narrative economy: each episode is characterised by an establishing scene, strong (causal) motivation, hooks to the next episode, and a tag. Taken as a whole, the commercials develop a clear and deliberate narrative line, finding opportunity not only to incorporate themes and reprise elements – such as Cooper's rescue of Annie Blackburn (Heather Graham) from the Black Lodge and the electrical disruptions that accompany it – from the television series, but also to recycle musical motifs: not only the main '*Twin Peaks* Theme', but also 'Dance of the Dream Man', and 'Audrey's Dance' (see Malkinson: np.). Above all, the Georgia Coffee advertisements present as one of the most linear works in the Lynch canon, not only following a logico-temporal order, but also providing the strongest sense of closure found anywhere in the *Twin Peaks* storyworld. In this conservative instance of sequelisation, *Twin Peaks* provides a backwards looking model, and the process by which the Georgia Coffee mini-series remakes familiar signs and characters, and closes each episode with a flourish, serves ultimately to diminish its difference – its potentiality. As Roland Barthes describes (as though he were writing in anticipation of *Twin Peaks* and its *Return*) the Georgia Coffee advertisements serve to limit a 'difference which does not stop and which is articulated upon the infinity of texts [. . .] a difference of which each text is the return' (Barthes 1974: 3). Although fashioned by Lynch himself, the closed set of four episodes demonstrates the logic of the 'marketplace' (Nochimson 2014), a commercial investment in 'reality' that divests the Georgia Coffee series of the intensities and permutational possibilities explored elsewhere in the Lynch canon.[6]

The insistent linearity – and associated investment in detection – evident in the Georgia Coffee advertisements is generically consistent with at least one aspect of the *Twin Peaks* television series – the police procedural – but it is undertaken almost entirely at the expense of the circularity – the open 'tabularity' (Barthes 1975) – of its melodramatic network. This rendering of sensation (and affect) is far more evident in another short film work: 'Premonitions Following an Evil Deed', Lynch's contribution to the omnibus film, *Lumière and Company* (1995). Produced to coincide with and commemorate the centennial of cinema, *Lumière and Company* was comprised of a series of single-shot films (each of which was no more than 55 seconds long), commissioned from an international group of forty filmmakers, including Theo Angelopoulos, Sarah Moon and Zhang Yimou. Each filmmaker worked with an original, hand-cranked Lumière camera (with a small wooden magazine holding 55 seconds of film), and within specific constraints: no more than three takes, no artificial lighting, no stopping of the camera. In order to achieve his vision for the short work, Lynch constructed an elaborate set and Dolly track, and devised a hood for the camera which would enable him to create five (non-chronological) 'shots' by momentarily blinkering the camera as it tracked from one part of the set to the next (Lynch and McKenna 2018: 349–50).

'Premonitions Following an Evil Deed' is an oneiric work. Shot in half-light, somewhere between dream and waking, its series of five panels (fragments) do not destroy narrative entirely but create a whole – a constellation – that *resonates* without closing. In the first 'shot', three uniformed police officers walk toward a female body lying on the ground in an open area; the screen cuts to black. Next, a woman, seated in her living room, looks with concern to the right of frame; again, the screen cuts to black. In the third shot, a beautiful young woman is drawn away from a couch outdoors, where she has been sitting with two other girls, and walks forward and to the right of screen; the image is engulfed in a flash of smoke and white light. As the smoke clears, the camera pans along three hooded and uniformed, alien-looking men who circle a naked woman suspended in a medical tank filled with water; the pan moves across the structure that supports the tank to rest in front of a diaphanous paper screen, which erupts in flames to reveal the same living room as before. The final 'shot' has the woman and her husband, now visible next to her, rise from their seats as a police officer enters and removes his hat. The series of 'shots' plays out against an audio track that consists of pensive music and the mechanical clanking of industrial noise.

'Premonitions Following an Evil Deed' plays out like a ruinous sequel. It takes up the coordinates of *Fire Walk with Me*, not in order to re-present it, but (as Werner Spies observes, with reference to *Eraserhead*) to *repeat* it in 'an ambiguous play of forgetting, [and] writing over, [as] a palimpsest of [melodramatic] experience' (Spies 2010: 23). Nieland specifically comments on this scratchy film's investment in melodramatic repetition, stating that 'Premonitions Following an Evil Deed', which 'begins in death [the discovery of a body] and the mysteries of absence, reduces melodrama to its gestural essence' (Nieland 2012: 80). These shots do not return the viewer to the self-same, but instead 'suggest that Lynchian melodrama is not just a durable emotional template but also a seemingly undying one, with its surfeit of bad homes and girls in trouble and its penchant for a grandiosity of gesture and passion' (Nieland 2012: 80). As in the case of *Fire Walk with Me*, and *Blue Velvet* before it, the domestic experience, the ambivalence of home, connects with unconscious drives and desires that play out in the tensions between filiation and affiliation, negativity and positivity, darkness and light: 'Domestic experience, these [works] remind us, is famously warped and fissured, shot through with contingency and replayed in various modes of medial reanimation in Lynch's work' (Nieland 2012: 81). Perhaps one of the most striking examples of this remediation of domestic space is *Untitled* (2007), a work commissioned for the exhibition, 'David Lynch: The Air Is on Fire' (Paris, 2007). Lynch's full-scale replica of a living room, *Untitled* (2007) was closely modelled on a drawing from the late 1970s, *Untitled* (c. 1977), its porticos literally leading patrons through the void to somewhere dark and unexpected (see Silva 19–21). In *Fire Walk with Me* this embodied threshold finds expression in the picture, and picture within a picture, that Laura hangs on her wall and which she later herself enters.

'Premonitions Following an Evil Deed' refigures the melodramatic coordinates of *Fire Walk with Me* and ends with the man and woman (the parents) backing away from the police officer, joining hands as they await the words they desperately do not want to hear. As with *Twin Peaks* and *Blue Velvet*, the normality of domestic settings and familiar objects only serves as a means through which to bring darkness to the surface. It is tempting to see Laura's scream, prominent in the punishing cabin and boxcar segments toward the end of *Fire Walk with Me*, as an expression of horror and existential pain, but it might also be the case that Lynch leads us through this representation of suffering (the 'spectacle' of violence) in order, ultimately, to reach a *sensation* of joyful affirmation. In the film's final segment (and to the strains of Badalamenti's 'The Voice of Love') Laura, seated in the Red Room with Cooper standing at her side, shudders with tears of sadness and laughter and joy. As Deleuze describes it, 'beyond the [darkness of] the scream there is the smile' (2003: 28):

> Life screams at death, but death is no longer this all-too-visible thing that makes us faint; it is this invisible force that life detects, flushes out, and makes visible through the scream. Death is judged from the point of view of life, and not the reverse. (Deleuze 2003: 62)

Like Deleuze's favoured examples of Bacon, Beckett and especially Kafka – 'the one artist that I feel could be my brother' (Lynch in Rodley 2006: 56) – Lynch is not an artist who 'believes' in death: 'His is indeed a figurative *misérabilisme*, but one that serves an increasingly powerful Figure of life' (Deleuze 2003: 62, capitalisation in original). Following Deleuze's assessment, the same homage should be paid to Lynch as to Bacon, Beckett or Kafka: 'In the very act of "representing" horror, mutilation, prosthesis, fall or failure, they have erected indomitable Figures, indomitable through both their insistence and their presence. They have given life a new and extremely direct power of laughter' (Deleuze 2003: 62).

The final shots of *Fire Walk with Me* offer affirmation, but not closure. The ending does not provide a 'new foundation' – upon which to (say) build a third season of *Twin Peaks* – but rather (as Deleuze describes) works to create an event that 'engulfs all foundations, it assures a universal breakdown . . . but as *a joyful and positive event,* as an un-founding' (Deleuze 1990: 263, emphasis added). As in Michel Foucault's account of genealogy, which records the 'singularity of events outside of any monotonous finality', *Fire Walk with Me* becomes *effective*: 'it introduces discontinuity into our very being' (Foucault 1986: 76, 88). In the words of Foucault, Lynch's ruinous prequel 'deprives the self of the reassuring stability of life and nature. . . . It [uproots] its traditional foundations and relentlessly disrupt[s] its pretended continuity. This is because knowledge is not made for understanding; it is made for cutting': for punching holes (Foucault 1986: 88). Rather than reduce the world of *Twin Peaks* to a set of essential traits and final meanings, Lynch's *Fire Walk with Me* presents as a swarm and tangle of events: 'If [the world] appears as a "marvelous motley, profound and totally meaningful", this is because it began and continues its secret existence through a "host of errors and phantasms"' (Foucault 1986: 89).[7] For all of those who recognised the radical experimentation of *Fire Walk with Me*, it would have come as no surprise that when *Twin Peaks* did eventually 'Return', it did so not with ressentiment, but with the force of the will: the eternal joy of becoming.[8]

Notes

1. Discussed in further detail below, this notion of 'ruinous' prequels (sequels and remakes) is taken, in the first instance, from Stephen Heath's formulation that Nagisa Oshima's *Empire of the Senses* (*Ai no korida*, 1976) is a 'direct and ruinous remake' of Max Ophüls' *Letter From an Unknown Woman* (1948) (Heath 1981: 146).

2. In Deleuze's ninth rubric, the force that disrupts re-presentation is complicated by a *multiplication* of elements, or for Lynch the combination of sound and image. At the beginning of rubric nine, Deleuze writes: 'It is a characteristic of sensation to pass through different levels owing to the action of forces. But two sensations, each having their own level or zone, can also confront each other and make their respective levels communicate. Here we are no longer in the domain of simple vibration, but that of resonance' (2003: 65).

3. Aligned with the sexual drives, which always remain more or less unsatisfied, the flame recurs across *Blue Velvet* and other works.

4. This expansion is principally, but not exclusively, Badalamenti's, and includes contributions such as 'Requiem In C Minor' (Luigi Cherubini), 'The Pink Room' (Lynch) and 'Best Friends' (Lynch and David Slusser).

5. For a different account of the w/hole in Lynch's work see Jennifer Pranolo who writes: '*Inland Empire* [2006] does not form a narrative whole so much as a Byzantine assemblage of [recycled] conventions, tropes and stock character types' (Pranolo 2011: 482, and by way of its conclusion makes note of 'the various "holes"' in the film (ibid.: 492).

6. For a related point, see Matt Hills (2020) on franchising and anti-franchising in *The Return*.

7. Foucault's quotations are from F. W. Nietzsche, *Human, All Too Human*, no. 16 (1878).

8. Special thanks to Marcel Hartwig for inviting me to present a version of this chapter at 'Canonizing David Lynch' (Siegen, September 2019) and, before that, to Julie Grossman for bringing me along to Snoqualmie (March 2019) and subsequently for her comments on this essay.

Bibliography

Atkinson, Michael. *Blue Velvet*. British Film Institute, 1997.

Barthes, Roland. *The Pleasure of the Text*. Translated by Richard Miller. Farrar, Straus and Giroux, 1975.

Barthes, Roland. *S/Z*. Translated by Richard Miller, Hill and Wang, 1974.

Chion, Michel. *David Lynch*. 2nd edition, translated by Robert Julian. BFI, 2006.

Corliss, Richard. 'The Fantasy Film as Final Exam'. *Time*, 17 December 1984, 53.

Creed, Barbara. 'A Journey through *Blue Velvet*: Film, Fantasy and the Female Spectator'. *New Formations*, vol. 7, 1988, pp. 5–15.

Deleuze, Gilles. *Cinema 1: The Movement-Image*. Translated by Hugh Tomlinson and Barbara Habberjam. University of Minnesota Press, 1986.

Deleuze, Gilles. *The Logic of Sense*. Translated by Mark Lester with Charles Stivale, Constantin V. Boundas (ed.). Athlone, 1990.

Deleuze, Gilles. *Francis Bacon: The Logic of Sensation*. Translated by Daniel W. Smith. New York: Continuum, 2003.

Foucault, Michel. 'Nietzsche, Genealogy, History'. *The Foucault Reader*, Paul Rabinow (ed.). Penguin, 1986, pp. 76–100.

Grossman, Julie and Will Scheibel. *Twin Peaks*. Wayne State University Press, 2020.

Hainge, Greg. 'Neither Here nor There: Lynch Dissolves'. *David Lynch: Between Two Worlds*. Queensland Art Gallery, 2015, pp. 31–41.

Hallam, Lindsay. *Twin Peaks: Fire Walk with Me*. Auteur, 2018.

Hawker, Philippa. 'Blue Velvet'. *Filmviews*, no. 136, 1988, pp. 7–8.

Heath, Stephen. 'The Question Oshima'. *Questions of Cinema*. Macmillan, 1981, pp. 145–64.

Hills, Matt. 'Understanding *Twin Peaks: The Return* as a "Film Reboot" via Anti-Franchise Discourses Within Media Franchising'. *Film Reboots*, Daniel Herbert and Constantine Verevis (eds). Edinburgh University Press, 2020, pp. 97–110.

Lynch, David and Kristine McKenna. *Room to Dream*. Text Publishing, 2018.

McGowan, Todd. *The Impossible David Lynch*. Columbia University Press, 2007.

Malkinson, Agnes. '"Damn Fine Coffee" Advertising: David Lynch's TV Commercial Adaptation of *Twin Peaks*'. *Senses of Cinema*, no. 79, 2016, https://www.sensesofcinema.com/2016/twin-peaks/26839/ (last accessed 14 November 2021).

Martin, Adrian. 'Ruinous Sequels'. *Reading Room*, 3, 2009, pp. 48–63.

Martin, Marie. 'Le remake secret: généalogie et perspectives d'une fiction théorique'. *CiNéMAS*, vol. 25, no. 2–3, 2015, pp. 13–32.

Metz, Christian. *Psychoanalysis and Cinema: The Imaginary Signifier*. Translated by Celia Britton, et al. Macmillan, 1982.

Nieland, Justus. *David Lynch*. University of Illinois Press, 2012.

Nochimson, Martha P. *The Passion of David Lynch: Wild at Heart in Hollywood*. University of Texas Press, 1997.

Nochimson, Martha P. 'Interview'. *Lost in the Movies*, 2014, https://www.lostinthemovies.com/2014/11/opening-door-conversation-with-martha.html (last accessed 14 November 2021).

Norelli, Clare Nina. *Soundtrack from* Twin Peaks. Bloomsbury, 2017.

Pranolo, Jennifer. 'Laura Dern's Eternal Return'. *Screen*, vol. 52, no. 4, 2011, pp. 477–92.

Rodley, Chris (ed.). *Lynch on Lynch*. Revised edition. Faber and Faber, 2005.

Said, Edward W. *The World, The Text and the Critic*. Harvard University Press, 1983.

Silva, José Da. 'The Dweller in the Threshold'. *David Lynch: Between Two Worlds*. Queensland Art Gallery, 2015, pp. 17–29.

Spies, Werner. 'Dark Splendor – David the Painter'. *David Lynch – Dark Splendor: Spaces, Images, Sound*, Werner Spies (ed.). Max Ernst Museum, Brühl des LVR, 2010, pp. 19–45.

Žižek, Slavoj. 'Grimaces of the Real, or When the Phallus Appears'. *October*, no. 58, 1991, pp. 45–68.

Filmography

Blue Velvet. Directed by David Lynch, performances by Kyle MacLachlan, Isabella Rosselini, Dennis Hopper, and Laura Dern, Dino De Laurentiis Entertainment Group, 1986.

Dune. Directed by David Lynch, performances by Kyle MacLachlan and Sean Young, Dino De Laurentiis Company, Estudios Churucusco Azteca, 1984.

Eraserhead. Directed by David Lynch, performances by Jack Nance and Charlotte Stewart, American Film Institute, Libra Films, 1977.

HollyShorts Greeting. Directed by David Lynch, performances by David Lynch, Emily Stofle, Ariana Delawari and Jenna Green, 2007.

Industrial Symphony No. 1: The Dream of the Brokenhearted. Directed by David Lynch, performances by Laura Dern and Julee Cruise, Polygram, 1990.

Premonitions Following an Evil Deed. Directed by David Lynch, performances by Jeff Alperi and Michele Carlyle, Fox Lorber, 1995.

The Elephant Man. Directed by David Lynch, performances by John Hurt and Anthony Hopkins, Brooksfilm, 1980.

Twin Peaks. Directed by David Lynch et al., performances by Kyle MacLachlan and Mädchen Amick, Lynch/Frost Productions et al., 1990–1.

Twin Peaks: Fire Walk with Me. Directed by David Lynch, performances by Sheryl Lee and Ray Wise, CIBY Picture, 1992.

Twin Peaks: The Return [on DVD and BluRay *Twin Peaks: A Limited Event Series*]. Directed by David Lynch, performances by Sheryl Lee and Kyle MacLachlan, Showtime, 2017.

Wild at Heart. Directed by David Lynch, performances by Laura Dern and Nicolas Cage, PolyGram Filmed Entertainment and Propaganda Films, 1990.

Other Media and Sources Cited

Badalamenti, Angelo. *Soundtrack from* Twin Peaks. Warner Bros. Records, 1990.

Cruise, Julee. *Floating into the Night.* Warner Bros. Records, 1989.

Lynch, David. *Ricky Board/ Bee Board.* 1987–8, 'David Lynch: My Head is Disconnected', HOME Gallery, Manchester, 2019.

Lynch, David. *Untitled.* 'David Lynch: The Air Is on Fire', Fondation Cartier, Paris, 2007.

Lynch, David. *Untitled.* c.1977, 'David Lynch: My Head is Disconnected', HOME Gallery, Manchester, 2019.

CHAPTER 5

'Is it future or is it past?' Visual Effects in *Twin Peaks: The Return*

Jannik Müller

Introduction

The much-anticipated third season of *Twin Peaks* (2017) marks the first time David Lynch has made extensive use of computer-generated imagery (CGI) in a film or series. During his eleven-year hiatus from film and television, the technical aspects of film production have changed significantly. Over the course of the 1990s and 2000s, CGI had become mainstream in big-budget movies, but remained a rarely used tool in low- or medium-budget productions. During the 2010s, the use of CGI became feasible even for low-budget film productions. A case in point is the science fiction film *Ex Machina* (Garland 2014), which won the 2016 Oscar for 'Best Visual Effects' with a budget of only $15,000,000 against contenders such as *Star Wars: The Force Awakens* (Abrams 2015), *The Martian* (Scott 2015) and *Mad Max: Fury Road* (Miller 2015). Digital technologies have advanced to a point where photorealistic visual effects are everywhere, regardless of a production's size or budget.

Lynch, who was very outspoken about the creative freedom brought by the use of digital cameras in *Inland Empire* (Lynch 2006; Todd 2012: 129; Lynch and McKenna 2019: 435), was now able to add CGI to this newfound liberty. CGI enables the filmmaker to manipulate or generate images independently, separate from the confines of the film set and shooting schedules. During post-production, digital technology allows the filmmaker to change a scene over and over again until satisfied. With a reportedly high budget for *Twin Peaks: The Return* (Lynch and McKenna 2019: 477, 499), audiences could assume high-standard visual effects for a TV-series from 2017.

The effects, however, were controversial. As Sébastien Chauvin wrote in his *Cahiers du Cinéma* article on *Twin Peaks: The Return*, the visual effects were '[. . .] one of the big surprises of season 3'[1] (Chauvin 2017: 22). On the pop culture blog *Polygon*, Julie Muncy writes: 'What's most striking about all these special effects, however, isn't their content, but their composition: Most of them are terrible' (2017: n.p.). The conflict seems to arise between the aesthetic expectations for visual effects on the one hand, and David Lynch's artistic style on the other hand. According to Allister Mactaggart, 'Lynch's films straddle a number of borders between film and fine art. The films reference avant-garde artistic practice and they also operate within mainstream cinema, although at its edges' (2010: 18). Mactaggart suggests studying Lynch's films as 'film paintings'. Instead of relying 'upon Hollywood narrative and generic structures', Lynch focuses on the audiovisual construction of 'films which looked like moving paintings' (ibid.: 12; Chion 2006: 9). Referring to Lev Manovich, Mactaggart highlights digital filmmaking as a technology that allows Lynch 'to treat a film image as an oil painting' and thus 'redefines what can be done with cinema' (Mactaggart 2010: 144; Manovich 2001: 305). This raises the question of how Lynch incorporates contemporary technology to create digital visual effects into his work and what aesthetic conventions he either follows or disregards.

This chapter aims to categorise different types of visual effects in *Twin Peaks: The Return* by approaching the series from the perspective of film and animation studies. Situated within the discourse of realism in computer-animation, it examines the visual phenomena audiences perceive as realistic and unrealistic – or hardly even recognise at all – with attention to the aesthetic conventions and technological tools generating them. In this context, the influence of mainstream animation technology can be understood as pervasive not only in blockbuster productions, but also in auteurist productions associated with a distinctly un- and surrealistic visual style.

Realism in Visual Effects

The quality of visual effects is often judged in comparison with and in relation to recorded, live-action footage. Therefore, the question of realism arises not only with digital visual effects, but also with the ontology of the moving image in general. As Michael Lommel and others point out in their introduction to *Surrealismus und Film: Von Fellini bis Lynch*, film is commonly associated with 'realism' (Lommel et al. 2008: 7). Theorists and practitioners have claimed an indexical relationship between the recorded image and the real world since it captures the events unaltered as they happen in front of the camera, instead of interpreting them. Contrary to this realist film ontology, formalism regards film as a constructed work of art. It is not an authentic recording of the 'real' world, but a technologically constructed work that is 'distinct from everyday perception by means such as montage, framing or the absence of color and language' (Elsaesser and Hagener 2010: 15). Although helpful for examining the facets of the photochemical image, both of these attributions are inherently reductionist: no live action film is completely realist, depicting real life without any artistic decisions to influence it, nor is it completely formalist, without referencing the actual moment of recording.

One can easily see this in the earlier works of David Lynch. As a surrealist, his films lean in the direction of formalism. However, even his most surreal film *Inland Empire* is recorded in a profilmic world, with actors on sets or on location. The captured material refers indexically to the moment of recording. Lynch's formalist approach emerges through editing techniques, sound design and analogue special effects, which remove the recorded imagery from the realistic situation captured in front of the camera.

The discourse surrounding realism and formalism is even more problematic in regards to digital visual effects. These images are completely fabricated on a computer, with no indexical tie tracing back to the moment of recording in the profilmic world. However, Lev Manovich points out a steady 'progression towards realism' in the computer graphics industry (2001: 184). In Manovich's terms, realism can be understood as the point where a computer-generated image is indistinguishable from a photographic image. Arguing with Maureen Furniss, one can add that visual effects continually strive for mimesis, an imitation of the way humans perceive the real world, while, like all animation, they have the potential for abstraction from realist concepts (2014: 6).

Stephen Prince discussed the implications for film ontology in his 1996 paper on 'perceptual realism'. Computer-generated imagery can appear realistic without having any indexical relationship to reality. In other words, it can look like it has been recorded even though a recording never took place. Prince illustrates this with scenes from *Forrest Gump* (Zemeckis 1994) in which Tom Hanks is composited into historical footage to appear alongside John F. Kennedy or John Lennon (Prince 1996: 30). Therefore, realism can no longer be linked only to the indexical relationship to the 'real' world but should also encompass the human visual perception of what is real (ibid.: 28). As an example, Prince mentions the dinosaurs in *Jurassic Park* (Spielberg 1993): Scientists cannot know for sure what dinosaurs looked like; they can at most formulate theories. For this reason, the images in Spielberg's film cannot be called realistic. However, the filmmakers used certain visual cues, for example detailed skin texture, lighting models and motion blur, to make the dinosaurs appear perceptually realistic. The images are not real, but visual cues in the images correspond with the audience's real-life and filmic experiences in a way that makes them seem real (Prince 1996: 31).

To achieve perceptual realism, the digital images need to blend in with the recorded material by mimicking light conditions, textures and so on, but also need to simulate analogue filmic standards like motion blur and film grain (Flückiger 2008: 334; Flückiger 2015).

Still, it remains difficult to tell how exactly these visual effects are perceived and in what way we can call them realistic or not realistic. Shilo T. McClean has developed a helpful taxonomy that serves as the basis for this analysis. Rather than only regarding the degree of photorealism of the computer-generated images, a concept which is constantly redefined since the audiences' perception of it changes over time, her taxonomy describes the 'narrative purposes of usage' (McClean 2007: 73). It consists of documentary, invisible, seamless, exaggerated, fantastical, surrealist, new traditionalist and hyperrealist visual effects (ibid.). The documentary mode is used to explain concepts or theories visually to the audience, for example via infographics. Invisible and seamless effects are so convincing that they are not detectable or only detectable because the audience knows the images could not have been filmed without the use of computer graphics. Exaggerated visual effects can look perceptually realistic, but portray improbable or even physically impossible events. Fantastical effects show supernatural elements in real-world settings. While invisible, exaggerated and fantastical effects do not disrupt the diegetic world, surrealist effects are often deliberately unrealistic. They portray mental states or dreams or show the diegetic world in a highly stylised fashion. Finally, new traditionalist and hyperrealist effects are found in completely computer-animated sequences or films. The former make use of a rather abstract and cartoonist approach and the latter aim at highly realistic graphics, which in their extreme can appear uncanny (ibid.: 69–102).

On the basis of McClean's taxonomy, this analysis develops three categories of visual effects that can be identified in *Twin Peaks: The Return*. Hyperrealist and fantastical effects are merged into the first category of perceptually realistic effects. The second category consists of surrealist effects and the third describes an effect that borders on seamlessness or invisibility. Documentary, new traditionalist and exaggerated visual effects are not present in the series and can be disregarded, since they mainly serve the narratives of documentary films, computer-animated films with a cartoonist approach or superhero movies. A study of the various categories of visual effects proves to be especially relevant in the discussion of Lynch as a film painter: in certain cases, he defies Hollywood conventions of realism, yet follows them in others. Especially in the combination of these categories, Lynch employs a wide aesthetic range that is exceptional in contemporary film and television.

Perceptually Realistic Effects

One of the most famous CGI shots of the new series is the nuclear explosion in 'Part 8'. The two-minute long scene, shot in black-and-white, begins with a documentary-style title card that reads 'July 16, 1945; White Sands, New Mexico; 5:29 AM (MWT)' which lets audiences who are well-versed in history identify the scene as a representation of the Trinity test, the first ever detonation of a nuclear bomb. The camera hovers over a mountain range and, with the explosion, begins to push in towards the forming mushroom cloud (Figure 5.1). It then moves into the cloud, where narrative and visual logic break down into abstract images. The computer animation in this scene is perceptually realistic. The landscape and the clouds appear realistic enough that they could be perceived as actual recordings. Disregarding the lack of film grain, the images of the forming mushroom cloud could be perceived as archive footage from the 1940s or 1950s. The only unrealistic element in this scene is the camera movement: Because of the energy released by the explosion, no physical camera could approach the mushroom cloud this closely without melting away. By slowly pushing in towards and eventually into the mushroom cloud, the scene reveals itself not to be archive footage, but a computer-generated shot, since actual footage of nuclear explosions is always static (Chauvin 2017: 23).

One could make the argument for the nuclear explosion being a seamless effect, since visual cues render it perceptually realistic. The audience

Figure 5.1 White Sands Mushroom Cloud from *Twin Peaks: The Return*, 'Part 8' (Screenshot from *Twin Peaks: A Limited Event Series*, Blu-ray, © Paramount Pictures (Universal Pictures))

identifies it as a computer-generated scene because it could not have been made otherwise (McClean 2007: 83). Since the scene is completely computer-animated, it creates what is called a hyperrealist effect. The nuclear explosion 'is in keeping with the narrative intentions of Invisible [sic] and Seamless [sic] usages. Only the impossibility of the camera move reveals the digital substance of the shot [. . .]' (ibid.: 101). In computer animation, the virtual camera is not constrained by physical laws, but can move as freely as the animator wants. According to Richard Rickitt, though, spectacular 'roller-coaster rides through the artificial environment of the computer' can distract the audience. Therefore, virtual cameras tend to emulate the more restrained camera work of physical cameras (Rickitt 2006: 233–4). A more extreme form of virtual camera movement would be, for example, the impossible tracking shot through a keyhole in *Panic Room* (Fincher 2002). The virtual camera movement towards the nuclear explosion, however, is a simple, straightforward tracking shot. It defies the laws of physics, but visually adheres to perceptual and filmic conventions and thus seems perceptually realistic.

There are several other effects that are perceptually realistic, but much more fantastical. Later in 'Part 8', a hybrid creature, a cross between a frog and a moth, emerges from an egg in the desert and eventually crawls into the mouth of a girl. The 'Frogmoth' is perceptually realistic, although no such creature exists outside the series' diegesis. Among the visual cues which generate perceptual realism, Prince names lighting, texture and movement as the most important (Prince 1996: 33). The lighting of the creature's body matches the rest of the scenery. Its texture is largely reminiscent of the slightly shiny skin of a frog, while its forelegs and wings are similar to those of insects. The creature's movements also match the audience's real-life and filmic experiences. For instance, its movements are clumsy and restricted by its bodyweight, which creates the impression of the 'Frogmoth' having a physical presence in the environment it was digitally placed in. Additionally, the filmic convention of motion blur makes the creature blend in with the rest of the image. The computer-generated 'Frogmoth' meets all three criteria and is therefore perceived as realistic. Since this perceptually realistic effect visualises a supernatural hybrid creature which could not exist in the real world, it is a fantastical effect (McClean 2007: 89).

Hyperrealist and fantastical effects are both perceptually realistic, although they actually portray impossible phenomena. The nuclear explosion is a realistic event that could not have been filmed the way it is shown, and the supernatural 'Frogmoth' is an unrealistic creature that is made to appear realistic. In both cases, the perceptual realism of the animation is used as a spectacle since the quality of the effects is measured by how similar to the real world they look (McClean 2007: 89, 102). For that reason, McClean's categories of hyperrealist and fantastical effects are combined into the category of 'perceptually realistic effects'. Such high-end visual effects were not present in David Lynch's work previously, but they cannot be described as 'one of the big surprises' of *Twin Peaks: The Return*. Despite Mactaggart pointing out that digital technology allows filmmakers to gain painterly control over their images, free from narrative and generic restrictions, Lynch's perceptually realistic effects nevertheless strongly adhere to the aesthetic conventions of both Hollywood and the visual effects industry.

Surrealist Effects

The surprising effects of the series are those that do not look perceptually realistic at all, even though scenes like the nuclear explosion clearly show that the filmmakers were capable of approaching photorealism. One scene worth discussing here is Dougie Jones' death scene in the Red Room in 'Part 3'. First, Dougie Jones, sitting in an armchair, appears to shrink. His hands grow smaller, which causes his green ring to fall off. Suddenly, his head explodes and smoke rises from his neck. Out of the smoke emerges a golden orb, which hovers around for a while (Figure 5.2). Dougie's body deflates and his clothes fall to the ground. In his place, a distorted grey shape levitates above the armchair, surrounded by black smoke. Its distortion decreases and the golden orb pushes out of the grey shape. The grey mass swirls down to the armchair and – with a lot of lightning and smoke – disappears. What remains is the golden orb on a black cushion.

Figure 5.2 Dougie Jones disintegrates, from *Twin Peaks: The Return*, 'Part 3'
(Screenshot from *Twin Peaks: A Limited Event Series*, Blu-ray,
© Paramount Pictures (Universal Pictures))

In his *Sight & Sound* article, Michael Ewins calls effects like these 'uncannily synthetic' (Ewins 2018: 33). This assessment conveys irritation with the visual effects, just as Julie Muncy (2017: n.p.) deems such effects 'terrible'. Much of these backlashes might be due to the uncommon use of surrealist visual effects in mainstream media. Due to their financial burden, visual effects are rarely employed in order to break with realist conventions. This warrants a closer look at what makes these effects – the visual cues of lighting, texture and movement Lynch employs – not perceptually realistic, but worthy of being noted by someone like Ewin as uncanny.

The light reflection on the golden orb in Fig. 5.2 does not change, which it should when moving left and right, up and down in space. This is because the orb is a two-dimensional still frame and not an animated three-dimensional object. When it moves without the reflection moving, the illusion is broken and the image is revealed to be flat and not part of the actual scene. The textures of the effects do not seem natural as well. While the shrinking effect on Dougie's hand looks relatively realistic, the smoke does not: It seems to levitate rather than to disperse and when the body collapses, the smoke collapses with it and leaves no residual smoke behind. Lastly, the movement in the effects inhibits perceptual realism: The smoke and the orb seem to hover unnaturally in the air and the grey object distorts in only two dimensions instead of three. This gives the audience the impression that the objects are not really part of the recorded image but are – like the golden orb – flat images. Additionally, Dougie's collapsing clothes seem to have been realised with a stop motion effect, which creates a jerky movement because of the lack of motion blur.

Considering Lynch's reputation as a surrealist filmmaker (Lommel, Maurer Queipo and Roloff 2008: 10), the above effects can be classified as surrealistic. As McClean points out, surrealist visual effects are often used to visualise mental states and dream sequences or act as visual metaphors (93–8). This, however, is not the case in *Twin Peaks: The Return*. In the first season, the 'Red Room' was established as a location Cooper only visited in a dream. In season 2, it was rationalised as an actual, albeit supernatural place one could enter through a portal in Ghostwood Forest outside of Twin Peaks (Glaubitz and Schröter 2008: 288). In season 3, it is further explored as one of many supernatural places connected with each other and accessible from many different locations.[2] Therefore, the surrealist effects do not visualise dreams or metaphors, but represent the 'Red Room' as an otherworldly place.

This, however, does not sufficiently explain the use of surrealist effects, since they not only visualise events in the theatrical 'Red Room', but also in the diegetic 'real' world. After his otherworldly odyssey in 'Part 3', Cooper enters reality through a power socket. Surrounded by hovering dark smoke, Cooper's body stretches out of the power socket like rubber and levitates towards the ground, where the smoke disperses and Cooper's body resumes its normal shape. The lighting looks fairly realistic because Cooper's stretched body casts a shadow on the wall while emerging from the power socket. The texture and movement however do not seem perceptually realistic: The smoke seems to stick to Cooper instead of dispersing in the air and his body gets distorted to an absurd degree. Such an effect is likely to be perceived by audiences as odd and unrealistic. Using McClean's categorisation again, the surreal quality of the effects does not reflect mental or dream states, but is a highly stylised creative visualisation fitting for an idiosyncratic filmmaker like Lynch (McClean 2007: 96–8).

This is further demonstrated by a scene from 'Part 11' in which Gordon Cole, Albert Rosenfield and Tammy Preston inspect a trailer park where a supernatural incident has supposedly taken place. Gordon Cole discovers a vortex to another dimension that opens up in the sky. It could be argued that the vortex is a fantastical effect, since it represents a supernatural phenomenon occurring in the diegetic 'real' world (McClean 2007: 90–1). But although it is narratively framed as a real occurrence, the lack of perceptual realism exposes the effect's digital composition: the lighting is inconspicuous, but the texture and movement are once again irritating. Instead of appearing as an object in the three-dimensional diegetic world, with the sky behind and the trees and power lines in front of it, the vortex distorts the two-dimensional filmic image itself (Figure 5.3). The sky, the trees and

Figure 5.3 A vortex in the sky, from *Twin Peaks: The Return*, 'Part 11' (Screenshot from *Twin Peaks: A Limited Event Series*, Blu-ray, © Paramount Pictures (Universal Pictures))

the power lines appear to be sucked into the vortex as one flat surface, which creates a highly stylised effect characteristic of McClean's surrealist category (Chauvin 2017: 23; McClean 2007: 96–7).

The reason for a lack of perceptual realism is often attributed to a production's budget. It is known that Lynch almost dropped out of the project due to budgetary constraints, but subsequent negotiations between Lynch and the producing network Showtime gave Lynch free range to realise his vision (Lynch and McKenna 2019: 477, 499). However, on-set confrontations shown in a making-of documentary reveal Lynch complaining about time restrictions and a lack of creative flexibility, leading back to budgetary issues (Jason S.: *A Pot of Boiling Oil* 2017). Even though Lynch stated he would not have done the project if his creative vision had been impaired, it is possible that a limited budget was at least part of the reason why some visual effects do not seem convincing enough.

Another explanation, however, is that Lynch decided not to follow the rules of photorealistic CGI in order to generate different aesthetic experiences for the audience. The surrealist effects of Dougie's death in the 'Red Room', Cooper emerging from the power socket and the vortex in the sky support Mactaggart's argument on viewing Lynch's work as film paintings. Since computer animation allows the artist to translate virtually any idea into filmic images, they are an ideal tool to create a film (or in this case a television series) like a painting rather than a conventional film production (Mactaggart 2010: 141; Manovich 2001: 304–7).

Many of the visual effects were created by the French visual effects studio BUF, a company that worked on CGI-centred productions such as *The Matrix* sequels (Wachowski and Wachowski 2003) or *Blade Runner 2049* (Villeneuve 2017). According to BUF's website, the studio overall worked on 213 shots, or 40 minutes for the show, ranging from perceptually realistic shots like the nuclear explosion to surrealist sequences like Dougie's death. In an interview with *Cahiers du Cinéma*, the special effects supervisor Pierre Buffin talks about working with David Lynch:

> It wasn't always easy to meet his demands. We worked quite a while on the scene where Dougie blows up in the 'Red Room'. Lynch had basically told us: the character sits in his chair, he begins to shrink, he loses his ring, then he collapses and turns into pizza dough. We then made some kind of pizza dough but it was ridiculous. [. . .] When we arrived at those kinds of dead ends, he took over with 2D effects. (Buffin in Chauvin 2017: 22)[3]

According to Buffin, BUF only corresponded with Lynch himself, while on other productions the visual effects artists talk to a supervisor and are almost never in direct contact with the director (ibid.: 22–3). The visual effects thus emerged through a trial-and-error approach where Lynch gave BUF instructions and reference material (mostly from his own works of fine art), the VFX artists worked out a shot and then Lynch revised it. Sometimes an effect did not work, so Lynch adjusted his wishes for the scenes or worked on his own 2D-effect shots. Although visual effects supervisor Pierre Buffin concedes that blockbuster-style effects do not fit Lynch's aesthetic (ibid.: 22), Buffin claims to have been irritated by the final product:

> At first, I was pretty lost. We had much more sophisticated effects, and right there I was seeing some pretty old-school effects for 2017. Maybe our weakness is that we always try to create impressive effects. But Lynch doesn't care about that. (ibid.: 23)[4]

From this quote we can conclude that Lynch's views as a film painter were sometimes in conflict with the aesthetic conventions of the mainstream effects studio that sought to create perceptually realistic spectacles.

Many of the surrealist effects, like the vortex or Dougie's death, were created by BUF, but some effects were done 'in-house' (Lynch and McKenna 2019: 502), in the studio with direct supervision by Lynch. Those primarily 2D-animated shots were often based on Lynch's works as a fine artist. Chrysta Bell, who plays Tammy Preston on the show and who collaborated with Lynch for several years as a musician, states: 'I didn't know until I saw the show that it included all of David's animations, sculptures, paintings – all of the stuff he'd been working on for years' (ibid.: 491).

Although reminiscent of Lynch's artworks, the surrealist effects still stirred up controversy. Ryan Coogan is certainly right to point out that '[t]he world of *Twin Peaks*, detailed though it may be, is demonstrably weird from the outset' (Coogan 2019: 137). The weirdness of the original *Twin Peaks*, however, stems mainly from the characters and the rules of its world and less from the visuals. Along with the world of *Twin Peaks* that is explored further in *The Return* (Sanna 2019: 10), the surrealist visuals and their realisation with computer-generated imagery bring an additional layer of weirdness and complexity to the series.

Another reason for the confusion surrounding the visual effects is the combination of different kinds of effects in the series. Given the high resolution of the digitally filmed images and the perceptually realistic rendition of the nuclear explosion or the 'Frogmoth', the surrealist effects stick out more in comparison. Synthetic looking visual effects are commonly associated with a lack of budget or talent. Since Lynch is known as a highly professional technician (Todd 2012: 111), the audience's normative preconceptions of 'good' and 'bad' visual effects are challenged. While Hollywood's hyperrealist spectacle adheres to the industrial standards of computer animation, the surrealist effects are directly inspired by David Lynch's experimental artworks and thus defy the conventions of mainstream visual effects. Although they apply to aesthetically different categories, what perceptually realistic and surrealist effects have in common is that they are recognisable as visual effects. There is another category, however, that aims to remain unnoticed.

Seamless to Invisible Effects

Twin Peaks: The Return features several characters that appeared in both the previous seasons and the film *Twin Peaks: Fire Walk with Me* (Lynch 1992), and are shown in season 3 as they appeared in the early 1990s. For instance, the evil spirit Bob, played by Frank Silva, who died in 1995, is integrated by using stock footage from the original series, since the character was an integral part of the story. In *Twin Peaks: The Return* he therefore appears not in human form, but as a black orb showing his face inside it. According to BUF, they 'could only use some very limited footage from the first seasons that matched the desired acting. A CG model of Bob was created for this purpose, and we used the selected Bob's images to help the texturing' (BUF). Through digital technology Bob, or rather Bob's face, is made to appear exactly the way he looked 25 years ago, even though no new scenes were filmed.

The same holds for the character of Major Garland Briggs, who Lynch incorporated into the story even though the actor Don S. Davis passed away in 2008. On their website, BUF notes:

> The main challenge was to recreate a CG head of Major Briggs, who says 'Blue Rose' while moving from right to left through dark clouds and stars. As the actor Don S. Davis died in 2008, and as David Lynch wanted the same face (but stretched and a bit transparent) as in the two first seasons of the show, we just had pictures from this period to recreate the full head and animate it. (Ibid.)

Instead of moving images, Major Briggs' head was animated on the basis of still images alone. This creates a surreal effect, which is fitting since his floating head is seen in supernatural environments like near a black box floating in space or inside the Fireman's house.

In addition to these idiosyncratic resurrections of deceased actors, Lynch also follows the contemporary Hollywood trend of digitally altering a living actress's appearance. In 'Part 17', Cooper travels back in time to save Laura Palmer from being killed. First, we see a scene with Laura Palmer and James Hurley from the film *Twin Peaks: Fire Walk with Me*.

The archive footage is filtered in black-and-white[5] and is cross-cut with new scenes of present-day Cooper hiding in the bushes. This scene is followed by a scene in which the present-day Cooper talks to the young Laura Palmer, who looks like she did in the early 1990s (Figure 5.4). To make this interaction possible, BUF used digital de-ageing technology.

> The great challenge of these shots was to make the actress Sheryl Lee look 25 years younger, in order to match the footage from the first season. It was quite tricky to find an effect that makes her naturally young, and does not look like a 'plastic surgery'. We used a mixed technique with 2D morph and hand-painted key frames interpolated by the 'optical flow'. (BUF)

Here, Lynch uses state-of-the-art technology. After more or less success-ful uses in *X-Men: The Last Stand* (Ratner 2006) and *The Curious Case of Benjamin Button* (Fincher 2008), de-ageing technology has become increasingly sophisticated in the last decade. It has been applied in several films of blockbuster franchises like the Marvel Cinematic Universe and *Star Wars* and was recently used as the central gimmick in films like *The Irishman* (Scorsese 2019) and *Gemini Man* (Lee 2019), where stars such as Robert De Niro and Will Smith played old and young versions of the same characters (Parker 2020: 37).

Pierre Buffin calls Laura Palmer's de-ageing the 'only "invisible" effect that we had to deal with'[6] (Buffin in Chauvin 2017: 23) and hereby uses

Figure 5.4 Cooper meets the young Laura Palmer, from *Twin Peaks: The Return*, 'Part 17' (Screenshot from *Twin Peaks: A Limited Event Series*, Blu-ray, © Paramount Pictures (Universal Pictures))

the same terminology as McClean. Wells summarises McClean's category of invisible effects as 'deliberately concealed, undetectable interventions preserving the reality of the diegetic world, where the audience must not suspect or detect effects use' (Wells 2012: 468). McClean elaborates that the

> detection of the techniques is considered by effects artists to be a failure to achieve the necessary standard. Indeed, invisibly introducing effects into a film and having them go unnoticed is considered to be 'the best' use of this type of DVFx. (2007: 76)

Invisible effects are not meant to be seen but are only able to be discussed with background knowledge of the production. As a prominent example, McClean names the technique of sky replacement as a means of 'preserving narrative integrity' which otherwise might have been disrupted due to a lack of continuity in editing (ibid.: 77). Computer-generated or -manipulated environments, however, are much less noticeable compared with human faces, since the human brain is trained to examine facial movements much more closely. Creating a photorealistic face has been and is still seen as one of the hardest tasks in CGI. According to Rickitt, '[w]e are all experts in what faces of all shapes, shades and emotions look like and are not easy to fool with any form of synthesized performance' (Rickitt 2006: 213). That is why de-ageing, although intended to be invisible, is rarely undetectable. By showing off their technological achievements through extensive close-ups, many blockbusters unintentionally give away the imperfections and artificiality of the effects.

The seamless to invisible effect has a less painterly quality. Although it is a digital tool with which Lynch has painter-like control over the image, the de-ageing effect is an almost clichéd effect for contemporary Hollywood productions. Many recent blockbusters show flashbacks with younger versions of famous actors first and foremost because it is technologically possible to do so. In contrast to most of these blockbuster movies, however, Lynch uses the effect very subtly. In 'Part 17', Laura Palmer is shown in a medium long shot. As the scene progresses, the camera gets closer to an American shot and eventually to a medium shot. Additionally, she is shown in very low-key lighting and mostly in black-and-white, which obscures the image and helps to disguise imperfections one might see in a well-lit image or in a close-up. While it is perhaps too uncritical to call the effect truly invisible, it certainly is on the threshold between seamless and invisible. As noted by McClean, '[t]he Seamless [sic] use of effects is continuous with Invisible usage, but seamless effects are discernible if subjected to scrutiny and consideration' (McClean 2007: 78). On the one hand, after thoroughly studying the above scene audiences may find imperfections in the images and detect the visual effects to be visible after all. On the other hand, from a narrative point of view, the effect aspires to be invisible.

The mise-en-scène and the camera work in 'Part 17' do not draw attention to the de-ageing effect and aim to convince the audience that they are seeing the Laura Palmer they know from the past. Blockbusters often advertise a film's use of de-ageing technology and show the digitally manipulated faces in long close-ups. Lynch instead obscures Laura Palmer's face and does not advertise her de-aged mien. Audiences and fans know of the technology's usage by way of David Lynch's precirculated statements. Still these audiences would not have noticed the effect just on the basis of the images. Without any contextual knowledge, one could therefore think the shots of young Laura Palmer were unused footage from the film *Fire Walk with Me*, intercut with new footage of Agent Cooper. Therefore, the de-ageing of Laura Palmer constitutes a third category of visual effects in *Twin Peaks: The Return* where computer animation is used very subtly and defers attention from its production process. The almost invisible effect is not only perceptually realistic, but almost indistinguishable from the indexical realism of recorded imagery.

Conclusion

Using McClean's taxonomy of visual effects, this chapter aimed to show which aesthetic conventions for computer-generated imagery are followed or disregarded in *Twin Peaks: The Return*. The visual effects can be categorised into (1) perceptually realistic effects that follow mainstream trends, (2) surrealist effects that defy these trends and (3) seamless to invisible effects that explore the possibilities of defying the age or even the death of actors. Therefore, one of the most repeated phrases of the series, 'Is it future or is it past?', also applies to the usage of visual effects: While the hyperrealist and fantastical effects like those of the nuclear explosion or the 'Frogmoth' creature represent contemporary visual effects that can be seen in many films and TV-shows, Lynch's surrealist effects point to the past. They adapt motifs from Lynch's previous artworks and were received as 'old school' or 'uncannily synthetic' (Ewins 2018: 33) due to their lack of perceptual realism. They refer back to a time when CGI was not able to mimic recorded photographic images.[7] With the de-ageing of Laura Palmer, Lynch applies a seamless to invisible effect. This technology has been used in a number of productions in the last 15 years, but has only recently become sophisticated enough to approach invisibility. The de-ageing effect used on Sheryl Lee points toward the future of visual effects, since the technology opens up new technical possibilities as well as ethical questions about the future use of likenesses of ageing or even deceased actors (Parker 2020: 37). In *Twin Peaks: The Return*, audiences can see precursors of these issues in the form of Frank Silva's and Don S. Davis's likenesses being reused in the form of archive footage. Being now able to convincingly de-age Sheryl Lee to look 25 years younger heralds the possibility of recreating entire performances via CGI. Interestingly however, Lynch chooses not to re-create deceased actors' likenesses with this technology – be it for ethical or aesthetic reasons – which in itself warrants a more detailed discussion elsewhere.

Within the context of Lynch's work as film paintings, the visual effects reflect the conflict between the mainstream aesthetic conventions of visual effects and Lynch's style as an auteur. *Twin Peaks: The Return* is unique in using distinctly different visual effects styles within a single series. Depending on the intended purpose of the effect, certain aesthetic conventions are either followed or disregarded. In perceptually realistic effects, certain unrealistic properties such as camera movement or subject matter are permitted or even required to immerse the audience in the audiovisual spectacle. In the example of the nuclear explosion, a surrealist effect such as animated still images or stop motion animation would not create both a sense of awe due to the spectacle and the impression of witnessing an actual historic event.

Other effects, however, show surrealist qualities because they portray strange or even impossible occurrences. They probably could have been rendered more perceptually realistic, but as Buffin described in his interview, it might have been even more distracting and limiting to Lynch's dreamlike and surrealist style. The surrealist effects are a transmedial continuation of David Lynch's artworks within contemporary digital technology. As a different kind of spectacle, they defy the convention of perceptual realism and provoke the audience to critically reflect the filmic reality.

The perceptually realistic and surrealist effects are primarily used to create an aesthetic experience, either an immersive or an irritating one, which supports Mactaggart's argument that Lynch's film paintings favour the visual and acoustic over narrative or generic conventions (2010: 12). Both these categories make audiences aware of the effects' artificiality. In the case of the almost invisible de-ageing effect, however, it is essential to make the viewer believe the images are real. Any unrealistic or even slightly distracting element would have drawn the attention away from the narrative towards the production process of the effect. Thus, the audience would have been distracted from a key scene in which it is imperative for the audience to believe they are seeing Laura Palmer alive shortly before they know her death to take place. The twist of Cooper changing history by saving Laura is so emotionally resonant, I would argue, because the audience is led to believe they are watching footage from decades ago. Therefore, the seamless to invisible effect is employed not to emphasise the visual aspect of a film painting, but to serve the emotionally resonant narrative. While most visual effects in *Twin Peaks: The Return* support Mctaggart's argument, the de-ageing effect is a demonstration of Lynch also following current trends in mainstream Hollywood productions.

The unique status of the series' visual effects, and the reason for their controversial reception, I would argue, is not only due to the perceived quality of the effects, but also to the combination of different categories: perceptually realistic, surrealist and almost invisible effects co-exist within the same series, sometimes even in the same episode. The exclusive use of perceptually realistic and seamless to invisible effects would have made the CGI itself unremarkable. It would have made them spectacular and technically impressive, but also interchangeable with any other mainstream production. At the same time, only non-perceptually realistic effects would have given the impression that Lynch did not know how to use modern technology. They might have underlined Lynch's reputation as a creator of weird worlds (Sanna 2019: 10–11) but might also have caused the series to seem outdated.

As Manovich attested in the early 2000s, visual effects are occupied by a progression towards realism. In combining the past, present and possible future visual effects, Lynch uses the full potential of computer animation and thus challenges mainstream Hollywood conventions and viewer expectations. On the one hand, he demonstrates his ability to keep up with modern developments in technology by fulfilling the expectations for mainstream visual effects. On the other hand, he remains consistent with his painterly style by breaking established aesthetic conventions. Through this strategy, Lynch makes the audience aware that the highly standardised aesthetics of visual effects need not remain within the confines of realism. Rather, as *Twin Peaks: The Return* reminds us, digital animation is a virtually limitless source of creative possibilities.

Notes

1. Own translation. Original: '*une des grandes surprises de la saison 3.*'
2. The 'Red Room' appears to Bad Cooper in the middle of a highway. Mike tries to reach Dougie Jones from the 'Red Room' in different places, such as a casino, an office building and at Dougie's/Cooper's hospital bed.

3. Author's own translation. Original: '*Ce n'était pas toujours facile de répondre à ses demandes. Ainsi on a passé pas mal de temps sur la scène où Dougie devait exploser dans la Red Room. Lynch nous avait dit en substance: le personnage est assis sur son fauteuil, il se met à rétrécir, il perd sa bague, puis il s'effondre et se transforme en pâte à pizza. On a donc fait uns sorte de pâte à pizza mais c'était vraiment risible. [. . .] Quant nous arrivions à ce genre d'impasses, c'est lui qui prenait le relais avec des effets 2D.*'

4. Own translation. Original: '*Au départ j'étais plutôt déboussolé. Nous avions fait des effets bien plus sophistiqués et, là, je voyais des effet vraiment old school pour 2017. Nous avons peut-être un défaut, qui consiste à chercher à faire des effets impressionants. Alors que ça, Lynch s'en fiche pas mal.*'

5. A whole paper could probably be written about the significance of the black-and-white filter in *Twin Peaks: The Return*. During the series, several key scenes are in black-and-white, from the very first scene of 'Part 1' and most of 'Part 8' to Gordon Cole's 'Monica Bellucci-Dream' in 'Part 14' and Cooper changing history in 'Part 17'. Not only does it refer back to the legacy of monochrome film, it also suggests intervention, be it a nuclear bomb's, the Fireman's, or Cooper's intervention in the natural order of the world. Because the aesthetic convention of a black-and-white filter abstracts the originally coloured image, it could also provoke doubt about the reality of the monochrome scenes. As Monica Bellucci's and Gordon Cole's monologue ('We are like the dreamer who dreams and then lives inside the dream') suggests, the black-and-white scenes could indicate dream scenes. Even more radical, they could reveal these scenes or indeed the whole series as a constructed work of fiction inside the fiction. Thanks to Andreas Rauscher for the valuable suggestion.

6. Own translation. Original: '*Le seul effet "invisible" que nour avons dû gérer*'.

7. It must be noted that these effects refer to the past CGI-aesthetic that Lynch himself did not use in the 1990s. While it would be tempting to suggest that Lynch uses old-fashioned CGI to evoke nostalgia for the original series, this disregards the fact that the original show almost never used digital visual effects. If Lynch intended these effects as a comment on nostalgia, it would have made sense for him to use them in the most nostalgic scenes: those that take place on the night of Laura Palmer's death. On the contrary, these scenes rely on the most sophisticated effects in the show.

Bibliography

BUF. 'Twin Peaks'. *BUF*, 2017, https://buf.com/films/twin-peaks/ (last accessed 8 December 2020).

Chauvin, Jean-Sébastien. 'Primitif. Entretien avec Pierre Buffin, créateur des effets spéciaux'. *Cahiers du Cinéma*, no. 737, 2017, pp. 22–3.

Chion, Michel. *David Lynch*. 2nd edition. BFI, 2006.

Coogan, Ryan. '"Here's to the Pie That Saved Your Life, Dougie": The Weird Realism of *Twin Peaks*'. *Critical Essays on Twin Peaks: The Return*, Antonio Sanna (ed.). Palgrave Macmillan, 2019, pp. 135–48.

Elsaesser, Thomas and Malte Hagener. *Film Theory. An Introduction through the Senses*. Routledge, 2010.

Ewins, Michael. 'The Stars Turn and a Time Presents Itself'. *Sight & Sound*, vol. 28, no. 1, 2018, pp. 33–6.

Flückiger, Barbara. *Visual Effects. Filmbilder aus dem Computer*. Schüren, 2008.

Flückiger, Barbara. 'Photorealism, Nostalgia and Style. Material Properties of Film in Digital Visual Effects'. *Special Effects. New Histories/Theories/Contexts*, Dan North, Bob Rehak and Michael S. Duffy (eds). BFI, 2015, pp. 78–96.

Furniss, Maureen. *Art in Motion. Animation Aesthetics*. Revised edition. John Libbey, 2014.

Glaubitz, Nicola and Jens Schröter. 'Surreale und surrealistische Elemente in David Lynchs Fernsehserie *Twin Peaks*'. *Surrealismus und Film: Von Fellini bis Lynch*, Michael Lommel, Isabel Maurer Queipo and Volker Roloff. Transcript, 2008, pp. 281–300.

Lommel, Michael, Isabel Maurer Queipo and Volker Roloff. 'Einleitung'. *Surrealismus und Film: Von Fellini bis Lynch*, Michael Lommel, Isabel Maurer Queipo and Volker Roloff (eds). Transcript, 2008, pp. 7–18.

Lynch, David and Kristine McKenna. *Room to Dream*. Canongate Books, 2019.

McClean, Shilo T. *Digital Storytelling. The Narrative Power of Visual Effects in Film*. MIT Press, 2007.

Mactaggart, Allister. *The Film Paintings of David Lynch. Challenging Film Theory*. Intellect, 2010.

Manovich, Lev. *The Language of New Media*. MIT Press, 2001.

Muncy, Julie. '*Twin Peaks* Uses Glitches, New Technology to Bring Lynch's Madness into a New Age'. *Polygon*, 2017, https://www.polygon.com/2017/5/31/15713068/twin-peaks-vhs-technology (last accessed 8 December 2020).

Parker, Kate. 'Rolling Back the Years. Is De-Aging Tech the Future of Film-Making?' *Engineering & Technology*, vol. 15, no. 2, 2020, pp. 34–7.

Prince, Steven. 'True Lies. Perceptual Realism, Digital Images, and Film Theory'. *Film Quarterly*, Vol. 49, No. 3, 1996, pp. 27–37.

Rickitt, Richard. *Special Effects. The History and Technique*. Aurum, 2006.

Sanna, Antonio. 'Entering the World of Twin Peaks'. *Critical Essays on Twin Peaks: The Return*, Antonio Sanna (ed). Palgrave Macmillan, 2019, pp. 2–21.

Todd, Anthony. *Authorship and the Films of David Lynch. Aesthetic Receptions in Contemporary Hollywood*. I. B. Tauris, 2012.

Wells, Paul. 'Computer Animation. Margins to Mainstream'. *The Wiley-Blackwell History of American Film, Volume IV, 1976 to the Present*, Cynthia Lucia, Roy Grundmann and Art Simon (eds). Wiley-Blackwell, 2012, pp. 448–71.

Filmography

A Pot of Boiling Oil (Impressions: A Journey Behind the Scenes of Twin Peaks). Directed by Jason S. Showtime, 2017.

Blade Runner 2049. Directed by Denis Villeneuve, performances by Ryan Gosling, Harrison Ford, Ana de Armas, and Robin Wright, Alcon Entertainment, Columbia Pictures, 2017.

Ex Machina. Directed by Alex Garland, performances by Domhnall Gleeson, Alicia Vikander, and Oscar Isaac, A24, Universal Pictures, 2014.

Forrest Gump. Directed by Robert Zemeckis, performances by Tom Hanks, Robin Wright, Gary Sinise, and Sally Field, Paramount Pictures, 1994.

Gemini Man. Directed by Ang Lee, performances by Will Smith, Mary Elizabeth Winstead, Clive Owen, and Benedict Wong, Paramount Pictures, 2019.

Jurassic Park. Directed by Steven Spielberg, performances by Sam Neill, Laura Dern, Jeff Goldblum, and Bob Peck, Universal Pictures, 1993.

Inland Empire. Directed by David Lynch, performances by Laura Dern, Jeremy Irons, Justin Theroux, Harry Dean Stanton, StudioCanal, 2006.

Mad Max: Fury Road. Directed by George Miller, performances by Tom Hardy, Charlize Theron, Nicholas Hoult, and Riley Keough, Village Roadshow Pictures, Warner Bros., 2015.

Panic Room. Directed by David Fincher, performances by Jodie Foster, Forest Whitaker, Jared Leto, and Kristen Stewart, Columbia Pictures, Sony Pictures Releasing, 2002.

Star Wars: The Force Awakens. Directed by J. J. Abrams, performances by Daisy Ridley, Oscar Isaac, Harrison Ford, and Adam Driver, Lucasfilm Ltd., Walt Disney Studios, 2015.

The Curious Case of Benjamin Button. Directed by David Fincher, performances by Brad Pitt, Cate Blanchett, Mahershala Ali, and Tilda Swinton, Paramount Pictures, 2008.

The Irishman. Directed by Martin Scorsese, performances by Robert De Niro, Al Pacino, Joe Pesci, and Ray Romano, TriBeCa Productions, Netflix, 2019.

The Martian. Directed by Ridley Scott, performances by Matt Damon, Jessica Chastain, Kristen Wiig, and Jeff Daniels, 20th Century Fox, 2015.

The Matrix Reloaded. Directed by Lana Wachowski and Lilly Wachowski, performances by Keanu Reeves, Laurence Fishburne, Carrie-Anne Moss, and Hugo Weaving, Warner Bros, 2003.

The Matrix Revolutions. Directed by Lana Wachowski and Lilly Wachowski, performances by Keanu Reeves, Laurence Fishburne, Carrie-Anne Moss, and Hugo Weaving, Warner Bros., 2003.

Twin Peaks. Directed by David Lynch et al., performances by Kyle MacLachlan and Mädchen Amick, Lynch/Frost Productions et al., 1990–1.

Twin Peaks: Fire Walk with Me. Directed by David Lynch, performances by Sheryl Lee, Kyle MacLachlan, and Ray Wise, CIBY Picture, 1992.

Twin Peaks: The Return [on DVD and Blu-ray *Twin Peaks: A Limited Event Series*]. Directed by David Lynch, performances by Sheryl Lee and Kyle MacLachlan, Showtime, 2017.

X-Men: The Last Stand. Directed by Brett Ratner, performances by Hugh Jackman, Patrick Stewart, Ian McKellen, and Famke Janssen, 20th Century Fox, 2006.

CHAPTER 6

That Gum You Like *Isn't* Going to Come Back in Style: *Twin Peaks* 1990–1/2017, Nostalgia and the End of (Golden Age) Television

Bernd Zywietz

Introduction

The leading question of this contribution stems from a personal endeavour: How can one come to terms with *Twin Peaks* season 3 a.k.a. *Twin Peaks: The Return* (2017) or, for short, *The Return*. The original *Twin Peaks* series is important to me, both personally and professionally. In searching for clues on how Lynch and Frost thought to continue Dale Cooper's story after what was, emotionally, the worst possible ending of season 2, I started researching and reading books such as Chris Rodney's *Lynch on Lynch* in an early German edition (Lynch and Rodney). This was the start of my career in film studies, which I followed up with a short film *Lünsch* – as part of my degree programme – about two young and aspiring student film makers kidnapping Lynch in order to force him to explain his movies to them. My first engagement in lecturing at a university as a student assistant was a David Lynch film course (together with one of the editors of this volume) and my final one, years later, offered a thorough study of *Twin Peaks*, much to the despair of some of my students. After that, I took a turn to a broader field of interest in media studies and left 'academia' in 2020 for the time being. However, the very personal, even intimate, significance of the original show stuck with me.

So, naturally, I was thrilled when in 2014 Lynch himself (or whoever is behind his official Twitter account) hinted in a tweet that he and Frost were about to revisit – or to revive – *Twin Peaks*. He did so by quoting a famous character of the series, the otherworldly Man from Another Place: 'Dear Twitter Friends: That gum you like is going to come back in style! #damngoodcoffee' (Lynch).[1] Yet three years and eighteen episodes later I could not help but wonder: Had Lynch been wrong – or even outright lying – concerning his announcement back then? A great many people loved and appreciated the limited television event, which aired in 2018, but I am convinced that I was not alone in having a different (or limited or conservative) *taste* about season 3. Even though Lynch announced in his tweet the return of 'the gum you like', it was not my favourite 'gum' which came back 'in style' in 2018. Admittingly, 'style' is not 'taste', but what 'style' are we talking about anyway?

In between the many weekly recaps, avid celebratory online discussions and dissections of every aspect and episode of *The Return*, some viewers openly expressed their concerns with the show. Several writers, writing in places ranging from established news outlets to simple message boards, stressed the importance *Twin Peaks* had to their lives (as I did in the opening of this chapter). Like me, these writers tried less to make sense of the show's shenanigans than of their own felt inaptitude or deficiency to praise, love and embrace the widely acclaimed show. One of them was Matt Armitage, who 'set out to investigate my own and others [sic] problems with *The Return*' (Armitage 2017a). In his two-part online essay (Armitage 2017a and 2017b), the Director of Operations at 25YL Media states:

> I'll begin with a confession – I was disappointed in *The Return*. Go on, you can boo, hiss, and throw your Funko Dale Coopers at me. I know, I deserve it. I need to go and learn my Lynch as I clearly don't understand the genius that I witnessed. [. . .] I should also state that I didn't dislike *The Return*, I just didn't really love it. I wanted to love it. I tried really hard to love it. (Armitage 2017a)

In general, any criticism comes across as personal expression of uneasiness. However, I think there was and is more to this attitude than intentionally reducing the risk of attacks and defamation from within the respective 'interpretative communities' or even facing an expulsion from these communities (see Fish 1980; Laverty 1995). In this chapter, I will discuss three interlinked approaches to explain, not *The Return* per se, but my relationship with the show. None of these three approaches or perspectives accounts for every single challenging aspect. However, as they are connected via the concept of nostalgia, this chapter might at least serve as a short illustration of the value such an auto–ethnographic approach could have for analytical purposes in film and media studies.

Detachment and 'Nostalgia'

Let us begin with the elements *The Return* actually or purportedly got 'wrong'. For me, there was too little 'Twin Peaks' in *Twin Peaks: The Return*. By this I am not only referring to the eponymous town and its characters but also to the series' previous seasons. The story lines and the cast, previously located in one setting, now were scattered across the United States (Las Vegas, New York City, Buckhorn in South Dakota etc.).

Linked together only by a muddled storyline in the style of *The X-Files*, which at the same time revealed and explained too much (undoubtedly Mark Frost's main contribution), while giving little insight into the story. Further, the show offered no relatable characters like Special Agent Dale Cooper, with whom audiences could have explored the show's settings and narrative. Even though all of these realistic or otherworldly tableaus were marvellously composed and displayed, they remained, most of the time, detached and empty – due to the lack of a guiding identification figure or a conventional narrative grounding.

Most of all it was the overarching tonality that bothered me. *The Return* was closer to *Twin Peaks: Fire Walk with Me* (F/USA 1992), one of the most riveting films I have ever encountered. However, the surreal, bizarre, grotesque, self-aware and silly as well as sentimental *Lynchian* approach grows into monotonous *l'art pour l'art* over the eighteen hours running time of season 3. This is due to its missing perspectivation: the show lacks a contrast with the 'original' daily soap cheesiness, naiveté, and prime time melodrama of *Twin Peaks*, whether heartfelt or tongue-in-cheek. Again, there is no character (not even a Laura Palmer, as in *Fire Walk with Me*) who held it all together.

There are valid readings considering those conventionalist 'flaws' as merits, as Debra Minoff and Susannah McCullough argue in their YouTube video essay *Twin Peaks: The Return – A Critique of Nostalgia*. According to them, Lynch is not up to cash in on the fan nostalgia with *The Return*. Rather, they argue, he prefers teasing and refusing or even withholding information about our favourite characters to shine a light on the nature of 'pandering entertainment'. To do that, he delivers 'static, disconnected Lumiere-like vignettes' instead of a tight episodic structure. *The Return* is about 'rediscovering the old', but also about destroying it.

David Sweeney (2019: 294) points in the same direction when he writes:

> Nostalgia undoubtedly accounts for part of the appeal of *The Return* to certain elements of its audience; however, Lynch and Frost do not pander to this desire. Instead, *The Return* interrogates the form of the TV series' 'revival', just as the original series subverted the generic conventions of the soap opera.

This initially makes sense, particularly as it accounts for the uncertainties of what to call *The Return*: a 'sequel', a 'third season', a 'new series' or a 'revisitation'. Or is it all at once or something completely different? Such arguments (or rhetoric) often actualise a common topos in 'Lynch Studies': Lynch as an avant-garde 'auteur' who narrates his films on a 'meta'-level; his films, videos and TV series are reflections about films, videos and TV series. As true as it may be to a certain extent, such a perspective on Lynch's work and its meaning seems sometimes unsatisfying or problematic. It immunises *Twin Peaks* against conventional but perhaps legitimate critique as it belittles regular audiences who 'didn't get it' (for example because they allegedly do not see that this is *art*, not entertainment). Ironically, such a take on what *Twin Peaks* is about renders implicitly even some positive, enthusiastic reactions towards the show as deficient. From this point of view, most forms of *Twin Peaks* fandom and fan practices are at odds with Lynch's (ascribed) artistic interventionalist intentions, destructive even. See, for example, the narrative about how audience demands and television executives' decisions in 1990 spoiled Lynch's very idea of never revealing Laura Palmer's murderer in the first place. Lynch meant to refuse closure, as not to reduce Laura Palmer's (Sheryl Lee) character to being just another victim of weekly murder mystery and consumable TV violence. Therefore, *The Return* itself is, again, deliberately negligent to fan expectations or TV audience's demands, because these ruined the 1990s-project *Twin Peaks* in the first place.[2] How convincing and well-founded this may sound or be: the imaginary antagonism between an innovative, deconstruction artist (Lynch) versus disappointed, ignorant fans does not hold up, particularly when considering *nostalgia* in both positions.

Although initially considered as a disease in the 17th century, the term nostalgia combines two Greek words: *nóstos* [νόστος] for 'return' or 'home coming' and *álgos* [ἄλγος] for 'pain' (ailment). Associated with homesickness, nostalgia is well researched as a psychological and cross-cultural phenomenon (Batcho 2013; Boym 2001; Hepper et al. 2014) and used to study consumerism (Holbrook and Schindler), including television franchise revivals (Hassler-Forest 2020; see also his chapter in this volume) and fan practices (Geraghty). Nostalgia can be described as 'a sentimental longing or wistful affection for the past' (Rosen). Such a view would understand nostalgia as a kind of bitter-sweet emotional state (a mood or 'Stimmung') or subjective emotional reaction (an emotion) as it is both an experience and a response at the same time: a warm, positive modulated affection for something personally significant which is chronologically remote and thus associated with loss or a sense of loss. However, it is unclear what nostalgia (primarily) refers and is attached to: a certain time, place, experience, person, some material or immaterial object, a stored mental representation, or an idealising ex-post (re)creation of the above.

Nostalgia might be deemed an ideologically and politically suspicious concept for being a catch-all term for any sentimental, romantic and reactionary (at least affirmative) attachment to something from the past (or something that was overcome). However, this would be a limited, normative conception, as there are several different ways to engage with nostalgia. Even the postmodern irony or analytical deconstruction often ascribed to Lynch and his work (for example in *Blue Velvet*, but sure enough in *Twin Peaks*) can be considered as a reflexive form or both a processing and a negotiation of nostalgia. Despite his artistic preferences for deadpan humour, aesthetic strangeness and formal symbolism, Lynch might be more wholehearted and sympathetic to his characters, their oddities, relationships, and worlds than initially thought. This might be especially the case with *Twin Peaks* and *The Return*, as

> nostalgia seems to be a concept that fits without restrictions the structural character- istics of televisual seriality. Series can never (this is the hypothesis) not evoke a feeling of nostalgia, because they are based on the imperative to always leave a void. The void is inevitably present, whether in the form of the temporal gaps between episodes and seasons, the void a long-watched series leaves when it finally ends, or the never- arriving closure of an unfinished narrative. (Niemeyer and Wentz 2014:134)

Hence, nostalgia offers both the possibility of and the necessity for a reflection on mediation, media, their respective technologies (Boym) and vice versa (Niemeyer and Wentz 2014). *The Return* might be a '*Critique of*' (The Take, emphasis added) or even, with its last episode, '*the Ultimate Argument Against Nostalgia*' (Willmore, emphasis added). That does not imply, however, that the show is devoid of or not *about* it.

Meta-television and Doubled Nostalgia

If *Twin Peaks* 1990–1 is about television, the same would hold for *The Return*, even though the latter is 'metatextual' on a second, third or even fourth order. The first two seasons were already an ambivalent venture, albeit located somewhere in-between the creators' and the audiences' nos- talgic repurposing of – for example – classical Hollywood movies of the 1940s and television culture from the 1950s up to its then present form (from Formica tables to TV dinners; see *Twin Perfect* 2019). Such a read- ing may allude to the show's referential aesthetic means of expression or its reflection of certain contemporary issues such as self-stylisation.

Twenty-five years later, *The Return*, released in a media historical con- text that might be labelled as 'meta-nostalgia' or 'retro-postmodernism', is a take on early 1990s *Twin Peaks*. At the same time, it considers all of the pop-cultural 'Americana' elements preserved and transcended within its object of reference. Two more dimensions may be added, as the 1940s film noir or cinematic biker stereotypes the original *Twin Peaks* drew on by then have already been both established products and instruments of cultural imaginative fashioning. Finally, there is *Twin Peaks*' life of its own, as it developed, expanded and changed over the past quarter-century – namely by way of fan festivals and fan fiction, DVD editions, a plethora of allusions in and inspirations for other series and films.

Therefore, the notion of *The Return* as a kind of auto-aggressive palimpsest, as a commentary on the old series and as a tease-and-denial-game with an audience's nostalgia is only partly convincing. This is not only because the original series is far less 'ironic' and 'pastiche' (Lockhurst 2008: 199) than interpretative discourses make us believe. Sure, in *The Return* we find ironically exaggerated reminiscences of what was already considered hyperbole in *Twin Peaks*, such as, for example, Cooper's excessive coffee addiction. Beyond the typical doubling motifs in Lynch's cinema, that is *tulpas* and doppelgangers (Good-/Bad-Cooper, Laura/Maddie, reminiscent of Fred/Pete and Renee/Alice in *Lost Highway*, etc.), *The Return* offers a further mode of doubling. In the first two *Twin Peaks* seasons, character James Hurley (James Marshall) typifies the sensitive biker, linking him back to Marlon Brando's iconic Johnny Strabler in *The Wild One* (USA 1953). In 'Part 4' of *The Return*, Wally (Michael Cera), adult son of police deputy Andy Brennan (Harry Goaz) and Twin Peaks Sheriff's Department receptionist Lucy (Kimmy Robertson), picks up the reference by way of caricature (in the sense of 'iconographic style') via pose and pathos: he sports a motorcycle, leather jacket and a vintage cap in the same manner as Marlon Brando did in *The Wild One*. Wally has no 'existence' beyond this very scene; we learn nothing more about him and he has no further narrative importance or meaning. It remains unclear if he is to be conceived of as something of a 'real' fictional person who had modelled himself after a fictional movie character or if his appearance is an exclusive meta-fictional pun on another ontological level. But that is of as little (narrative) significance as Dougie Jones'/Cooper's picaresque antics in the world of insurance frauds, mobsters, murder assaults, marriage problems and the conundrums of contemporary office life. Above all, there is still the character of James Hurley present in *The Return*. A character whose life – like that of his aunt Nadine (Wendy Robie), uncle 'Big' Ed (Everett McGill) and other characters in *Twin Peaks* (and those of their actors) – went on over the past twenty-five years.[3]

When James first appears in the Roadhouse tavern in 'Part 2', it is a moment as crucial and iconic as the one with Wally in 'Part 4', albeit in an entirely different way. The former high school biker, now a security guard with short-cropped hair at the Great Northern Hotel, is spotted by Double-R-Diner waitress Shelly (Mädchen Amick) as he enters the eatery, looking for someone. Watching him from a distance, Shelly briefly talks about him with her friends. 'James is still cool,' Shelly says, smiling affectionately, though in *Twin Peaks* (1990–1) the two characters hardly interacted with each other. There is a bitter-sweet melancholy to this scene for both the creators and the audience. Reminiscence here is merely an intra-fictional experience (yet at the same time also meta-fictional, as I will show later): the referential object of nostalgia is that of *The Return*'s own past. Revisiting the town of Twin Peaks is about fragmentation and dominance of form or allusion. At the same time, it is about coherence and continuation as well. Even when this concerns characters who are present in their absence, like Laura Palmer was in the first one and a half seasons of *Twin Peaks* (1990–1).

Late Style

In a 2017 article for the *Los Angeles Review of Books*, Jonathan Foltz wrote about 'David Lynch's Late Style' (Foltz 2017). He draws on the term 'late style', first developed by Theodor Adorno in a 1937 essay fragment on Ludwig van Beethoven and later used by Edward Said in his studies of the works by writers and composers such as Thomas Mann, Giuseppe Tomasi di Lampedusa, Samuel Beckett and Richard Strauss (Said 2006). For Said (2006: 8), while referring to Adorno's take on Beethoven (here, Beethoven's third period), late style constitutes

> a moment when the artist who is fully in command of his medium nevertheless abandons communication with the established social order of which he is a part and achieves a contradictory, alienated relationship with it. His late works constitute a form of exile [. . .]

According to Adorno (1997: 566):

> The power of subjectivity in the late works of art is the irascible gesture with which it takes leave of the works themselves. It breaks their bonds, not in order to express itself, but in order, expressionless, to cast off the appearance of art. Of the works themselves it leaves only fragments behind, and communicates itself, like a cipher, only through the blank spaces from which it has disengaged itself.

This holds true (and Foltz is aware of this) not only for Lynch's recent late works but his œuvre in general. Yet in its fragmented, disconnected, and digressive style *The Return* for Foltz is a 'late work' in particular:

> The new season challenges us most in the way it seems to undo the story it is telling [. . .]. Instead of the nostalgic recreation of a familiar form, Lynch gives us broken

bits of what we loved, collaged together in surprising, often baffling ways. The series rejects smooth pacing, narrative efficiency, and well-defined character arcs. Plot threads are introduced and abandoned seemingly at will. Unexplained gaps in the story are the norm. The show plays inconsistent games with chronology, running roughshod over narrative continuity.

However, there is not just fragmentation, detachment, and other forms of narration that in other contexts would be considered as 'bad storytelling'. There are uncanny moments of the show's self-awareness. For example, after Killer Bob (as an anthropomorphic flying orb) is finally destroyed in 'Part 17', Dale Cooper faces his friends and colleagues who are lined up like actors on a theatre stage at the curtain call. A close-up on Cooper's face is superimposed on this theatrical moment and offers another layer of (depicted) perception. At this moment, we might get the most striking glimpse into the experience of mortality as described by Foltz, Adorno and others:

> [L]ate works are born from the awareness that our subjective relationship to death can never enter artworks, which survive too long to record this mortifying knowledge. For this reason, late style is the result of an artist who has abandoned the very conceit of expression itself. (Foltz 2017)

Such a reasoning is reminiscent of Roland Barthes' description of how death is evoked by photography in *Camera Lucida* (as a most nostalgic medium). Indeed, there is something in our appreciation of several characters from *Twin Peaks* (or rather actors) who we assumed have been forever young for almost thirty years, up to *The Return*. With *The Return* they suddenly grew terrifyingly old, including FBI Deputy Director Gordon Cole/ David Lynch himself. As a result, there is a perceived disconnect between presentation and representation. Lucy's and Andy's Kimmy Robertson and Henry Goaz, for example, appear too old and distinguished for reprising their comic *Twin Peaks* characters, so that you cannot un-see the actors behind their roles' funny façades – another kind of 'superimposition'. On the one hand, we might read this as a deliberate choice in the sense of artistic expression aimed at conveying meaning. On the other hand, this might bring to light a new dimension in Lynch's work as regarding its self-awareness about technical possibilities and their fundamental insufficiencies in capturing something ephemeral.

Towards a Phenomenology of Nostalgia

Where does this leave us with "nostalgia"? There are already academic in-depth studies of *The Return* that look at the TV series' structural and aesthetic level as informed by nostalgia. Rife und Wheeler (2020: 424), for example, argue that the series' resistant treatment of nostalgia demonstrates a 'critical mode of theorizing nostalgia as containing inherent multiplicity and duplicitousness,' that is 'a theorizing of nostalgia itself as doppelganger.' While this is a fascinating reading, particularly as it takes Lynchian allegorism into account, I would propose to even go further: In Lynch's *The Return* (and not so much in Frost's) all of the presented fragmentations that at the same time inform an audience's detachment as it causes frustration in meaning making processes are not to be understood as purely autotelic effects. They are artistic devices to explore and represent, if not even *reify* nostalgia phenomenologically. Therefore, I concur with Sweeney when he notes that '[t]he audience's return to Twin Peaks, and to *Twin Peaks*, is problematised through acts of estrangement' (Sweeney 2019: 294). Although, at least in my point of view, the Lynchian nostalgic is not necessarily considered as problematic per se. Rather it is addressed as an experience of unattainability in itself. While Lynch's film discourses are often characterised by a surreal piecemeal narrative, *The Return* as an inherently nostalgic television series employs said narrative mode to create a haunting encounter with nostalgia or rather the mental and emotive 'event' of nostalgia. Such an experience of nostalgia is a 'hauntological' one in a Derridean sense[4] due to its character of a nostalgia fulfilled and thus it offers both a collision with and a disassociation from the (in)tangible object that is *Twin Peaks* (in the sense of an incongruence of the superimposition): The beloved and longed for nostalgic object or place is split into, on the one hand, the version we idealise, store, filter and fixate on either in or as our imagination and, on the other hand, into the once real but dynamic (changed, gone), irretrievable object or unattainable place. Both objects cannot be merged for they are not only temporally and ontologically (as in 'real' vs. imagined) disjunct: The relationship between both can be understood as the one between a media or semiotic code and what is mediated or encoded. Thus, the nostalgic recreation or reimagination is not the result of the encoding process, but rather the endless iterative process of encoding and re-coding itself. This resembles the process of a renewed rewriting of memories.

This is the frightening mortality Adorno and in following him also Foltz warned about: the terrifying knowledge that one cannot hold and capture the past as one cannot hold and capture something that is gone or ever changing. As Foltz (2017) writes: 'Lynch knows that the world has moved on from *Twin Peaks*', so he 'insists upon a form of watching that leads us endlessly back to the helpless fact of watching.' Lynch expressively (re-)constructs, and with *The Return* evokes what some of us might undergo when visiting our hometown (our first 'Heimat') after leaving for good a long time ago. Such is the experience of re-entering the town of Twin Peaks in 2017: what was formerly so well-known is found to be inconsistent, oblique and in some strange way 'inaccessible'. A similar experience is created by the many stories and characters in *The Return*: they are absent and present at the same time, just as Laura Palmer was in the first one and a half seasons of *Twin Peaks*. In the vastness of the ensemble cast, the happenstance of events, we randomly run into some unknown characters while others exist only by way of reference in the dialogues of other characters – characters whom we also hardly know, if at all.

One of those haunting, absent figures is the ominous 'Billy', enunciated only in the conversations of his friends and acquaintances, minor characters such as Megan (Shane Lynch), Sophie (Emily Stofle) and Audrey Horne (Sherilyn Fenn). This is particularly frustrating: Audrey was and is one of the most beloved, plot-driving characters in *Twin Peaks* 1990–1. Yet, in *The Return*, besides the reprise of 'her' dance at the Roadhouse (one of the autotelic self-referential, self-aware 'highlights' of the show), Audrey's appearance is limited to arguing with her husband Charlie (Clark Middleton) about searching for Billy. That is even more irritating as Audrey's (and 'Mr C.'s a.k.a. Evil-Cooper's) son Richard (Eamon Farren) is way more important (or at least present) in *The Return*. This, however, is only revealed, or rather hinted at, in a faint, word-of-mouth relation to her. References to the 'Billy story' or 'stories' are spread across several episodes. Somehow, Billy vanished, someone has seen him last or is heard of having seen him last. Something has happened, but we just cannot figure out what and why and how these people are related to each other.

All of this is a pretty accurate 'mediatisation' – in the sense of the Hegelian 'concept of the reconstructive analysis of today's media-related transformations' (Krotz 2017: 106), in this case that of the experience of a nostalgic 'clash'. It tells us that the old Twin Peaks – however much it may have changed and moved on – is still there. It is still a town with all the old elements, but also with a lot of new dark or heart-warming, quirky, soapy, bizarre characters and their stories. Yet we, the audience, no longer have access to all of that. We, not Twin Peaks, went away for twenty-five years and now we return as strangers. As with former friends we left in our hometowns and lost touch with, those characters had lived their lives just as we did, changed, and lost sight of each other. In the short time we now revisit Twin Peaks, we only catch glimpses of the town's surface. We only get bits and pieces of information about its residents from a distance and by eavesdropping on patrons at the Roadhouse. In comparison and despite their surreal metaphorical and enigmatic nature, the places that were once strange and otherworldly, such as the Black Lodge, the tower in the sea of 'non-existence' or the fortress of Senorita Dido (Joy Nash) and the 'Fireman' (Carel Struycken), now feel closer, more welcoming, understandable and comforting.

Lynch's biggest offence to, or betrayal of, the fans in the audience is to put them in the role of a stranger, while they felt that they have 'stayed in' the town of Twin Peaks and thus true to the *Twin Peaks* series over those many years. David Lynch and Mark Frost can artistically (even if not legally) do with *Twin Peaks* whatever they want and feel to be the best. However, even though I can personally ignore Frost's poorly written tie-in books *The Secret History of Twin Peaks* (Frost 2016) and *Twin Peaks: The Final Dossier* (Frost 2017) as non-canonical,[5] *The Return* is a completely different matter. When I encountered *Twin Peaks* for the first time, it was not as a time-bound 'product' of necessities, circumstances and contingencies, of certain creative minds, media business parameters, fan involvement. It was a television series but, then again, it transcended every one of those aspects. *Twin Peaks* was simply *there*, at least for me (and *for me*). It had an auratic quality to it, although it was not a distinct embodied artefact and was without a unique praxeological and cultural locality.[6] It had a spiritual value. I am, for example, still convinced that if there is any kind of 'beyond', Under-, Nether- or Otherworld, it is formatted, structured and presents itself (aesthetically, 'coded') like the supernatural in *Twin Peaks*.

> We've all moved on, and I've moved on since my sixteen-year-old self who sat transfixed every week watching this strange show unfold before me. [. . .] *Twin Peaks*, that's precious to me, I feel a sense of ownership, and in that it has been part of my life for so long, a strange sense of authorship as well. [. . .With *The Return* s]omething seismic has occurred to an underlying structure of my sense of self, and it bothers me. (Armitage 2017a)

This feeling might be intentional, as it is made the subject of artistic analytical expression. *The Return* as something driven by a disenchanted but haunted nostalgia. From that perspective Lynch's 'late style of the new *Twin Peaks* is nowhere more evident than in the giddy profanation of its own aesthetic legacy, which openly trivialises the visceral power of the original show's vast symbolic repertoire' (Foltz 2017). However, there is an inconsistency in Lynch's relation to the audience of *Twin Peaks* (and not primarily that of *David Lynch* as film auteur). On the one hand, he – regularly – refuses to give any hints or clues on how to read his work because he does not want to guide (and, thus, limit) the audiences' individual interpretations and ways of experience. On the other hand, every revisitation or reimagination (starting with *Fire Walk with Me*) inevitably does create such limitations. This brings us back to the issue of an inherent nostalgic seriality to the media format of TV series, the medium of television itself – or, eventually, what we could label 'media' or specifically 'television nostalgia'.

Television (Media) Nostalgia

When the original show aired in the early 1990s *Twin Peaks* was celebrated as both an innovation and avant-garde television. It also was broadcast in the context of the decline of traditional television formats. In his seminal study *Television's Second Golden Age* (1996), Robert J. Thompsons describes how, starting in the 1970s, shows such as *Hill Street Blues* (1981–7, directed by *Twin Peaks* co-author Mark Frost) and *St. Elsewhere* (1982–8) constituted a new era of 'Quality TV'. Adding an air of decadence and deterioration to the show he writes:

> *Twin Peaks* had an overall negative effect on the quality drama. By so strikingly taking the quality formula to its extreme only to alienate most of its once dedicated audience by the middle of its second season, *Twin Peaks* sent a message to network programmers that boundless experimentalism alone couldn't sustain a series over the long haul. (Thompson 1997: 178)

A quarter-century later we have another comparable situation. Old *Twin Peaks* is now, in hindsight, regarded not as an end but as a starting point (or at least a major inspiration) for modern complex television fictions and the rise of a third – and today maybe even a fourth – Golden Age of Television with decisive American companies such as HBO, Netflix and Amazon Prime. At the same time *Twin Peaks* returned to television, some critics sensed, yet again, another end of an era: The end of auteur-driven television. One indication was that Netflix was said to wind down investments and cut costs of its own productions. Another is that high-profile series like Nicolas Winding Refn's *Too Old to Die Young* (2019, Amazon) were cancelled (Collins 2019; Pilarczyk 2019).

To this day, however, the output of high value fictional and serial content remains enormous, due to, for example, new video-on-demand and streaming services such as Disney+ and HBO Max, competing for attention and new subscribers. *The Return's* major artistic problem would not be that it was too ambitious and challenging for the audience. Instead, it aired in a time where new series might have become too foreseeable and overambitious in their efforts to create something idiosyncratic (for example Cary Joji Fukunaga's *Maniac* (2018)).

Today there are, to put it simply, way too many *Twin Peaks* released too frequently on too many platforms (see Halskov 2021: Chapter 4). One strand of fictional television had become permanently exceptional, a nev-erending prolific string of events and singularities, of quality, exception-ality, and artistic endeavours we can hardly overlook. For the audience, but maybe also Lynch, *The Return* is (about) a twofold disappointment in media (or in this case 'television') nostalgia, both on the level of the artwork ('content') and on the level of the cultural-technological apparatus or *dis-positif*. On the first level, as previously stated, *The Return*'s problem is not that it is being viewed a quarter-century later, but rather that it returned after *Twin Peaks* (1990–1) had *happened* and *made* a lasting impression on televised serial narration. After *Twin Peaks* (1990–1) there were more con-ventional, family-friendly derivates. These repurposed the idea of a small rural town with odd characters and strange occurrences, including murder mysteries such as David E. Kelley's *Picket Fences* (1992–6) or *Due South* (1994–9). Also owing much to *Twin Peaks*, Chris Carter's *The X-Files* (1993–2002, 2016–18) presents two FBI agents with their own kinds of tulpas or doppelgangers, including aliens, conspiracies, and secret govern-ment branches. David Duchovny, the same actor who played Dale Cooper's colleague Denis/Denise Bryson, portrays protagonist Fox Mulder in *The X-Files*. The series was revived in the same year as *The Return*.

Other mystery, science-fiction or genre-blending shows with vast nar-ratives or supernatural aspects like *Lost* (2004–10) are hardly conceivable without *Twin Peaks* and its commercial and cultural success. But these are TV shows which negotiated the essential elements of the show on their own terms, those of prime-time television storytelling and aesthet-ics, modes of production and perception. This would be something that David Lynch would neither have an interest in nor, most likely, be capable of emulating. *Twin Peaks* 1990–1 was – as were *Picket Fences, Due South, The X-Files* and *Lost* – a weekly show in the context of 'mainstream' television and its audiences. These audiences also watched *Dallas* (1978–91) or *Murder, She Wrote* (1984–91) and later, perhaps, *The Walking Dead* (2010–). Even as these were not the consumers who became and stayed fans throughout the years, they resembled the target audience Lynch's and Frost's series was originally created for (and the target of Lynch's artistic interventionist endeavour, according to Sweeney or Twin Perfect and others). The original *Twin Peaks* marked or foreshadowed a bifurcation: it was meant to inspire either 'regular' network TV enter-tainment or, from another perspective, ambitious authored contents or 'events' often created by established and celebrated film 'auteurs' like David Fincher, Martin Scorsese or Woody Allen. *The Return* was 'aired' in weekly episodes and as a 'Showtime Original Series'. As such it was listed among ambitious and high-quality shows that also pushed and probed genre boundaries like *Weeds* (2005–12), *Dexter* (2006–14, 2021–) or *Homeland* (2011–20). More an eighteen-hour David Lynch movie than a TV series (declared as 'the best film of the decade' by the prestigious *Cahiers du Cinéma* in 2019), *The Return* was an artwork in its own right, but it was not an entertainment product of and within a mass media context. As aesthetically bold and experimental as *The Return* was and is, the show dodged its cultural 'arena' and did not challenge its competition. Instead, it stayed in its confined artsy niche to preach to the converted choir (in this case: Lynch aficionados). In doing so it turned out significantly more timid and affirmative (not to say 'reactionary') than the original *Twin Peaks* did in 1990–1. To be fair, it can be asked whether there was an 'arena' to fight in or a television to challenge and to comment on in the first place.

There were so many things happening while the good Dale Cooper was lost in the Black Lodge. On a political historical level there was the dissolution of the Soviet Union, '9/11' and the 'War on Terror'. Barack Obama became the first African American US President, and he was then followed by Donald J. Trump. On a media cultural and technological level, VHS and USENET (relevant for 1990s *Twin Peaks* 'cult', see Jenkins 1995) were replaced by DVD and BluRay, the World Wide Web, streaming platforms and then social media (blogs, Facebook, Twitter, YouTube – where *The Return* as object of debate and exegesis primarily 'took place'), while television became a thing of broadband transmission rates and smart phones.[7] Cooper (and 'our' Twin Peaks) misses how TV became the new cinema or how both cinema and television faded into oblivion as outdated concepts in a pervasive digital *media convergence*, where content is marked by its *spreadability* and the work of *participatory cultures* (to use just some of media scholar Henry Jenkins' descriptive terms – Jenkins 2008, 2009; Jenkins et al. 2013). When and how, exactly, did Cooper's (or Twin Peaks') world's aspect ratio turn from the classic four-by-three television standard – what was 'in style' back then – to *The Return*'s 'cinematic' sixteen-by-nine? Also, the 'content' we talk about, when we talk about *Twin Peaks* or what became of it, is nowadays no longer really 'aired' or 'broadcast' but offered for non-linear, on-demand consumption and potential binge-watching.

Twin Peaks was and is defined in relation to the standards, limits and constrains of the medium of television. With that I refer, on the one hand, to the technical and socio-cultural apparatus which held once a time-specific agency in our living rooms. On the other hand, there is television as content and programme: stories, setting, characters, a distinct generic and symbolic form, with a distinct range of aesthetics and narrativity, modes of production and of perception. So even if the 'water cooler effect' has not yet vanished (Manly 2019) but lives on in the discourse of social media, I would not say that *The Return* works properly as the advertised 'Limited Event Series' in terms of an actual return to or reflection of Twin Peaks/ *Twin Peaks*. The 2018 show simply lacks both the consumer environment of the mundane and the collective pop-cultural run-of-the-mill background of another era. This is something which not only television but also the whole media ecosphere no longer provide, as converged and fragmented as they are. Hence, *The Return*'s television nostalgia is different to 'nostalgic television' which denotes TV shows set in bygone times or reimagines a respective aesthetic period.[8] *The Return* is about and expresses the longing for and the experience of a loss of a way of watching – and of being watched by a show. In that sense *Twin Peaks* has simply lost its home the same way as the US North-Western 'Brigadoon' Twin Peaks has lost its homeliness.

Conclusion

Driven by an individual necessity of coming to terms with *Twin Peaks: The Return*, I sketched out three interlinked analytical or explanatory approaches in this chapter. *The Return* can be investigated as a combination of several 'hauntings' of – sometimes even conflicting types, modes or dimensions (for example epistemological, phenomenological) – nostalgia. However, the suggested perspectives remain insufficient, even disappointing, in so far as they do not take into account the disappointment as an artistic experience or effect. By way of narrative fragmentation, allusions, re-cast actors or the current television ecosphere and its modes of reception *The Return* is not merely about the unattainability of the nostalgic object: it is set to evoke on different structural levels the frustration and estrangement we feel when trying to align with what is past. Instead, we are left with what is revisited and re-imagined. Inasmuch it is regarded as part of Lynch's late work, *The Return* is great Lynch (for Lynch aficionados), but a poor *Twin Peaks* for *Twin Peaks* fans.

Then again, the significance of one's own intuition is irrefutable in both Lynch's words (or the lack of them) and his artworks. So, one cannot acknowledge one (Lynch, 'art', self-awareness, second- and third-order nostalgia, postmodernism) without the other (medium with a life of its own, mundane 'entertainment', first-order nostalgia, romanticism). Therefore, of the many media and forms of expression that David Lynch masters (including music and design), television might be the one that evades him.

Notes

1. https://twitter.com/DAVID_LYNCH/status/518060411690569730 (last accessed December 23, 2020).
2. See for this narrative and interpretation for example the four and a half hour long, compelling video essay *Twin Peaks ACTUALLY EXPLAINED (No, Really)* by a YouTuber only known as 'Rossetter' (Twin Perfect 2019).
3. *Twin Peaks* co-creator Mark Frost provides (his version of) these characters' background stories in *Twin Peaks: The Final Dossier* (Frost 2017).
4. Derrida 2006. This comes rather close to what Rife and Wheeler (2020) describe as *doppelgangerian*.
5. To this day I refuse to read what Frost (and maybe Lynch in that case) thought of what had happened to Cooper's love interest Annie (Heather Graham) after the final episode of season 2, thus defying their authority of and power over the diegetic universe of *Twin Peaks*.
6. The actual VHS tapes I recorded *Twin Peaks* on are an entirely different topic.
7. It is remarkable how post-'Dougie' Cooper, after he awakens at the hospital, self-confidently demands and understands (that is: takes for granted) Bushnell Mullins' (Don Murray) mobile phone.
8. Regarding the 1980s and early 1990s, one can mention pastiches or period pieces such as *Stranger Things* (2016–) or *Glow* (2017–19) or subtle or limited (to, for example, costumes or music) stylised reminiscences like *13 Reasons Why* (2017–) or *I Am Not Okay With This* (2020).

Bibliography

Adorno, Theodor W. 'Late Style in Beethoven'. *Essays on Music. Selected, with Introduction, Commentary and Notes by Richard Leppert*, Theodor W. Adorno (ed.). University of California Press, 2002, pp. 564–68.

Armitage, Matt. 'Something Is Missing: Criticisms of *The Return* – Part One'. *25YL*, 05 October 2017, https://25yearslatersite.com/2017/10/05/something-is-missing-criticisms-of-the-return-part-one (last accessed 15 November 2021).

Armitage, Matt. 'Something Is Missing: Criticisms of *The Return* – Part 2'. *25YL*, 12 December 2017, https://25yearslatersite.com/2017/12/12/something-is-missing-criticisms-of-the-return-part-2/ (last accessed 15 November 2021).

Batcho, Krystine Irene. 'Nostalgia: The Bittersweet History of a Psychological Concept'. *History of Psychology*, vol. 16, no. 3, 2013, pp. 165–76.

Boym, Svetlana. *The Future of Nostalgia*. Basic Books, 2001.

Collins, Sean T. 'Netflix's Bright Future Looks a Lot like Television's Dim Past'. *Deadspin*, 18 March 2019, https://theconcourse.deadspin.com/netflixs-bright-future-looks-a-lot-like-televisions-dim-1833056161 (last accessed 15 November 2021).

Derrida, Jacques. *Spectres of Marx. The State of the Debt, the Work of Mourning and the New International*. 1994. Routledge, 2006.

Fish, Stanley Eugene. *Is There a Text in This Class? The Authority of Interpretive Communities*. Harvard University Press, 2000.

Foltz, Jonathan. 'David Lynch's Late Style'. *Los Angeles Review of Books*, 12 November 2017, https://lareviewofbooks.org/article/david-lynchs-late-style/ (last accessed 15 November 2021).

Frost, Mark. *The Secret History of Twin Peaks*. Macmillan, 2016.

Frost, Mark. *Twin Peaks: The Final Dossier*. Macmillan, 2017.

Geraghty, Lincoln. *Cult Collectors: Nostalgia, Fandom and Collecting Popular Culture*. Routledge, 2014.

Halskov, Andreas. *Beyond Television: TV Production in the Multiplatform Era*. University Press of Southern Denmark, 2021.

Hassler-Forest, Dan. '"When you get there, you will already be there": *Stranger Things*, *Twin Peaks* and the Nostalgia Industry'. *Science Fiction Film and Television*, vol. 13, no. 2, 2020, pp. 175–97.

Hepper, Erica G et al. 'Pancultural Nostalgia: Prototypical Conceptions across Cultures'. *Emotion*, vol. 14, no. 4, 2014, pp. 733–47.

Holbrook, Morris B. and Robert M. Schindler. 'Nostalgic Bonding: Exploring the Role of Nostalgia in the Consumption Experience'. *Journal of Consumer Behaviour*, vol. 3 , no. 2, 2003, pp. 107–27.

Jenkins, Henry. '"Do You Enjoy Making the Rest of Us Feel Stupid?": alt. tv.twinpeaks, the Trickster Author, and Viewer Mystery'. *Full of Secrets. Critical Approaches to Twin* Peaks, David Lavery (ed.). Wayne State University Press, 1995, pp. 51–69.

Jenkins, Henry. *Convergence Culture. Where Old and New Media Collide*. New York University Press, 2008.

Jenkins, Henry et al. *Confronting the Challenges of Participatory Culture. Media Education for the 21st Century*. MIT Press, 2009.

Jenkins, Henry, Sam Ford and Joshua Green. *Spreadable Media. Creating Value and Meaning in a Networked Culture*. New York University Press, 2013.

Krotz, Friedrich. 'Explaining the Mediatisation Approach'. *Javnost – The Public*, vol. 24, no. 2, 2017, pp. 103–18.

Laverty, David. 'Introduction: The Semotics of Cobbler – *Twin Peaks*' Interpretive Community'. *Full of Secrets. Critical Approaches to Twin Peaks*, David Lavery (ed.). Wayne State University Press, 1995, S. 1–21.

Lockhurst, Roger. *The Trauma Question*. Routledge, 2008.

Lynch, David and Chris Rodley. *Lynch über Lynch*. Translated by Marion Kagerer, Verlag der Autoren, 2002.

Manly, Lorne. 'Post-Water-Cooler TV'. *The New York Times*, 9 August 2013, https://www.nytimes.com/2013/08/11/arts/television/how-to-make-a-tv-drama-in-the-twitter-age.html (last accessed 15 November 2021).

Minoff, Debra and Susannah McCullough. '*Twin Peaks: The Return* – A Critique of Nostalgia'. *The Take*, 29. November 2017. https://youtube/juiJLAfqt7k (last accessed 15 November 2021).

Niemeyer, Katharina and Daniele Wentz. 'Nostalgia Is Not What It Used to Be: Serial Nostalgia and Nostalgic Television Series'. *Media and Nostalgia. Yearning for the Past, Present and Future*, Katharina Niemeyer (ed.). Palgrave Macmillan, 2014, 129–38.

Pilarczyk, Hannah. 'Aufräumen im Serienangebot'. *Der Spiegel*, 28 July 2019, https://www.spiegel.de/kultur/tv/amazon-prime-video-neues-ueber-herr-der-ringe-transparent-aus-fuer-winding-refn-a-1279380.html (last accessed 15 November 2021).

Rife, Tyler S. and Ashley N. Wheeler. '"I'll see you again in 25 years": doppelganging nostalgia and *Twin Peaks: The Return*'. *Critical Studies in Media Communication*, vol. 37, no. 5, 2020, pp. 424–36.

Rosen, Lisa. 'A Sentimental Longing or Wistful Affection for the Past'. *Medium*, 30 November 2018, https://medium.com/@lisarosentv/a-sentimental-longing-or-wistful-affection-for-the-past-bb5ae9581b15 (last accessed 15 November 2021).

Said, Edward W. *On Late Style. Music and Literature against the Grain*. Bloomsbury, 2006.

Sweeney, David. '"I'll Point You to a Better Time/A Safer Place to Be": Music, Nostalgia and Estrangement in *Twin Peaks: The Return*'. *Critical Essays on* Twin Peaks: The Return, Antonio Sanna (ed.). Palgrave Macmillan, 2019, pp. 281–96.

Thompson, Robert J. *Television's Second Golden Age:* From Hill Street Blues *to* ER. Syracuse University Press, 1997.

Twin Perfect. '*Twin Peaks* ACTUALLY EXPLAINED (No, Really)', 21. October 2019, https://www.youtube.com/watch?v=7AYnF5hOhuM (last accessed 15 November 2021).

Willmore, Allison. '"Twin Peaks" Was The Ultimate Argument Against Nostalgia'. *Buzzfeed*, 6 September 2017, https://www.buzzfeed.com/alisonwillmore/what-year-is-it (last accessed 15 November 2021).

Filmography

Blue Velvet. Directed by David Lynch, performances by Kyle MacLachlan, Isabella Rosselini, Dennis Hopper, and Laura Dern, Dino De Laurentiis Entertainment Group, 1986.

Dallas. Directed by Leonard Katzmann et al., performances by Barbara Bel Geddes and Jim Davis, CBS, 1978–91.

Dexter. Directed by James Manos Jr. et al., performances by Michael C. Hall and Julie Benz, Showtime, 2006–21.

Due South. Directed by Paul Haggis et al., performances by Paul Gross and David Marciano, Alliance Communications, 1994–9.

Homeland. Directed by Alex Gansa et al. performances by Claire Danes and Damian Lewis, Showtime, 2011–20.

Hill Street Blues. Directed by Michael Kozoli et al., performances by Daniel J. Travanti and Veronica Hamel, NBC, 1981–7.

Lost. Directed by J. J. Abrams et al., performances by Naveen Andrews and Maggie Grace, ABC, 2004–10.

Lünsch. Directed by Bernd Zywietz, performances by Gerald Haffke and Anette Rücker. Produced by Bernd Zywietz, 2004.

Murder She Wrote. Directed by William Link et al., performances by Angela Lansbury and Peter S. Fischer, CBS, 1984–96.

Maniac. Directed by Cary Joji Fukunaga et. al., performances by Emma Stone and Jonah Hill, Netflix, 2018.

Picket Fences. Directed by David E. Kelley et al., performances by Tom Skerritt and Kathy Baker, CBS, 1992–6.

St. Elsewhere. Directed by John Falsey et al., performances by Ed Flanders and David Morse, NBC, 1982–8.

The Wild One. Directed by László Benedek, performances by Marlon Brando and Mary Murphy, Columbia Pictures, 1953.

The X-Files. Directed by Chris Carter et al., performances by David Duchovny and Gillian Anderson, Warner Bros., 1993–2018.

The Walking Dead. Directed by Frank Darabont et al., performances by Andrew Lincoln and Jon Bernthal, AMC, 2010–.

Too Old to Die Young. Directed by Nicolas Winding Refn, performances by Miles Teller and Cristina Rodio, Amazon, 2019.

Twin Peaks. Directed by David Lynch et al., performances by Kyle MacLachlan and Mädchen Amick, Lynch/Frost Productions et al., 1990–1.

Twin Peaks: Fire Walk with Me. Directed by David Lynch, performances by Sheryl Lee and Ray Wise, CIBY Picture, 1992.

Twin Peaks: The Return [on DVD and BluRay *Twin Peaks: A Limited Event Series*]. Directed by David Lynch, performances by Sheryl Lee and Kyle MacLachlan, Showtime, 2017.

Weeds. Directed by Jenji Kohan et al., performances by Mary-Louise Parker and Justin Kirk, Showtime, 2005–12.

CHAPTER 7

'Two Birds, One Stone': Transmedia Storytelling in *Twin Peaks*[1]

Dan Hassler-Forest

The twenty-first-century media landscape is governed by transmedia franchises: massive entertainment juggernauts that expand across media platforms, encourage audience participation, and are owned and operated by massive transnational media conglomerates. In this context, the parallel rise of media convergence and corporate consolidation has resulted in a growing variety of transmedia storytelling (Jenkins 2006: 97–8). But before transmedia franchises like *Star Wars*, *Harry Potter* and the Marvel Cinematic Universe took over our entertainment ecosystem, David Lynch and Mark Frost's *Twin Peaks* pioneered the productive use of transmedia, creatively interweaving multiple media platforms to construct a single coherent storyworld.

By supplementing the original series' television episodes with meaningful expansions in other media, *Twin Peaks* in the early 1990s prefigured a trend that would come to dominate the convergence culture industry in the twenty-first century (Scott 2019: 12). Over the years, the series has repeatedly adopted transmedia forms for serialised storytelling and worldbuilding in ways that further develop the franchise's own cultural legacy while also embracing contemporary media-industrial practices. Though relatively limited in terms of the number of media texts, these practices illustrate the rich potential for the transmedia expansion of franchises that exist primarily within a single medium. This indicated how media properties can use transmedia forms for the layered construction of complex storyworlds, while at the same time demonstrating the inherently collaborative nature of these complexly networked franchises.

In this chapter, I will describe the ways in which *Twin Peaks* employed transmedia storytelling forms to enhance its narrative world and foster active and long-term participation amongst the series' fans. This chapter will show how transmedia expansions combined contemporary forms of merchandising with innovative forms of storytelling. As the only major serialised storyworld in David Lynch's career, these media-industrial experiments also shed light on the work of an artist and cinematic 'auteur' figure who has inspired tremendous speculation amongst fans, especially in the connections between different works and across different media. Finally, by contrasting the original series with the expansions that accompanied the return of *Twin Peaks* a quarter century later, the chapter will shed light on changing possibilities and limitations within specific media-industrial periods.

In order to map out the key transmedial connections within this rich and surprisingly diverse franchise, I will first offer a few terms that help distinguish basic forms of transmedia multitexts (Parody 2011: 210–18) from each other, before moving on to a more detailed analysis of the transmedia forms that have come to surround, enhance and enrich *Twin Peaks* in its different incarnations and historical periods.

Transmedia Models

In his essay 'Transmediality and the Politics of Adaptation', Jens Eder suggested a basic typology of transmedia multitexts (or 'constellations') that provides a helpful entrance for this discussion. While Henry Jenkins' oft-cited but rather broadly worded description of transmedia storytelling gave media scholars a provocative starting point, it also clearly exaggerated the degree of organised and consistent cross-platform development of fictional storyworlds, which are in practice only rarely integrated in the way the term's definition suggests. Eder's model adds much-needed emphasis on the hierarchical structures that we inevitably encounter both within the various transmedia franchises, and in the industries and audiences that engage with them. Eder's typology distinguishes between four basic models: 'integration', 'supplementation', 'participation' and 'multiple exploitation' (2015: 75–7).

The form of transmedia storytelling that Jenkins foregrounded in *Convergence Culture*, with *The Matrix* (1999) as his primary example, constitutes what Eder's essay describes as 'integration': different media texts form a single and more or less coherent narrative whole, with each medium making the most of its medium-specific qualities and affordances. While this model is frequently cited as a kind of ideal or even default definition of transmedia storytelling, it is important to note that it is also fairly rare, as it requires a tremendous amount of planning and coordination. Far more common is the 'expansion' model, in which one primary media text (often referred to as the 'mothership') is expanded via a range of 'satellite texts'. Most commonly, the mothership would be a costly, labour-intensive, and high-profile mass media production, like a feature film, television series, or AAA video game, while the expansions are less expensive secondary texts that function simultaneously as world-building expansions and as entrance points to the franchise. A third model is the 'participation' strategy, in which audience activity is integrated into the production cycle, as with game shows where audiences use apps, websites or other satellite media to vote on or otherwise affect the ongoing narrative. Finally, 'multiple exploitation' indicates a form of multitext in which a theoretically limitless number of transmedia texts exist alongside each other, without depending on any of the others to create meaning – a model for which a predominantly non-narrative transmedia brand like *Hello Kitty* is a fitting example.

Clearly, these four paradigms are neither exhaustive nor entirely mutually exclusive. But they do help to emphasise the diverse forms transmedia multitexts can take, as well as the fact that each of these is thoroughly embedded within the context of residual and emerging media-industrial practices. Thus, Eder's typology helpfully foregrounds the inherent connections between transmedia as a narrative form – 'transmedia storytelling' – and the political economy in which it circulates – 'transmedia franchising' (Johnson 2013: 55). In the case of *Twin Peaks*, the forms of transmedia expansion that were pioneered in both incarnations of the series effectively combine transmedia storytelling forms with historically specific media-industrial forms and the cultural forms of participatory fan culture (Booth 2016: 25).

Twin Peaks: Pioneering Transmedia

When the *Twin Peaks* pilot premiered on US network television on April 8, 1990, it broke ratings records and became a massive pop-culture phenomenon. The first season's mere eight episodes, ordered from Lynch/ Frost Productions by the overly cautious ABC network, struck a nerve with television audiences. But its delirious cliffhanger finale also left fans deeply frustrated: not only did the series climax refuse to answer the show's central mystery – 'Who killed Laura Palmer?' – but it also left uncertain the fate of more than half the main cast.

I have strong personal memories of the series' original broadcast, and the seemingly interminable gap between the first and second seasons of *Twin Peaks*. As a sixteen-year-old film and television enthusiast, I had been wholly captivated by those eight episodes, which simultaneously critiqued and reproduced familiar American TV tropes. Like millions of others, I was dazzled by the skill with which David Lynch and Mark Frost had masterminded such a richly layered and strikingly cinematic storyworld, which constantly hinted at an even more elaborate, possibly supernatural mythology. The show gave us a fictitious small town full of mysteries that spiralled outwards from the murder of Laura Palmer.

Scrambling to meet fans' insatiable demand for more *Twin Peaks* while the show's producers were preparing a much longer second season, David Lynch's 22-year-old daughter Jennifer authored a spin-off book that was rushed into stores that summer. But *The Secret Diary of Laura Palmer* turned out to be more than just a cleverly timed merchandising opportunity. The bestselling book gave a first-person account of the series' absent protagonist, the life of small-town teenager Laura Palmer. Palmer, broadly outlined in the series' ongoing murder investigation, sprang to vivid life in the secret diary's pages. Faithful in every detail to the series' geography and cast of characters, the book gave the reader access to a text that seemed to have escaped from the fictional world of the series to arrive as a physical object in our own reality.

It is important to note that Laura Palmer's secret diary was an important plot point in the first season. Several of the characters investigating her murder had established that Laura had kept a secret diary that might contain clues to her murderer's identity, and one of the plot threads left dangling in the season finale concerned a bungled attempt to retrieve it. Millions of eager *Twin Peaks* fans like myself therefore quickly made the book a bestseller in the summer of 1990. The diary's contents impressively fleshed out Laura Palmer's background and inner life as a character, thereby laying much of the groundwork for the later prequel film *Twin Peaks: Fire Walk with Me* (1992). At the same time, plot spoilers for the developing narrative were carefully avoided, as crucial information in the final sections of the diary was omitted, and several blank pages marked only with the words 'PAGE RIPPED OUT (as found)'.

Later that year, as the second season developed, the secret diary was retrieved, only to reveal that crucial pages from the diary had indeed been torn out. The hunt in the show therefore now turned to those missing entries. Thus, eager fans were simultaneously granted advance insight into future narrative developments while also being denied answers to questions that could only be answered by watching further episodes. Similarly, the publication of spin-off books such as *The Autobiography of F.B.I. Special Agent Dale Cooper: My Life, My Tapes* (1991) and *Welcome to Twin Peaks: Access Guide to the Town* (1991), as well as the audio cassette tape *'Diane . . .': The Twin Peaks Tapes of Agent Cooper* (1990), added further background and depth to the TV series' ongoing storyworld by offering more details about characters, locations and back story.

While these other transmedia were less central to the unfolding plot than *The Secret Diary of Laura Palmer*, they did stimulate fans' imagination and deepened their involvement with the series' storyworld. As early expressions of online fandom at the time illustrated, the growing franchise's cross-fertilisation of input across media inspired a tremendous amount of elaborate speculation in the early internet's Usenet groups (Jenkins 2006: 121). As a vital part of this cult text, the publication of these transmedia expansions strengthened the idea that the *Twin Peaks* storyworld extended beyond the boundaries of a single media platform, instead constituting what Matt Hills describes as a 'hyperdiegesis': 'a vast and detailed narrative space, only a fraction of which is ever directly seen or encountered' (Hills 2002: 104).

While the television series would come to an untimely end as audience interest waned during the second season, this early investment in transmedia storytelling would help feed the dedicated fan culture that would thrive over the years. *Twin Peaks* showed that immersive and complexly layered hyperdiegetic storyworlds could spread across media platforms, yielding constellations of media texts that were remarkably integrated. For even if the initial transmedia spin-offs followed the expansion model as satellites to the TV show's obvious 'mothership', the subsequent release of the *Fire Walk with Me* feature film destabilised this hierarchy, moving the franchise as a whole further towards the integrated model of transmedia storytelling.

Twin Peaks: The Return – Twenty-first-century Transmedia

Blossoming briefly in the early 1990s, *Twin Peaks* was a vital precursor of digital fan culture that in many ways foreshadowed the emergence of convergence culture. By the time Mark Frost and David Lynch cryptically announced the return of the beloved series in early 2014, the production practices of the television industry were defined in the first place by their transitional character. Since the early 2010s, both television networks and cable channels have faced growing pressure from industrial 'disruptors' like Netflix, Hulu and Amazon, which offer increasingly competitive video-on-demand (VOD) services (Lotz 2014: 132–3). Besides the obvious advantages of accessibility, mobility and individual control, a key innovation that many of these VOD services have embraced is the 'full-drop season' (Mittell), which does away with the traditional week-long wait between episodes. Taken alongside the long-term decline of traditional television audiences, the rise of cable-cutting and other digital entertainment alternatives, and the ongoing growth of 'on-demand culture' (Tryon 2013), broadcasters embedded within television's traditional industrial framework are forced to innovate in order to attract sufficient advertisers and/or subscribers.

Within this hyper-competitive media environment, traditional television networks have been using cross-platform strategies to lure viewers back to weekly programming. In her analysis of the transmedia campaign surrounding the niche-marketed breakout TV hit *Glee*, Valerie Wee showed how the clever combination of licensed Twitter accounts and carefully timed releases of musical tracks via Apple's iTunes Store helped the Fox network transform the weekly episodes into minor media events (Wee 2006: 314–15). While social media and other new digital services are generally seen as obvious competitors for traditional media platforms, *Glee*'s innovative use of transmedia practices shows that they can also be employed to increase viewers' engagement with weekly broadcasts.

When American premium cable channel Showtime finally returned fans to the world of *Twin Peaks* in an 18-episode weekly series airing from 21 May to 3 September 2017, the franchise promised to revive the characters, locations and mythology so fondly remembered by the show's original viewers, as well as the later generations who had discovered *Twin Peaks* via reruns, VHS recordings, DVD and Blu-ray discs, or video streaming services. Identified variously as *Twin Peaks: The Return*, *Twin Peaks: Season Three*, and *Twin Peaks: A Limited Event Series*, the new series (hereafter *The Return*) appeared in a media-industrial context where the revival of nostalgic television favourites has become both fashionable and lucrative (Hassler-Forest 2020: 176–7).

In a marketplace where many platforms are frantically vying for audience attention and engagement, reviving existing storyworlds with dedicated fan cultures offers an obvious competitive advantage (Weinstock 2016: 14–16). At the same time, *Twin Peaks* seemed especially appropriate to revisit, having been singled out so often as an early paradigm for the twenty-first century's alleged 'Golden Age of Television' (Telotte 2016: 64). As a spectacularly short-lived pop-culture phenomenon, *Twin Peaks* quickly became a jealously guarded cult favourite, watched over by a dedicated global fandom. But its influence on twenty-first-century television culture is often explained by the series' combination of long-form storytelling and cinematic style with a complex and ever-expanding mythological deep structure, alongside its then-unusual emphasis on television authorship in the figure of 'auteurist' film director David Lynch.

As a more recent high-profile television production designed to be a media phenomenon for the cultural elite, *The Return* used similar methods to facilitate what Matt Hills has described as 'just-in-time fandom': a carefully regulated form of fan culture in which the most invested viewers are constantly forced to keep up with shifting production and distribution practices in order to stay abreast of the cultural conversation (Hills 2002: 140–1). As the convergence culture industry developed in the digital age, facilitated by the proliferation of connective social media platforms, this kind of just-in-time fandom grew ever more important. For *The Return*, this involved not only the meticulous synchronisation of digital music releases, but also the publication of two separate novels that elegantly bookended the new season's broadcast.

The first of these books, *The Secret History of Twin Peaks*, was published in October 2016, six months ahead of the new season's premiere. Rather than introducing any of the third season's new characters or filling in the blanks between the original series and the revival, the book instead expanded the storyworld in the opposite direction. Presented as a secret dossier made up of an elaborate collection of annotated historical records, *The Secret History of Twin Peaks* begins with facsimiles of 'historical documents' dating back to the early nineteenth century, before proceeding to map out a wide-ranging mythological superstructure for the franchise that spans two centuries of American history. Simultaneously foreshadowing the third season's more expansive narrative framework and embellishing the franchise's mythological superstructure, the book gave readers new information about the organisation of the franchise's storyworld without even hinting at the new season's plot. Meanwhile, the simultaneous release of the audiobook featured the voices of multiple original cast members, thereby both authorising this transmedia expansion as consistent with the existing franchise and playing into the nostalgia that inevitably fuels most viewers' interest in these television revivals.

Almost a year later, and a mere six weeks after the final two episodes had been broadcast, the book's companion volume *Twin Peaks: The Final Dossier* was published. Similar in form but also shorter and less ambitious in narrative scope and graphic design, this second book consisted of a collection of FBI files on all major characters in the storyworld. These files, diegetically written and compiled by third-season newcomer Special Agent Tammy Preston, give plentiful background information on events preceding the third season, as well as providing some obvious hints about its enigmatic finale. Taken together, the two books perfectly match Eder's 'expansion' model: they not only expand and enrich the existing storyworld through transmedia storytelling, but they do so in such a way that the contents are carefully synchronised with the release of a serialised television event. The first book broadened the mythological framework while providing a more elaborate history for the storyworld but did so without 'spoiling' narrative developments in the third season, or providing essential information that would disadvantage more casual viewers. In this sense, its obvious similarity to *The Secret Diary of Laura Palmer* added further layers of nostalgia for forensic fans eager to re-immerse themselves in the *Twin Peaks* storyworld (Hallam 2020).

At the same time, the books also provided a convenient way to resolve a longstanding tension within *Twin Peaks* authorship (Abbott 2016: 175–6). While director David Lynch has most commonly been singled out as the defining 'visionary' behind the franchise, his co-writer Mark Frost has somewhat uncomfortably shared the credit for the series. Therefore, as Twitter campaigns and online fan activism demonstrated all too clearly that Lynch was indeed the single most vital ingredient for a return to *Twin Peaks*, the two books gave Frost an avenue to express his own authorship in ways that were emphatically his. The occasional public interviews and other paratexts clearly illustrated this practical division of authorial labour, with Lynch commenting at one point that he had not even read *The Secret History of Twin Peaks* and noting 'en passant' that the book represents 'his' (Frost's) history of Twin Peaks – whereas the episodes are, by implication, primarily Lynch's (Hibberd 2017).

While it is obviously very much possible to read both books after (or before, or during) one's first viewing of *The Return*, the books' narrative contents and their publication dates were deliberately synchronised with Showtime's broadcast schedule in ways that enhanced the show's serialised structure. As a franchise that has embellished the (more or less) linear narrative movement of its television 'mothership' with transmedia expansions largely dedicated to the series' pre-history, the novels bookending *The Return* underline the revival's 'event-ness' while also acknowledging and respecting the franchise's spoiler-averse fan culture. For just as the almost comically oblique series promotional trailers had reassured fans about the revival's authenticity while refusing to give even the slightest indication of what would happen, the first novel offered a deep dive into the storyworld's mythology without hinting at what lay ahead. By the same token, the second book offered forensic fans a post-broadcast coda with clear narrative closure, while Frost's ambiguous status as an author left them free to speculate about alternative meanings as well. Both novels thereby functioned as expansions that supported Showtime's broadcast of weekly episodes through cross-platform transmedia serialisation.

Similarly, the release schedule of *The Return*'s two separate soundtrack albums playfully participated in the larger strategy of encouraging fan speculation in response to Showtime's weekly broadcast schedule. The two soundtracks did this in different ways, and for slightly different reasons. One album contained the instrumental score, while the other was filled with tracks by a wide variety of popular artists. For both albums, the track list was kept secret until the release date, which closely followed the final episode's broadcast. However, fans who pre-ordered either of these albums via a digital music platform like Apple's iTunes Music Store would see new tracks become available on a week-by-week basis just after a new episode had aired.

For the instrumental soundtrack, keeping the track list secret served a clear purpose with regard to plot spoilers, as the names of instrumental cues on film soundtracks often reveal elements of the story. For instance, while actor Carel Struycken is a familiar face from the original two seasons of *Twin Peaks*, his appearance in the opening scene of *The Return* is decidedly ambiguous, and his character's name is pointedly referred to in the episode's end credits only as a series of seven question marks. The suggestion that this iconic actor's return represented a new mystery strongly encouraged fan speculation, while the question marks in the credits explicitly teased a reveal that may or may not be forthcoming as the series progressed.

The question in this case was answered by the incremental release of the soundtrack album long before it was confirmed within the text of the series proper: the character's second appearance, in episode 8, was again followed by end credits that identified him only with question marks. But the following day, a new track titled 'The Fireman' became available to those who had pre-ordered the digital soundtrack. Forensic fans within online communities like welcometotwinpeaks.com and the *Twin Peaks* wiki were quick to decode the seven question marks as representing the seven letters of the word 'Fireman' – and from there on, to theorise that his function within the series' overall mythology must be to combat the evil associated with fire (as expressed throughout the franchise with the phrase 'Fire Walk with Me'). Indeed, these fan theories were validated six weeks later after the character's third appearance, in episode 14, where the end credits identified him definitively as 'The Fireman'.

For the other soundtrack album, containing vocal performances of tracks featured in the series, a similar release strategy further encouraged online engagement and just-in-time fandom. One of the ways in which *The Return* departed from the original series was the novelty of ending most episodes with a live performance by a contemporary musical act at the Twin Peaks Roadhouse. While several of the names had been surmised from the cast list that was circulated widely amongst fans months long before the series premiered, it remained unknown at what point in the series any given artist would appear, or in what capacity.

Without an advance soundtrack album to guide viewers' expectations, every musical performance constituted a genuine surprise to first-time viewers. Thus, the appearance of high-profile artists like Nine Inch Nails and Eddie Vedder could be experienced with delighted shock, while fans were also rewarded for their weekly engagement with digital access to the song the day after its appearance via its addition to the pre-ordered album tracks. In both cases, the soundtrack release strategy thereby gave forensic fans another level of engagement with the series that benefited both Showtime's industrial practice of weekly broadcasts and the digital sales of non-narrative franchise expansions as another form or transmedia serialisation.

Conclusion

While *Twin Peaks* has been understandably celebrated (and criticised) for its divergence from television conventions, the new series also serves as a helpful and vivid case study for industrial practices of transmedia storytelling and cross-platform serialisation. Following the innovative ways in which the original series expanded its storyworld between seasons through transmedia expansions, *The Return* adapted these practices for its own media-industrial context. The accompanying books and soundtracks strongly emphasised the new series' 'event-ness', while at the same time contributing to the season's transmedia structure. The first book, preceding the third season, prepared forensic fans for the new series' elaboration of the storyworld's mythology, while the second, appearing right after the finale, tied up narrative loose ends and clarified the plot. Meanwhile, the soundtracks' incremental digital releases encouraged fan speculation, while also rewarding viewers for watching the episodes as they were broadcast. Thus, to quote the Fireman's cryptic instruction from the first episode, *The Return* managed to 'kill two birds with one stone' by using integrated transmedia storytelling to combine digital fandom and on-demand culture with the television industry's continued reliance on traditional broadcast schedules.

Note

1. A shorter version of this article appeared previously in *M/C Journal* vol. 21, no. 1 (2018) as part of a special issue on transmedia serialization, edited by Anne Kustritz. This expanded and revised version is included here with the kind permission and support of the journal editors.

Bibliography

Abbott, Stacey. '"Doing Weird Things for the Sake of Being Weird": Directing Twin Peaks'. *Return to Twin Peaks*, Jeffrey Andrew Weinstock and Catherine Spooner (eds). Palgrave Macmillan, 2016, pp. 175–91.
Booth, Paul. *Digital Fandom 2.0*. Peter Lang, 2016.

Eder, Jens. 'Transmediality and the Politics of Adaptation'. *The Politics of Adaptation: Media Convergence and Ideology*, Dan Hassler-Forest and Pascal Nicklas (eds). Palgrave Macmillan, 2015, pp. 66–81.

Frost, Mark. *The Secret History of Twin Peaks*. Flatiron Books, 2016.

Frost, Mark. *Twin Peaks: The Final Dossier*. Flatiron Books, 2017.

Frost, Scott. *The Autobiography of F.B.I. Special Agent Dale Cooper: My Life, My Tapes*. Simon & Schuster, 1990.

Hallam, Lindsay. 'Drink Full and Descend: The Horror of *Twin Peaks: The Return*'. *New American Notes Online*, February 2020. https://nanocrit.com/issues/issue15/Drink-Full-and-Descend-The-Horror-of-Twin-Peaks-The-Return.

Hassler-Forest, Dan. '"When You Get There, You Will Already Be There": *Stranger Things*, *Twin Peaks* and the Nostalgia Industry'. *Science Fiction Film and Television*, vol. 13, no. 2, 2020, pp. 175–97.

Hibberd, James. '*Twin Peaks*: David Lynch Holds a Weird Press Conference'. *Entertainment Weekly*, 9 Jan 2017, http://ew.com/tv/2017/01/09/twin-peaks-david-lynch-press-conference/ (last accessed 8 November 2021).

Hills, Matt. *Fan Cultures*. Routledge, 2002.

Jenkins, Henry. *Convergence Culture: Where Old and New Media Collide*. New York University Press, 2006.

Jenkins, Henry. '"Do You Enjoy Making the Rest of Us Feel Stupid?" alt.tv.twinpeaks, the Trickster Author, and Viewer Mastery'. *Fans, Bloggers, and Gamers: Exploring Participatory Culture*, Henry Jenkins (ed.). New York University Press, 2006, pp. 115–33.

Johnson, Derek. *Media Franchising: Creative License and Collaboration in the Culture Industries*. New York University Press, 2013.

Lotz, Amanda D. *The Television Will Be Revolutionized*. 2nd edition. New York University Press, 2014.

Lynch, David, Mark Frost and Richard Saul Wurman. *Twin Peaks: An Access Guide to the Town*. Pocket Books, 1991.

Lynch, Jennifer. *The Secret Diary of Laura Palmer*. Penguin Books, 1990.

Mittell, Jason. 'Mind the Gap: Brief Thoughts on Seriality from Berlin'. *Just TV*, 22 Jun 2016, https://justtv.wordpress.com/2016/06/22/mind-the-gap-brief-thoughts-on-seriality-from-berlin/ (last accessed 24 June 2021).

Parody, Clare. 'Franchising/Adaptation'. *Adaptation*, vol. 4, no. 2, 2011, pp. 210–18.

Scott, Suzanne. *Fake Geek Girls: Fandom, Gender, and the Convergence Culture Industry*. New York University Press, 2019.

Telotte, J. P. '"Complementary Verses": The Science Fiction of *Twin Peaks*'. *Return to Twin Peaks*, Jeffrey Andrew Weinstock and Catherine Spooner (eds). Palgrave Macmillan, 2016, pp. 161–74.

Tryon, Chuck. *On-Demand Culture: Digital Delivery and the Future of Movies*. Rutgers University Press, 2013.

Wee, Valerie. 'Spreading the *Glee*: Targeting a youth audience in the multimedia, digital age'. *The Information Society*, vol. 32, no. 5, 2016, pp. 306–17.

Weinstock, Jeffrey Andrew. 'Introduction: "It Is Happening Again": New Reflections on *Twin Peaks*'. *Return to Twin Peaks*, Jeffrey Andrew Weinstock and Catherine Spooner (eds). Palgrave Macmillan, 2016, pp. 1–28.

Filmography

The Matrix. Directed by Lana Wachowski, Lilly Wachowski, performances by Keanu Reeves, Laurence Fishburn, Carrie-Anne Moss and Hugo Weaving, Warner Bros., 1999.

Twin Peaks. Directed by David Lynch et al., performances by Kyle MacLachlan and Mädchen Amick, Lynch/Frost Productions et al., 1990–1.

Twin Peaks: Fire Walk with Me. Directed by David Lynch, performances by Sheryl Lee and Ray Wise, CIBY Picture, 1992.

Twin Peaks: The Return [on DVD and BluRay *Twin Peaks: A Limited Event Series*]. Directed by David Lynch, performances by Sheryl Lee and Kyle MacLachlan, Showtime, 2017.

CHAPTER 8

The World Spins: Transmedia Detours and Cinematic Configurations around *Twin Peaks*

Andreas Rauscher

An inspiring starting point for speculations concerning well-known auteurs are the 'what-if' scenarios of film history. Projects that were discussed or were even about to go into production but then got lost in development hell and never made it to the screen. An attractive sub-category of this phenomenon covers classic films that almost got picked up by one director, but then ended up in someone else's hands. What would the Marvel Cinematic Universe (MCU) look like today if Stan Lee had succeeded in getting his long-time friend, the French comic book connoisseur and avant-garde director Alain Resnais to direct an adaptation of *Spider-Man* in the 1970s? In what ways would Alejandro Jodorowsky's *Dune* project that already signed on Salvador Dali, Mick Jagger and Orson Welles as well as Pink Floyd and H. R. Giger have influenced the look of the science-fiction-genre? What would have happened in a galaxy far, far away if David Lynch had not served as a replacement auteur for Jodorowsky on *Dune* but had directed *Star Wars Episode VI – Return of the Jedi* (1983)?

Far from being just an anecdote, the meeting between George Lucas and the director of *Eraserhead* and *The Elephant Man* to discuss *Return of the Jedi* really took place. After having some food together at a traditional diner and taking a tour in Lucas' sports car, the common ground eroded quickly. Lucas presented the prototypes of the cuddly creatures that came to be known as the Ewoks to Lynch at his ILM (Industrial Light and Magic) visual effects workshop. Lynch missed the opportunity to make several million dollars, politely rejecting the offer of the film, horrified by the idea of directing an army of teddy bears. This strange encounter not only inspires speculations on how in 1983 Darth Vader almost discovered transcendental meditation, in hindsight the meeting between Lynch and Lucas also represents an exchange between two very different approaches at the crossroads of the artistic and cultural networks that media scholar Henry Jenkins called transmedia storytelling, 'stories, that unfold across multiple media platforms, with each medium making distinctive contributions to our understanding of the world' (2006: 293). The differences are not only to be found in the story, but also in both its narrative framing and immersive sonic and visual aesthetics. Pondering these allows for a detour from the traditional narrative and cognitive focus of transmedia storytelling. In following such a detour, this chapter will open up an alternative route not often taken in the discourse of transmedia studies.

This chapter examines the aesthetic choices in the process of world-making with reference to *Twin Peaks*. Other detours have already been discussed in relation to Lynch's take on the neo-noir in studies like *Detours and Lost Highways* by Foster Hirsch (Hirsch 1999). In contrast to the popular idea of postmodern irony in the interpretation of Lynch, this chapter's concept of audiovisual detours allows for an appreciation of isolated moments of aesthetic intensity. Detours significantly deviate from the traditional goal-oriented economy of episodic television storytelling. The horizontal structure of streaming a TV series allows for emotional affects and associative thoughts. The film *Twin Peaks: Fire Walk with Me* (1992) does not further a hive mind insofar as it adds only a few things to what has already been covered in both the series and its spin-off novels. Nevertheless, the sheer intensity of its emotional impact engaging with Laura Palmer's struggle, carefully avoided by the knee-slappers of postmodern irony, is the result of a detour taken back to the dark moods of domestic melodrama and classical film noir. The aesthetic experience of a narrative already familiar from, but not shown within, the *Twin Peaks* television series results from a reconfiguration of the setting from tongue-in-cheek soap opera to existential angst, from *Peyton Place* (1964–9) to Ingmar Bergman. The fracture resulting from the detour of going back to the previously suppressed beginning of the narrative enables future audiences to configure their experience of *Twin Peaks*. They can start off with *Fire Walk with Me* before watching the series, follow the iconographic scavenger hunt through an exhibition of David Lynch's paintings and fine art, and reflect upon the background mythology provided in the novels by Mark Frost while creating their own track list from the soundtracks by Angelo Badalamenti.

Media scholar Colin Harvey defines transmedia configurations as

> the processes of manipulation and negotiation by which participants engage with transmedia networks [. . .] This might extend to deciding which element of a transmedia network to engage with – for instance, whether to watch the animated television series *Star Wars Rebels* or play the console game *Star Wars Battlefront* – but also the configurative strategies required to engage with a particular element of the transmedia network in question. (Harvey 2019: 158)

In the case of 'Twin Peaks', transmedia configurations provide completely different experiences if you choose the film *Fire Walk with Me* or the television pilot as your point-of-entry. The series counts among the few pop-cultural phenomena that connect the art gallery with the water cooler talk, and state-of-the-art in modernist soundtracks with the nostalgic pleasures of digging up strange old pop-records in crates. Lynch's painting *The Angel of Totality* (2009) can be interpreted as the continuation of a central visual motif in *Fire Walk with Me*, much as the video clip that accompanied Julee Cruise's song *Falling* on MTV can be connected to the mainstream success of the first season. Strolling along these transmedia routes can provide an associative aesthetic experience without giving too much thought on narrative patterns.

The polyphonic mixing of different modalities and keys allows for playful, self-ironic genre deconstructions as well as the disturbing intensity of disruptive shocks, sometimes all within the same franchise. The show combines the talents of David Lynch, at the time of production already a well-established art house director, and Mark Frost, a pioneer of quality TV coming from the series *Hill Street Blues* that many scholars (for example Thompson) consider to be one of the most influential game changers in regard to establishing complex narratives and elaborated aesthetic concepts in a format that was known for run-of-the-mill-productions and talking heads.

This chapter considers the transmedia aesthetics of *Twin Peaks*. It traces the series' development from prime-time postmodernism to its reconfigurations in *Fire Walk with Me* to its embrace of associative detours as guiding principle in *The Return*.

Twin Peaks and Cinematic Television

The attractiveness of the detours around *Twin Peaks* comes as a direct result of its cinematic style. If there had not been an elaborated mise-en-scène and iconic visuals as well as seductive and disturbing soundtrack compositions, the deviations from the murder mystery concerning the case of Laura Palmer would have probably been considered to be preposterous. The first two seasons of *Twin Peaks* build upon the origins of so-called quality television in the 1980s. In hindsight, media scholar Henry Jenkins considered the series to define the 'cutting edge of what a decade later would be called transmedia entertainment' (2020: 33).

Television historian Robert J. Thompson comments on television's turn towards cinema in his study *From Hill Street Blues to Television's Second Golden Age*:

> The new artistic possibilities introduced by quality TV had begun to attract the notice of successful film directors by the mid-1980s. Throughout its history, of

course, TV had always been considered the gross aesthetic inferior of the cinema. Many aspiring directors would slum around in television only until their big chance came, at which point they'd quickly beat it for the more legitimate world of film. During the 1980s, however, the old TV neighbourhood began to look a lot classier. TV's audience was potentially more mature than the teen-skewing audience of most movies; the ongoing series offered narrative possibilities not available in a two-hour film; and both the networks and cable outlets were demonstrating an occasional willingness to let television makers experiment. (Thompson 1997: 150)

Thompson mentions the anthology series *Amazing Stories* (1985–6) produced by Steven Spielberg, and Michael Mann's and Anthony Yerkovich's *Miami Vice* (1984–9) as updating the political perspectives of film noir by adding elements from clip culture, employing the rather unusual sunshine setting of Florida and inspiring complete fashion wardrobes by their looks.

Following their colleagues from cinema to prime-time television, Lynch and Frost had been hired by the network ABC to compete with innovations enabled by cable channels like HBO and others. The term 'cinematic' has been applied in discussions and reviews to the production values, a sophisticated use of stylistic devices, and elaborate aesthetic concepts of television that reach beyond the American standard home of traditional sitcoms and the limited studio space of soap operas. In contrast to its omnipresence in discussions, the term 'cinematic' itself has been quite under-theorised. The cinematic is often considered in the context of larger theoretical reflections. Kara Keeling (2007: 3) refers to Deleuzian film-philosophy, warning about 'the risk of subsuming things specific to other audiovisual media, such as television, under the rubric of cinema.' In *Breaking Bad and Television*, one of the few studies to directly address the topic of cinematic television, Angelo Restivo (2019: 7), on the one hand, takes cues from Jacques Lacan and argues that the cinematic should be seen as:

a kind of interrupter within the regime of images [. . .] the cinematic will be the term I use to name these particular types of images. As such, it names the occurrence of 'an aesthetic event': one that opens onto the indeterminate.

On the other hand, Jason Mittell (2015: 2) in his poetics of *Complex Television* demands that television and its shift towards new concepts of storytelling must be understood on its own terms:

'Complex TV' is [. . .] exploring how television storytelling has changed and what cultural practices within television technology, industry, and viewership have enabled and encouraged these transformations. Often these changes are framed as television becoming more 'literary' or 'cinematic', drawing both prestige and formal vocabulary from these older, more culturally distinguished media; however, we can better understand this shift through careful analysis of television itself rather than holding onto cross-media metaphors of aspiration and legitimation.

Taking a middle-ground position between thinking cinema from the top-down perspective of established Deleuzian, Latourian or Lacanian theory and the bottom-up approach of theorising the artefacts themselves the following considerations understand cinematic television as an exchange of forms and stylistic concepts across media. Depending on the show-runner, the writers' room, the directors and the audiences, the cinematic frameworks can relate to the mise-en-scène and variations of styles as well as narrative modes and tropes, genre concepts, character types and settings. Instead of trying to accumulate cultural capital by adjusting the TV set to the demands of the cinema screen, a more precise and direct discussion of the aesthetic intersections between both can be helpful to gain a better understanding of the dynamic processes resulting in transmedia network structures.

David Lynch's ways of world-making are rather based on aesthetic associations, surreal soundscapes, and subversive sideways than franchise building and branding intellectual property. The motifs found on the detour from the main plot in his films and the series *Twin Peaks* are reminiscent of photographic impressions taken at the side of the road. Images of the dark woods in the Pacific Northwest, the blinking neon sign outside the Roadhouse bar or the traffic light dangling above a lonely street in the middle of nowhere (Röttger and Jacob 2006) provide for the atmospheric value and the iconic sights defining both the series *Twin Peaks* as well as Lynch's œuvre.

Passages through Postmodernism: The First Seasons of *Twin Peaks*

The first two seasons of *Twin Peaks* arrived at the peak of postmodernism in Western popular culture. Coming from a European art-house perspective, *Twin Peaks* was considered to be an extension of the subversive interpretation of weird Americana that had been on display in *Blue Velvet* and *Wild at Heart*. With *Eraserhead* Lynch had already become a favourite of the midnight movie circle that travelled from the seminal book on the subject by Jonathan Rosenbaum and Jay Hoberman (1983) across articles in magazines associated with subcultures and post-punk to the programming of several late night art-house screenings. The release of the *Eraserhead* soundtrack on punk cult label Alternative Tentacles as well as the stories about the monster baby created further interest in the film that has been shown in art house cinemas throughout the 1980s and 1990s.

When I first encountered *Eraserhead* on the big screen in the early 1990s, the projectionist mixed up the reels. The dreamlike quality of the film made it so that no one really noticed until the screening was interrupted and after a short break the film started again from the middle onwards. In a funny way the switched reels of *Eraserhead* echoed the cultural practices of the surrealists who entered cinema screenings at random in the 1920s creating their own imaginary film. Instead of waiting for the epiphany of a hierarchical structured narrative artwork the surreal practice of remixing sound and vision by moving in and out of movie theatres as well as the multimodal architecture of Lynch's films with their references to popular culture allowed for open interpretations. The cultural practices in their reception came much closer to the idea of Umberto Eco's open artwork, articulated in the late 1960s, demanding active forms of involvement and participation from the audience (see Eco 1989). Even though the idea of an imaginary whole had been stimulated by recurring iconic visuals and idiosyncratic sounds, in contrast to traditional ideas about high-cultural variations of the 'Gesamtkunstwerk', the records by Lynch's composer Angelo Badalamenti could be bought at every record store. The horizontal structure of participatory fan activities created a reception beyond the vertical hierarchy of traditional art consumption. Nevertheless, both cultural fields of reception, the high-brow-reception of Lynch in the art world and the popular practices of fandom, remained an integral part of the same network. The pop-cultural hype surrounding *Twin Peaks* and *Wild at Heart* resulted in the video clips of 'Falling' by Julee Cruise and 'Wicked Game' by Chris Isaak entering heavy rotation on MTV, as well as the experimental opera based on *Lost Highway* by Olga Neuwirth and Elfriede Jelinek being internationally performed by avant-garde ensembles.

The idea of interconnected Lynchian art works can already be found in Michel Chion's (1995: 83) description of Lynchtown in his seminal book on the director:

> Lynchtown is a cute, typically American, small town in the midst of an ocean of forest, [. . .] Lynchtown is the base camp for an adventure of the imagination, a place where you can come and be refreshed with a cup of coffee in a familiar place. It is also a surface, but with only one side, not a recto with a verso. It is a façade with nothing to hide, not even nothingness.

Another facet of the Lynchian œuvre that contributes to the multimodal construction of an artistic vision du monde is provided by the sound design and the music composed by Angelo Badalamenti, described by Chion (1995: 158) as a cine-symphony:

> Neither does Lynch's cine-symphony, or rather his electro-symphony, shy from bringing into play the maximum number of registers and dimensions, making them resound together, literally fulfilling the program announced by the musical term itself: 'sumphonia' (Greek for 'with sound'). This is what I meant when I labelled his style romantic, in the full, multiple senses of the term [. . .] in musical terms, Lynch attempts to play in every scale, whereas other filmmakers narrow their work down to two or three keys.

The multi-modality of Lynch's work creates connections between his films, records, and exhibitions as well as cultural contexts employing different practices resulting in a networked transmedia form of world-making. The overwhelming effect on the senses on watching his films on a large screen with sophisticated sound set-up implies a romantic work of pure cinema, but at the same time the network effect creates a hub of aesthetic motifs and cultural practices that rather corresponds with the open structure of the (post-)modern art life.

Regarding the supposedly superficial façade, which has often been object of debate in the critical reception of Lynch's films, one important aspect is often forgotten by cultural criticism accusing Lynch of pure pastiche. For example, Jonathan Rosenbaum (1995: 25), who enthusiastically wrote about *Eraserhead*, attacked the supposedly conservative attitude behind *Twin Peaks* upon its release: 'Lynch's social orientation becomes much clearer with *Blue Velvet* and *Twin Peaks*: it consists basically of an infatuation with 1950s small town Americana and its dirty little secrets, coupled with a view that essentially regards women as either madonnas or whores.' Contrary to a nostalgia for an age that never existed, the meaning of the signs spread across the surface can change depending on the context created by involvement of the audience. The cult concerning 'damn fine coffee', cherry pie and donuts can serve as a deconstruction and an abstract in-joke like René Magritte's famous drawing of a pipe that is accompanied by the signifying text, 'çeci ne pas une pipe'. In other contexts, from fan-conventions at the locations from the series to the annual cult screening of all 'Twin Peaks' episodes at film studies departments, the coffee, donuts and cherry pie provide the buffet, far from being a treachery of images. Even within Chion's 'façade with nothing to hide' (1995: 83) the images in Lynch's films and artworks can provide iconic cultural symbols and ambivalent floating signifiers at the same time.

In *Twin Peaks* the intentional confusion of the ontological levels becomes an important element in the depiction of the Black Lodge's forces. After solving the murder of Laura Palmer, the question of whether Killer Bob (Frank Silva) was a phantom made-up by the murderer to suppress his feeling of guilt or if it was an evil spirit taking possession of him remains open. Very often the symbols of the supernatural remain quite abstract and are not explained further but rather handed over to the imagination of the audience, from the owl symbol representing the lodges, and the green ring to the red curtains and the dimensional gateway appearing under the sycamore trees in the deep forest. It seems to be quite appropriate that in *Twin Peaks: The Return* the realm of the Fireman watching over the world reminds of an old movie palace from the days of silent cinema. The magic of characters disappearing into thin air and mysterious gateways to other dimensions created by paintings or evil forces materialising above convenience stores appears to be much closer to the movie tricks by Méliès than to the make-up prosthetics of modern horror cinema and the computer-generated-effects of recent film history. Nevertheless, the terror summoned from the Black Lodge can have the same disturbing effect as the cenobites released by the simple elegance of the puzzle box in Clive Barker's *Hellraiser* series (1987–). The abstract quality of the supernatural beings in *Twin Peaks* is reminiscent of the mysterious gathering on a lonely Swedish island in Ingmar Bergman's *Vargtimmen/The Hour of the Wolf* (1968) that welcomes the despairing painter Johan (Max von Sydow) at a castle in the early hours of the morning. After meeting the strange old lady who removes her face when taking off her hat, as well as Baron von Merkens and other illustrious surreal party guests, Johan is never to be seen again, just like the FBI agents Chester Desmond and Philip Jeffries in *Fire Walk with Me*. If the visuals of the Black Lodge are understood in the context of horror semantics or approached as abstract images with an artistic value of their own depends on the configuration chosen by the audience. The surreal images and inventions can be enjoyed on a very immediate level. If the viewers want to dig deeper into the references to Ingmar Bergman's *Vargtimmen*, Alfred Hitchcock's *Vertigo*, Billy Wilder's *Sunset Boulevard*, and the history of television dramas like *Peyton Place*, or to examine the tropes of the modern horror genre, they can decide this on their own.

Détour(nements) around *Twin Peaks*

The detours taken from *Twin Peaks*' main plot of who killed Laura Palmer provide a cinematic mise-en-scène of elaborated style in sound and vision. This not only adds to Lynch's blurring of boundaries between media formats and art forms (Jerslev 2021), it also provides a point-of-entry to the aesthetic experience of *Twin Peaks* based on the atmospheric value of sound and vision instead of narrative comprehension.

In the press kit accompanying *Blue Velvet*, Lynch explained his fascination for setting pictures in motion:

> I always sort of wanted to do films. Not so much a movie-movie as a film-painting. I wanted the mood of the painting to be expanded through film, sort of a moving painting. It was really the mood I was after. I wanted a sound with it that would be so strange, so beautiful, like if the Mona Lisa opened her mouth and turned, and there would be a wind, and then she'd turn back and smile. It would be strange.' (http://www.lynchnet.com/sixmen/)

Since *Eraserhead*, sound has been a crucial element in this creative process, that is situated somewhere between appropriation art, expanded cinema and cultural techniques like sampling. The often discussed, occasionally even by Lynch himself, references to Edward Hopper, Francis Bacon and Jackson Pollock are always accompanied by atmospheric soundscapes and ambiguous variations of pop-cultural acoustic tropes.

In discussion with Chris Rodley, David Lynch (Rodley 2005: 158) comments on the concept of *Twin Peaks*:

> The mystery of who killed Laura Palmer was the foreground, but this would recede slightly as you got to know other people in this town and the problems they were having. And each week would feature close-ups of some things. The project was a mix of the police investigation with the ordinary lives of characters. We had drawn a map of the town. We knew where everything was located and that helped us determine the prevailing atmosphere and what might happen there.

The close-ups mentioned by Lynch can be understood in a narrative way, but also as the devices of cinematic world-building used in the series. Motifs like the traffic light on the lonely nocturnal forest road are explored in more detail as well as themes and atmospheres on the soundtrack that had been arranged by Angelo Badalamenti as an acoustic collection of templates to build upon. The idea of an expanding mental map corresponds with the explorative structure of horizontal storytelling, defining for current serial formats on television and on streaming platforms. The unconventional creation and use of the soundtrack also reflect the horizontal construction of *Twin Peaks*.

On the one hand, there is the idea of leitmotifs such as 'Falling', 'Laura Palmer's Theme' or 'Audrey's Dance'. On the other hand, if compared with the poignant pulp symphonies by John Williams, Danny Elfman, James Horner and other (post-)modern soundtrack composers, Badalamenti's works appear to be much closer to the improvisation on standard templates in jazz or the deck of records and sounds selected for a DJ set. Clare Nina Norelli (2017: 13), in her study on the *Soundtrack from Twin Peaks*, contends:

> Badalamenti himself has created many pieces with David Lynch, that have utilized techniques found in 'musique concrète'. Since the early 1990s the pair have recorded long pieces of music that they call 'firewood'. These 'firewood' tracks are then altered and sometimes mixed together to create different soundscapes for Lynch's visuals.

The associative thematic and topographical approach taken by Lynch and Frost in constructing the setting and by Badalamenti in composing *Twin Peaks* rely on mood boards, the creation of a certain atmosphere by visual and/or acoustic cues, and a detailed mise-en-scène that goes beyond the pure functionality of simple props.

The associative match between David Lynch and his co-creator Mark Frost prevented *Twin Peaks* from becoming stale routine even though the later episodes of season 2 came dangerously close to succumbing to stale generic conventions with high school-comedy, beauty contests, and femme fatale tropes. Mark Frost remembers an anecdote about introducing the Giant who appears to the shot down Agent Cooper in the first episode of season 2 that also is quite instructive about Lynch's work as a visual artist:

> He [Lynch] would every once in a while call me and say something like, 'There's a giant in Cooper's room', or that he wanted Josie to end up in a doorknob [. . .] And because he's first and foremost a visual artist, he worked in visual ideas, like a giant or Josie in a doorknob. (Bushman 2020: 140)

Mark Frost also recalls a development that is often forgotten in favour of backward talking entities, songs about sycamore trees, and supernatural waiting lounges with red curtains: 'The show had progressively moved from the pilot – which is, for the most part, almost kitchen-sink realism in its bones. David played it very straight first time out' (Bushman 2020 124). In contrast to his creative partner, Frost rather tried to reflect complete genre settings (Bushman 2020 95). The creative synergies of different transmedia frameworks, with Lynch working from the associative ideas of visual art and Frost parrying with genre narratives brought to television a whole set of different cinematic configurations. Because of its open associative form, in hindsight, the series did not succumb to the noncommittal pleasures of the pastiche criticised upon its original release by several reviewers (see Rosenbaum 1995). Instead of getting lost in the simulacra of the timeless post-histoire, the series and its innovative

mixture of appropriated retro paraphernalia and supernatural mysteries has become a point-of-reference that is nowadays closely connected
to late 1980s and early 1990s pop-culture. Far from being isolated from
history in an ever-lasting now of 1950s diners and ethereal retro-songs,
Twin Peaks and Lynch's cinematic work in *Blue Velvet* and *Wild at Heart*
reflect their respective cultural contexts of the postmodern condition in
a very modern way.

Fire Walk with Me – Affects in a World of Blue

The intrinsic value of audiovisual extensions into other media from the
soundtrack to the visual motifs depicted in Lynch's fine art like *Douglas
Fir Lamp* (2002), *This man was shot 0.9502 seconds ago* (2004), *The Angel of
Totality* (2009), and *Boy Lights Fire* (2010) granted *Twin Peaks* a life beyond
the narrative exhaustion of the crime plot and tiresome postmodern in-jokes
in season 2 that did not play any more with expectations but turned into
clichés themselves. Instead of further developing the cliffhanger at the end
of season 2 with Cooper trapped inside the Black Lodge and replaced by his
evil doppelganger, Lynch opted to go back in time for the *Twin Peaks* feature film. *Fire Walk with Me* (1992) explores the intensity of affects brought
about by the dark moods and melancholy associated with the tragic death
of Laura Palmer. While the colour blue is crucial to the intense song 'Questions in a World of Blue' sung by Julee Cruise in a key scene from the film, it
is missing from the film's colour palette, with the exception of the blue rose
early in the film. The direction of photography prefers the intensity of red
light and curtains instead. The transmedia spin-off book *The Secret Diary
of Laura Palmer*, written by David Lynch's daughter Jennifer and published
in 1990 between seasons 1 and 2, provided the starting point for the prequel
film. Upon its original release the diary with pages torn out served as a clue
book providing additional hints and atmospheric value to the speculations
about the identity of the murderer. After the story arc came to an end in
the series, the diary took on another function. It did not build up any more
expectations regarding the solution of the murder case. In *Fire Walk with
Me* it provided the template for creating scenes that, almost like artworks
based upon familiar tropes and topics, offered alternative perspectives. The
film made the audience experience emotional intensities that were relegated
to the safe distance of the backstory in the series.

In contrast to the enthusiastic reactions after the first episodes of the
series, the film *Fire Walk with Me* was received with very negative reactions
after its premiere at the Cannes film festival in 1992, where *Wild at Heart*
had won the Palme d'Or two years previously. It quickly disappeared from

cinemas, if it had been scheduled at all, and was largely panned by the critics. A first reconsideration took place in the pages of the *Twin Peaks* fanzine *Wrapped in Plastic* that dedicated several detailed in-depth analyses to the film. Later, reappraisals by British film critic Mark Kermode and Nouvelle Vague director Jacques Rivette discussed the film. A book-length insightful study by Lindsey Hallam (2018) introduced different perspectives on the film through the lens of Lynch's œuvre, traumatic experiences, the horror genre, Laura's fight for her soul, and the world of the TV series. It appropriately called to attention the different complex layers of meaning and audacious audiovisual experimentation in the film that had been ignored by many critics upon its initial release.

A very symptomatic misunderstanding is already communicated by the German title of the film *Twin Peaks: Der Film* that would translate as *Twin Peaks: The Movie*. The few expectations remaining after season 2 disappeared from German television were focused on the building of a franchise like *Star Trek: The Motion Picture* (1979) or *X-Files: Fight the Future* (1998, also following the peculiarities of German 'Eigentlichkeit' known as *Akte X: Der Film*). The final episodes of season 2 were even broadcast by the small TV channel Tele 5 after mainstream channel RTL only aired the episodes until the arrest of Laura Palmer's murderer. Many of the mainstream reviews of *Fire Walk with Me* expressed either disappointment (Lynch biographer Robert Fischer called *Fire Walk with Me* 'a film with seven seals' in the journal *epd Film*) or open hostility. Andreas Kilb (1992) in the weekly newspaper *Die Zeit*, for example, accused the film of selling out and being not a film but 'the sad result of a typical business meeting between an unexperienced European producer and an overambitious American director'.

When David Lynch retrospectives were shown at art-house cinemas in my region near Frankfurt am Main, *Fire Walk with Me* had been left out or only included as a belated addendum. Many articles discussing David Lynch often treated both *Fire Walk with Me* as well as *Dune* as minor entries. Mentioning *Fire Walk with Me* at film studies conferences resulted in the somehow irritating comment that at least the cherry pie still tastes good, when indeed it was, as Lindsay Hallam remarks, wrapped in barbed wire (Hallam 2018: 5). In its radical mixture of claustrophobic domestic terror and surreal sequences, *Fire Walk with Me* proved to be as mesmerising as Bergman's *Vargtimmen* (1968), especially in regard to the gathering of the forces from the Black Lodge above a convenience store.[1]

In hindsight, *Fire Walk with Me* marks the turn towards the radical subjectivity, the disturbing affects and the ontology-boggling mind-game-puzzles that came to define Lynch's work from the 1990s onward. The soundtrack by Angelo Badalamenti already sets the tone for the deeply disturbing film. The tracks rearrange and improvise upon the compositions from the series, but not in the way of the pre-arranged sonic 'firewood' of musical soundscapes prepared for further use in the series. The arrangements create a melancholic mood in presenting a much darker version of themes from the series accentuating the important role of atmospheres and affects in the film.

One of the only reviews in the German mainstream press that recognized the peculiar lyrical qualities of *Fire Walk with Me* was a piece written by the late film critic Hans Schifferle for the *Süddeutsche Zeitung* with an underground sensibility for associations and style. He chose a key sentence from one of the first dialogues between Laura (Sheryl Lee) and Donna (Moira Kelly replacing Lara Flynn Boyle from the series) about falling in space, 'and the angels wouldn't help you', for the headline of his article. Besides pointing out references to Otto Preminger's film noir *Laura* (1944) he compared *Fire Walk with Me* to a long dark and sad song. The associative form of the review corresponded with the film and discussed it seriously at a time when many critics seemed to be overburdened by it. Schifferle noticed many aspects about the film that came to be discussed decades later, but very few cared about upon its initial release. Schifferle (1992) characterised the main part of the film depicting the last seven days of Laura Palmer to be 'deeply romantic [. . .] Where the narrative ends, poetry begins – and vice versa. One illuminates the other, the bisection of the film is as simple as brilliant.'

Without Mark Frost, his sparring partner in storytelling, David Lynch opted for the strategic collapse of the narrative architecture and blowing up the previous format. The opening credits to *Fire Walk with Me* are shown in front of white noise accompanied by an elegiac new theme music in minor by Badalamenti. After the credits, the film opens with both the murder of Teresa Banks in the dark and an exploding television set. The following investigation provides no real set-up, but rather deconstructs the ironic trademarks that defined the series. FBI deputy director Gordon Cole (David Lynch in a cameo that began in the series and gradually turned into a starring role in season 3) presents the instructions to his agents by way of a bizarre dancer (Kimberly Ann Cole). The FBI agents Chester Desmond (Chris Isaak) and Sam Stanley (Kiefer Sutherland) travel to Deer Meadow to investigate the murder of Teresa Banks (Pamela Gidley). The town proves to be a kind of anti-Twin Peaks. The local police force reacts with outright hostility to the arrival of the FBI agents and the town's residents behave in a very reserved manner. At the local diner, the only specialty is that there are no specials and one of the few guests at the bar loses himself in repeating the same phrases again and again. The trailer park tristesse of Teresa Bank's home does not provide any more clues, even though a helpful caretaker, Carl Rodd (Harry Dean Stanton), tries to support the agents as best he can. The set-up, which intentionally leads nowhere, gives way to the tragedy of Laura Palmer. In the second half of the film, her last days are told from a radically subjective point of view. From all the absurd clues presented in the beginning, only the enigmatic blue rose remains. The process of cracking the code, fundamental to the whodunit and the mystery genre, results in the implosion of the familiar semantic in the sequences around Deer Meadow. The crime investigation has hit a dead end.

The associations with dark romanticism implied by the blue rose provide a key visual for the downward spiral that follows in the main part of the film. The other key addition to the cinematic revisiting of the last days in the life of Laura Palmer is the mysterious ring with the green gem and the owl symbol. It is spotted on a photograph of the murdered young woman Teresa Banks and creates a connection to the Black Lodge. The ring is found by Chester Desmond at the Big Trout trailer park near the crime scene. Audiences familiar with the series will note that Carl Rodd's mention of the former residents being called 'Chalfonts' and the association of electricity with supernatural forces in Lynch's cosmology are as alarming as the music box chimes of the puzzle box in Clive Barker's *Hellraiser*. The grounding of these rather abstract motifs within the semantics of the horror genre already suggests the turn towards the supernatural and disturbing the film will take in its main section. In a truly inspired move Lynch does not explicitly show the transgression into the horror genre. The arrival of the forces from the Black Lodge is indicated both on a rather abstract narrative and on a symbolic level. Instead, the image fades to black and Chester Desmond disappears, almost as if he is being delegated to the replacement bench of FBI agents to make room for the belated entrance of Agent Dale Cooper.

The self-deconstruction caused by the first act sets up the following focus on the main story with its tragic ending already known to the audience. The body of Teresa Banks, wrapped in plastic and floating on water in one of the first shots of the film, foreshadows the fate of Laura Palmer. The whole structure of *Fire Walk with Me* is more comparable to a medieval miracle play than an exercise in the mystery genre that became popular in the 1990s. Coming from the future – or maybe even beyond time and space – Agent Cooper, held captive in the Black Lodge after the finale of the series, moves through the Red Room and into Laura's dreams like a helpless spectator. Even Annie Blackburn (Heather Graham), Cooper's future love interest in season 2, appears to Laura to give her clues about the events happening in the series and asks her to write those down in her diary. On a narrative level, these scenes about the darkness of the future's past may seem confusing for those who are not familiar with the series and rather redundant for others who have expected to find answers to the cliffhanger at the end of the series.

The narrative perspective does not really matter for the immediate experience of *Fire Walk with Me* even though it is based on the spin-off book written by Jennifer Lynch. The accentuated repetition and the rewriting of the story already told in another medium introduces the idea of a palimpsest and thus creates new cinematic configurations within the transmedia network. Allister Mactaggart uses the term of the palimpsest in his discussion of the aesthetic 'eigen'-value of Lynch's cinematic images in his study *The Film Paintings of David Lynch: Challenging Film Theory* (Mactaggart 2010: 9–22). In a profound analysis, which echoes Walter Benjamin's discussion of allegories as well as Aby Warburg's and Erwin Panofsky's iconological studies, he discusses *Fire Walk with Me*:

> If, as some critics argue, Lynch's work is all about empty postmodern play then there would be little point in going back to 'Twin Peaks', because it had been 'played' out. However, by doing so, the film presents an opportunity to extend our mourning period and mourning-play. (Mactaggart 2010: 30)

Even though Mactaggart discusses the palimpsest in relation to Lynch's œuvre in general and not specifically regarding *Fire Walk with Me*, the idea of rewriting and reconfiguring an already existing text provides a perfect template for understanding the largely ignored film.

In a plea for rethinking the sensual experience of watching a film, Mactaggart (2010: 27) notes, of *Fire Walk with Me*, that 'the film helps to create a more dreamlike logic to the overall narrative structure'. The dreamlike structure created by the intensive use of sound and the mesmerizing visuals are painted over the text of the already familiar background story of the TV series. The distanced and knowing cognitive pleasure enabled by the series gets absorbed into a maelstrom of affects and intensities. After the implosion of the ironic investigations, the cinematic return to *Twin Peaks* after the series' finale plays out very differently from the ironic double-coding of the first two seasons. The psychological coming-of-age-tragedy about a trauma victim enduring incest offers only minimal comfort by allowing Cooper to provide spiritual guidance to Laura from his imprisonment in the Red Room. The final transcendental image unites both in what could be interpreted as the White Lodge. A guardian angel, or maybe *The Angel of Totality* from Lynch's painting, which earlier in the film disappeared from a painting in Laura's room, is superimposed over the image of Laura and Cooper, finally at ease in the Red Room. Mactaggart (2010: 27) comments on the last scene from *Fire Walk with Me*:

> Is this scene to be read seriously, or ironically, or even in both ways at once and does it, therefore, offer different, possibly incompatible readings to different communities? I want to suggest that, within the narrative signified, there is another level of meaning, an excess that runs counter to that of the symbolic and which threatens to undo its manifest meaning, and to offer counter- and anti-narrative levels of signification.

The further levels of meaning are crucial to the scene and the film as a whole. Without the ironic safety net of *Wild at Heart* and the *Twin Peaks* TV series scenes like this final image could be easily dismissed as 'kitsch' from a top-down-perspective. Regarding the careful orchestration of affects and the radical subjectivity of the film, that is the thorough point-of-view narration of Laura Palmer, such a dismissal seems to be even more superficial than the worst postmodern pastiche.

The return to Twin Peaks forty minutes into the film presents the iconic establishing shot, but the subsequent travelling shot following Laura and Donna down the main road differs significantly from the images and the perspectives established in the series. It appears to be much closer to the shots of autumnal streets found in John Carpenter's *Halloween* (1978) than the inviting and idyllic scenery from the TV series. In contrast to the killer lurking behind the picket fences of suburbia, the threatening evil personified by Bob (Frank Silva) has already moved into the Palmer home. Form and content create disturbing and stirring effects when in the afternoon Laura and Donna discuss the experience of falling in space. With deep resignation Laura explains that one would go faster and faster until they burst into flames and the angels would not help them since they have all long gone. In a very peculiar position, the camera shows Laura and Donna from an angle that fits the perspective of the angel in the Red Room during the final scene. Compositions like the use of the guardian angel as a recurring motif demonstrate the thoughtful combination of existential 'kitsch' associated with the sign itself and its rather abstract, open meaning that informs the chosen camera angle. The presence of the sublime associated with the guardian angel directly influences in an abstract way the composition of shots and the compositions on the soundtrack without sticking to the signalling effect of the motif itself. The perspective of a safeguarding presence is not shown in the scene between Laura and Donna. Nevertheless, such a presence is suggestively integrated in the choice of the camera angle and hinted at on the soundtrack that accompanied by cosmic noise features a short segment from the 'The Voice of Love' theme.

In general, *Fire Walk with Me* seems to be organised along the changing rhythms and moods of the soundtrack by Angelo Badalamenti and David Lynch. A poignant example for the musical arrangements of the scenes and their emotional effect can be found in Julee Cruise's performance of 'Questions in a World of Blue' at the local club called the Roadhouse. The mise-en-scène employs the expressive use of the colours red and blue. Instead of creating musical appropriation art by reinterpreting 1950s songs or delivering pop-cultural set pieces suitable for circulation on MTV, the sad lyrics and the deep melancholy of the song correspond directly with the emotional unrest of Laura and the action on the screen.

After her encounter with the Log Lady, who reminisces about all goodness being thrown in jeopardy, Laura enters the Roadhouse for a meeting with two customers. She is followed by Donna. Laura's slow movement through the club and the crucial test for her friendship with Donna, who here encounters a previously unknown side of Laura, are transmitted by the staging of the atmosphere rather than traditional narrative techniques. The slowing down of narrative time and the dominance of the sound comes close to taking on the qualities of a tableaux vivant. The thematic association of the scene is played out by the movement of the characters and the accompanying musical performance. Scenes like the rite de passage of growing apart implied by the lyrics of 'Questions in a World of Blue' and its mise-en-scène take on an almost transcendental quality. The performance of the song echoes at the same time Julee Cruise's 'The World Spins' in *Twin Peaks* and the Club Silencio sequence in *Mulholland Drive*, as well as Audrey Horne performing her dance routine from the first seasons at the Roadhouse in season 3, and thus resembles a nightmarish loop. The mournful sadness of Julee Cruise's performance at the Roadhouse gives way to an orgiastic and at the same time lethargic party sequence in a bar close to the Canadian border in the following scene. The drone sounds of the minimalist guitar riff and bass pattern drown out every conversation, in many versions of *Fire Walk with Me* the dialogue of this sequence is shown in subtitles. The two scenes form a contrast without putting into question Laura's and Donna's behaviour. The contrapuntal associations of heightened melancholy and deafening neglect are arranged in associative compositions of visuals and sound, distinguishing Laura's point-of-view from the postmodern business-as-usual surrounding her. The tableaux vivant character of the scenes in the Roadhouse and at the club, just like the scenes in the Red Room, demonstrates the artistic technique of the palimpsest to add further cinematic configurations and layers of audiovisual experience to the already known narrative. In scenes like the meeting of Laura and Dale Cooper in the Red Room that takes place beyond the linear time of the story, the configurations create hubs for opening non-linear spaces. These scenes are like the song performances, moving through time from Laura's subjective point-of-view or the encounters in the Red Room, often starting out with strong arrangements of affects, providing room for philosophical reflections. Within the developing context of the transmedia network structure they can also be used as a base for further narratives. Laura Palmer promised Agent Cooper in the Red Room that they would meet again twenty-five years later. More than two decades later *Fire Walk with Me*'s final tableau vivant of Laura and Cooper in the Red Room was set into motion again. The dialectics between isolated intensities encountered in song performances and tableaux vivants and trance-like high-speed dynamics indicates one of the film-philosophical ideas in Lynch's œuvre that will be discussed in the next section.

Let's Talk about Judy – *Twin Peaks: The Return*

Allister Mactaggart notices a 'dialectic between stasis and movement, between painting and film, between the autonomous image and diachronic narrative' (Mactaggart 2010: 15) in the works by David Lynch. Illustrative examples for stasis can be found in the opening sequence of *Blue Velvet* with its white picket fences, the song performances at the Roadhouse in *Twin Peaks* or in *Wild at Heart* when Sailor and Lula encounter a tragic car accident along a lonely desert road in the middle of the night. Examples of movement that border on becoming a stand-still inform Fred Madison's painful transformations in *Lost Highway*, the nocturnal rides on deserted roads, or the sped-up woodsmen from *Twin Peaks: The Return*.

In the films by David Lynch after 1992, stasis and movement continually begin to merge. This process results in open forms emancipating themselves from the totality of an imaginary whole. The open-ended structure rather stimulates the mental participation of the viewer instead of allowing him or her to immerse themself in the pleasures of a congruent storyworld. The process of configuration in choosing between different possible ontological constructions of the world viewed becomes one of the key elements in actively involving the audience in Lynch's mind-game films. The worlds presented on screen in *Lost Highway* and *Mulholland Drive* can be understood according to principles of genre turning the psychological drama into a supernatural mystery. Nevertheless, they can also be regarded as psychological manifestations of a disturbed inner life without any supernatural beings involved. In contrast to purely abstract or minimalist art, the mind-game films seduce the audience into participating in figuring out and constructing the different levels of the diegetic world according to one of the indicated schemes like generic American horror story or more art-house orientated psychic profile without any supernatural shenanigans and mystery men.

The later films by David Lynch, are told from a radical subjective point of view, as exemplified by *Fire Walk with Me*. Sometimes his films are situated between different genres, for example between a crime story grounded in the real world and a supernatural horror film. The viewer can construct both ontological options without ever being sure if supernatural phenomena like the Mystery Man in *Lost Highway*, the Cowboy in *Mulholland Drive* or the inhabitants of the Black Lodge in *Fire Walk with Me* are real entities moving around the storyworld or if they are just projections of the suffering protagonists imagined on the verge of a nervous breakdown.

Film scholar Thomas Elsaesser (2021: 222) precisely characterises the logic of Lynch's mind-game films:

> The magic of Lynch's mind-games would then be how the director always finds new ways to shake up, play off against each other and asymmetrically distribute causes and consequences, actions and intentions, memories and anticipations: he makes it look as if no one is in charge and all the possibilities are open, while directing our gaze and attention to detail and instant, and thus keeping control over mood and moment – even as the world, the people and places are allowed to arrange themselves in ever different configurations.

Taking into consideration positions in film theory, the different configurations in *Twin Peaks* allow for traditional semiotic readings and their search for meaning, but they also enable 'breaks in flow and resistance to ordered conditions' (Viegas and Williams 2017: 24), defining for Jean-François Lyotard's concept of acinema. The French postmodernist 'distinguishes the "tableau vivant" (extreme immobility) and "abstraction" (extreme mobility) as the two opposite ways to analyze acinema' (Viegas and Williams 2017: 25). Lyotard himself often discussed acinema in relation to avant-garde films and Italian neorealism. In a comprehensive volume on his idea of the acinema, edited by Graham Jones and Ashley Woodward, a very instructive application to Lynch's work is provided in an article by the two editors. They consider the resistance in the images against explanation to be an important alternative in discussing Lynch's films:

> The predominant approach to Lynch's work in cinema studies is to attempt to explain the 'meaning' his films have, and what is more, to provide them with a unity and coherence that they purportedly 'lack', through extensive textual commentary and interpretative correlations. Perversely, this is to miss what is most distinctive and powerful about these films [. . .] their force lies in their inherent resistance to signification and narrative recuperation, which is precisely what Lynch seems to do so well. (Jones and Woodward 2017: 202)

Nevertheless, I would argue that the cinematic configurations of *Twin Peaks* allow for both perspectives depending on the context.

Watching *Fire Walk with Me* on a cinema screen, the interlude in the FBI headquarter provides a paradigmatic example for Lyotard's acinema. After Agent Chester Desmond has disappeared at Deer Meadow, Agent Dale Cooper visits Gordon Cole and Albert Rosenfield (Miguel Ferrer) in the office at the FBI headquarters in Philadelphia. The protagonist of the series reports that he is worried about a dream he had the night before. Before the details can be further discussed, Cooper's attention is drawn to a surveillance monitor. While moving between the camera and the monitor, suddenly the elevator door opens, the screen shows the entrance of FBI agent Philip Jeffries (David Bowie). Back in the office, Cole informs Cooper and Rosenfield that Jeffries had been missing for years. With theatrical gestures Jeffries gives mysterious fragmentary information about a meeting above a convenience store and declares that he is not willing to talk about Judy, without the film or the series having provided any reference who or what Judy could be. The already cryptic images are superimposed with a meeting of the forces from the Black Lodge, the Man from Another Place (Michael J. Anderson), Killer Bob (Frank Silva), Mrs Chalfont (Frances Bay), a jumping masked man in a red suit and a woodsman (Jürgen Prochnow) gathered around a table. Fragments of a conversation can be heard on the soundtrack, the Man from Another Place demands all his 'garmonbozia' (according to the subtitles standing in for pain and sorrow), praises the Formica table in front of him, and a small boy accompanying Mrs Chalfont desires a victim. Like a mantra the sentence, 'we live inside a dream,' can be heard again and again. The Man from Another Place and Bob exit through the red curtains familiar from the Red Room in the series, probably in search for pain and sorrow. Back in the offices of the FBI in Philadelphia, Jeffries suddenly disappears. Cole calls the front desk to learn that the missing agent has never been there in the first place.

The above sequence brings the narrative to a halt. The investigations concerning the murder of Teresa Banks hit a dead-end and the introduction of supernatural elements via the Black Lodge brings about a change in the register of genre and mood. Similar to previously discussed scenes of the film, the above segment creates a tableau vivant in presenting the Black Lodge residents superimposed over the gathering of the FBI agents. Lyotard's second term for analysing acinema, the process of abstraction created by extreme mobility can also be spotted in David Bowie's movements that literally go nowhere. The mise-en-scène of the cryptic scene establishes a rhythm and its countermovement that appears again in *Twin Peaks: The Return*. The much-discussed episode 8 with its camera movements through the mushroom cloud of an exploding atomic bomb provides another instant of acinema.

Besides the different film-philosophical implications, the sequence in the FBI headquarters also seduces the audience to participate in configuring its meaning via different indicated options. From the perspective of the series the scene hints at a background mythology around the blue rose cases. In comparison to the anthology character of *The X-Files* that leads to the discovery of the monster of the week or an evil alien conspiracy, the blue rose cases lead into the associative abstract. In contrast to traditional horror settings like Dracula's castle, a haunted mansion or even the circles of hell inhabited by the cenobites, the room above the convenience store takes on a dreamlike quality and it could be right next door to the bizarre nocturnal group gathered in Bergman's *Vargtimmen*. From a postmodernist perspective the scene provides some meta-levels, like the director himself becoming an actor participating in the investigations of the plot and the peculiar casting of several FBI agents with rock musicians from the larger ensemble around David Lynch's productions.

The interlude in the FBI offices operates as a multi-layered hub to be configured by the audience. It can be studied as a clip and as a fascinating piece of media art playing with associations from pop-cultural iconography (David Bowie, the convenience store, the FBI agents), Jungian psychology (the different incarnations of emotions represented by the Black Lodge residents) or the horror and fantasy genre (the mysterious ring, the wanderings between the worlds). Within the storyworld of *Twin Peaks*, the setting is moved beyond the small town in the Pacific Northwest, an explorative process continued in season 3 by adding North Dakota, Las Vegas and New York to the mix of locations.

Looking back from the third season, the sequence can also be contextualised within the overall narrative background-story that Mark Frost provides in his two books *The Secret History of Twin Peaks* and *Twin Peaks: The Final Dossier*. In contrast to *The Secret Diary of Laura Palmer* and *The Autobiography of FBI Special Agent Dale Cooper* published during the first two seasons, the new novels are much closer to a source book for a role-playing system explaining background mythology than to a traditional spin-off story.[2] The mythology created and compiled by Mark Frost for the two books adds information about Judy that could not have been guessed at in 1992. Frost connected the original onomatopoeia by Bowie and Lynch to ancient demons: 'I went through a list of Sumerian or Babylonian deities or demons and came across the name Joudy, and suggested we say it was distorted by Bowie's Southern accent and what he really was trying to say was "Joudy"' (Bushman 2020: 248).

When the narrative framing provided by Mark Frost is discussed by David Lynch as Gordon Cole and his team, consisting of returning agent Albert Rosenfield and new protagonist Tammy Preston in season 3, it sounds like the rehearsal of a theatre group or a live-action-role-playing guild preparing for their next campaign. The auteur has become an actor in his own artistic network. During *Twin Peaks: The Return*, Gordon Cole turns into a stand-in for the original Agent Cooper whose 'doppelgangers' have either gone over to the dark side or are suffering from amnesia. He brings the team back together when new clues about the disappearance of Agent Cooper twenty-five years ago turn up and he returns to Twin Peaks in the final episodes to support his old friend when he confronts his evil doppelganger. When Cooper's evil incarnation is killed by an Englishman with special powers, this plays out like a parody of the successful super-hero movies based on comic books by Marvel and DC.

Even the supernatural elements take on a rather abstract and material-ist quality with David Lynch leading the investigations as FBI Deputy Agent Gordon Cole. In several scenes the new episodes get haunted by *Fire Walk with Me* almost breaking the fourth wall by laying open the construction of the storyworld and its cinematic building blocks. In film-philosophy there may be ongoing discussions about the best theoretical lenses to discuss the cinema of David Lynch. The auteur-actor-director nevertheless pursues philosophical questions of his own. Almost as if lay-ers of the palimpsest that is called *Twin Peaks* broke off to expose the older scenes, in *Twin Peaks: The Return* one evening Gordon Cole is surprised by a knock on his hotel room door. He opens it and is confronted by an image of the young Laura Palmer breaking into tears on the doorstep of Donna's house. The scene, like all passages to the cinematic past in season 3 shown in black-and-white, is taken from *Fire Walk with Me* and edited together with the reaction shot of Gordon Cole. As the episode's title, 'Laura is the One', indicates, the story is not finished yet. In a certain way the haunting of *Twin Peaks: The Return* by its own cinematic past could be discussed in relation to the concept of Mark Fisher's hauntology (Fisher 2014) since the dead-ends of the ruinous prequel can be interpreted as a failed future for the series (also see Marcus Stiglegger's analysis of the Los Angeles trilogy in this volume).

The philosophical investigations instigated by David Lynch and his avatar Gordon Cole operate on a more direct level. The scenes from *Fire Walk with Me* are presented as configurable materials of film and not as traditional flashbacks. Comparable to bands working with samples of their own music or Jean-Luc Godard conjuring up the shadows of his own past in the French Nouvelle Vague in the *Histoire(s) du Cinéma* (1998),

Cole is visited by memories from *Fire Walk with Me* that could as well be personal recollections of the actor-director David Lynch. The philosophical question raised in *Twin Peaks: The Return* originates from a dream sequence: In contrast to the high postmodernism of the series, Cole does not encounter a backwards talking dancing little man and Laura Palmer in the Red Room. Rather, he finds himself in a Parisian café together with Monica Bellucci guest starring as herself. During the relaxed talk with Bellucci, Cole, who in this dream could also be the real director David Lynch, suddenly remembers the enigmatic sequence in the FBI headquarters from *Fire Walk with Me*. The following events not only pick up the plot and the dangling causes left from the prequel twenty-five years ago; Cole or Lynch elaborates further on the key phrase, 'we live inside a dream', from this scene by asking, 'but who is the dreamer?' After Cole reports the events to his task force, Albert Rosenfield mentions that now he can also remember the event. The philosophical question relating to the ontological constitution of fiction in a film is not only projected on the events. But it is also articulated by the form and the cinematic configuration itself, instead of being merely illustrated. In this regard, David Lynch as an acting auteur corresponds with Stephen Mulhall's (2008: 132) idea of film-philosophy in practice that considers the potential of sequels:

> A sequel by a gifted director is likely to exhibit just the reflective questioning of its basic resources that one would expect of the philosophy of film; and although those resources will certainly include matters of thematic content whose relevance to philosophical discussions is fairly self-evident [. . .] it will also include more formal questions – questions concerning the ways in which the content is conveyed cinematically, and so ones relevant to investigations in the philosophy of film.

After Bob is defeated and Evil Cooper safely sent back to the Black Lodge in the final episodes of *Twin Peaks: The Return*, Dale Cooper travels back in time via the mysterious convenience store. In a sequence created with the help of a state-of-the-art digital toolbox (see Jannik Müller's chapter in this volume) he goes back to the terrible night of Laura Palmer's murder. Before Laura can walk off to her doom she is headed off by Cooper. She recognises him to be the person from her dreams in the Red Room and follows him through the woods. Even though she gets lost on the way, her fate has significantly changed. The next morning is shown in the following scene, but in contrast to the iconic body wrapped in plastic there is nothing to be found at the lake when Pete Martell goes fishing. Like the configurative practices of a video game the whole storyline has changed.

Twin Peaks: The Return subverts the expectations no series could fulfil after more than twenty-five years in an innovative way. The film-philosophical questions about whose dream cinema is anyway goes beyond the big screen. It connects narratives and intensities across media, from the diary of Laura Palmer to *Fire Walk with Me*, from the poignant soundtrack compositions by Angelo Badalamenti to the illustrious appearances by performers like The Chromatics, Nine Inch Nails, Julee Cruise, and Rebekkah Del Rio at the end of each episode of *Twin Peaks: The Return*. Like Michel Chion (1995: 159) already noted three decades ago in regard to the presumed death of cinema: 'Through Lynch and a few others cinema is advancing and renewing itself [. . .] That the cinema is no longer what it used to be is in fact proof of the contrary, that it is alive.' Instead of sending film into the early retirement of post-cinema, the auteur-actor and the transmedia network collectively explored and configured in and around the series continue to think cinema as an idea, a cultural practice, and a transmedia hub for creative configurations across media.

Notes

1. I must admit that I never had to reevaluate *Fire Walk with Me* since I was completely overwhelmed by it watching it as a preview in August of 1992 at the 'Fantasy Filmfest' in Frankfurt a few days before its official release in German cinemas. The reports about the disastrous screening in Cannes had been alarming, but the film's experience had been even more surprising and striking than watching *Wild at Heart*, *Lost Highway*, *Mulholland Drive* and *Inland Empire* upon their initial releases. Only *Straight Story* had a similar irritating, but completely different effect since the title proved to be pro-grammatic without any surrealist escapades.
2. Their inclusion of documents, maps, and notes is also reminiscent of interactive books like *S./The Ship of Theseus* (2013) by Doug Dorst and J. J. Abrams.

Bibliography

Bushman, David. *Conversations with Mark Frost*. Twin Peaks, Hill Street Blues, *and the Education of a Writer*. Fayetteville Mafia Press, 2020.

Chion, Michel. *David Lynch*. British Film Institute, 1995.

Eco, Umberto. *The Open Work*. Harvard University Press, 1989.

Elsaesser, Thomas. 'Actions Have Consequences: Logics of the Mind-Game Film in David Lynch's Los Angeles Trilogy'. *The Mind-Game Film: Distributed Agency, Time Travel, and Productive Pathology*. Routledge, 2021, pp. 208–23.

Fischer, Robert. '*Twin Peaks* – Ein Film mit sieben Siegeln' *epd Film*, no. 8, 1992, pp. 26–30.

Fisher, Mark. *Ghosts of My Life. Writings on Depression, Hauntology, and Lost Futures.* Zero Books, 2014.

Hallam, Lindsey. *Twin Peaks: Fire Walk with Me.* Devil's Advocates. Auteur, 2018.

Harvey, Colin. 'Transmedia Genres. Form, Content, and the Centrality of Memory'. *The Routledge Companion to Transmedia Studies*, Matthew Freeman and Renira Rampazzo Gambarato (eds). Routledge, 2019, pp. 157–64.

Hirsch, Foster. *Detours and Lost Highways. A Map of Neo-Noir.* Limelight Editions, 1999.

Hoberman, Jay and Jonathan Rosenbaum. *Midnight Movies.* Da Capo Press, 1983.

Jenkins, Henry. *Convergence Culture. Where Old and New Media Collide.* New York University Press 2006.

Jenkins, Henry. 'Why *Twin Peaks?*'. *Mysterium Twin Peaks. Zeichen – Welten – Referenzen*, Caroline Frank and Markus Schleich (eds). Springer, 2020, pp. 28–36.

Jerslev, Anne. *Blurred Boundaries.* Palgrave Macmillan 2021.

Jones, Graham and Ashley Woodward. 'How Desire Works: A Lyotardian Lynch'. *Acinemas. Lyotard's Philosophy of Film*, Graham Jones and Ashley Woodward (eds). Edinburgh University Press, 2017, pp. 201–21.

Keeling, Kara. *The Witch's Flight: The Cinematic the Black Femme, and the Image of Common Sense.* Duke University Press, 2007.

Kilb, Andreas. 'David Lynch's *Twin Peaks* – Schlußverkauf.' *Die Zeit*, 28 August 1992.

Mactaggart, Allister. *The Film Paintings of David Lynch: Challenging Film Theory.* Intellect, 2010.

Mittell, Jason. *Complex TV. The Poetics of Contemporary Television Storytelling.* New York University Press, 2015.

Mulhall, Stephen. *On Film.* 2nd edition. Routledge, 2008.

Norelli, Clare Nina. *Soundtracks from* Twin Peaks. Bloomsbury, 2017.

Restivo, Angelo. Breaking Bad *and Cinematic Television.* Duke University Press, 2019.

Rodley, Chris. *Lynch on Lynch.* Revised edition. Farrar, Straus and Giroux, 2005.

Rosenbaum, Jonathan. 'Art and Politics of *Twin Peaks*'. *Full of Secrets. Critical Approaches to Twin Peaks*, David Lavery (ed.). Wayne State University Press, 1995, pp. 22–9.

Röttger, Kati and Alexander Jackob. 'Bilder einer unendlichen Fahrt. David Lynchs *Mulholland Drive* in bildwissenschaftlicher Perspektive'. *Bildtheorie und Film*, Thomas Koebner, Thomas Meder and Fabienne Liptay (eds). Edition Text und Kritik, 2006, pp. 572–84.

Schifferle, Hans. 'Und die Engel würden Dir nicht helfen. *Twin Peaks: Fire Walk with Me*'. *Süddeutsche Zeitung*, 24 August 1992.

Situationist International'.Definitions'. *Nothingness.org*, 1958, http://library.nothingness.org/articles/SI/en/display/7 (last accessed 22 November 2021).

Thompson, Robert J. *From* Hill Street Blues *to* ER. *Television's Second Golden Age.* Syracuse University Press, 1997.

Viegas, Susanna and James Williams. 'Why Lyotard and Film?' *Acinemas. Lyotard's Philosophy of Film*, Graham Jones and Ashley Woodward (eds). Edinburgh University Press, 2017, pp. 22–30.

Filmography

Blue Velvet. Directed by David Lynch, performances by Kyle MacLachlan, Isabella Rosselini, Dennis Hopper, and Laura Dern, Dino De Laurentiis Entertainment Group, 1986.

Dirty Dancing. Directed by Emile Ardolino, performances by Jennifer Grey and Patrick Swayze, Vestron Pictures, 1987.

Dune. Directed by David Lynch, performances by Kyle MacLachlan and Sean Young, Dino De Laurentiis Company, Estudios Churucusco Azteca, 1984.

Eraserhead. Directed by David Lynch, performances by Jack Nance and Charlotte Stewart, American Film Institute, Libra Films, 1977.

Halloween. Directed by John Carpenter, performances by Jamie Lee Curtis and Donald Pleasence, Falcon International Pictures, Compass International Pictures, 1978.

Hellraiser. Directed by Clive Barker, performances by Andrew Robinson, Clare Higgins, Ashley Laurence, and Doug Bradley, New World Pictures, 1987.

Histoire(s) du Cinéma. Directed by Jean-Luc Godard, Canal +, 1989–99.

Inland Empire. Directed by David Lynch, performances by Laura Dern and Grace Zabriskie, Studio Canal et al., 2006.

Laura. Directed by Otto Preminger, performances by Gene Tierney, Dana Andrews, and Vincent Price, 20th Century Fox, 1944.

Lost Highway. Directed by David Lynch, performances by Bill Pullman and Patricia Arquette, CiBi 2000, Asymmetrical Productions and Lost Highway Productions LCC, 1997.

Mulholland Drive. Directed by David Lynch, performances by Naomi Watts and Laura Harring, Les Films Alain Sarde et al., 2001.

The Naked Gun. Directed by David Zucker, performances by Leslie Nielsen, Priscilla Presley, Ricardo Montalban, and George Kennedy, Universal, 1988.

Star Wars Episode VI – Return of the Jedi. Directed by Richard Marquand, performances by Mark Hamill, Carrie Fisher, Harrison Ford, and Billy Dee Williams, Lucasfilm Productions, 1983.

Star Wars Episode VII – The Force Awakens. Directed by J. J. Abrams, performances by Daisy Ridley, Harrison Ford, Carrie Fisher, John Boyega, and Adam Driver, Lucasfilm/Disney, 2015.

Star Wars Episode VIII – The Last Jedi. Directed by Rian Johnson, performances by Daisy Ridley, Mark Hamill, Carrie Fisher, John Boyega, and Adam Driver, Lucasfilm/Disney, 2017.

Star Wars Episode IX – The Rise of Skywalker. Directed by J. J. Abrams, performances by Daisy Ridley, Oscaar Isaac, John Boyega, Adam Driver, and Billy Dee Williams, Lucasfilm/Disney, 2019.

The Straight Story. Directed by David Lynch, performances by Richard Farnsworth, Harry Dean Stanton, and Sissy Spacek, Asymmetrical Picture, Canal +, Channel Four Films, 1999.

Sunset Boulevard. Directed by Billy Wilder, performances by Gloria Swanson, William Holden, and Erich von Stroheim, Paramount Pictures, 1950.

Twin Peaks. Directed by David Lynch et al., performances by Kyle MacLachlan and Mädchen Amick, Lynch/Frost Productions et al., 1990–1.

Twin Peaks: Fire Walk with Me. Directed by David Lynch, performances by Sheryl Lee and Ray Wise, CIBY Picture, 1992.

Twin Peaks: The Return [on DVD and BluRay *Twin Peaks: A Limited Event Series*]. Directed by David Lynch, performances by Sheryl Lee and Kyle MacLachlan, Showtime, 2017.

Vargtimmen/The Hour of the Wolf. Directed by Ingmar Bergman, performances by Max von Sydow and Liv Ullmann, Cinematograph AB, Svensk Filmindustri, 1968.

Vertigo. Directed by Alfred Hitchcock, performances by James Stewart, Kim Novak, and Barbara Bel Geddes, Universal, 1958.

Wild at Heart. Directed by David Lynch, performances by Laura Dern and Nicolas Cage, PolyGram Filmed Entertainment and Propaganda Films, 1990.

The Wizard of Oz. Directed by Victor Fleming, performances by Judy Garland and Frank Morgan, MGM, 1939.

Part III

David Lynch's Transmedia Aesthetics

CHAPTER 9

Tracing the *Lost Highway*: Mythical Topography in David Lynch's Los Angeles Trilogy

Marcus Stiglegger

For a millennium, the space for the hotel room existed, undefined. Mankind captured it, and gave it shape and passed through. And sometimes when passing through, they found themselves brushing up against the secret names of truth.

David Lynch, *Hotel Room* (1993)

Haunted Spaces

In his Jacques Derrida-inspired late writings *The Weird and the Eerie* (2016) Mark Fisher lists David Lynch's *Mulholland Drive* and *Inland Empire* as examples for the pop-theoretical approach of the author, linking these films with the concept of 'Hauntology' (Fisher 2016: 53–9). In doing so Fisher follows his idea that postmodern popular culture, especially pop music and cinema, are haunted by ghostly sounds, images and moods from the past or another timeframe. While referring back to Jacques Derrida's concept of hauntology (in *Specters of Marx*, 1994), this term originally combines the concepts of haunting and ontology (the doctrine of beings) in a neologism. According to Derrida hauntology signifies the presence (or the 'obvious non-present') of ideas, theories and ideologies from the past, which, even if they fail in practice, are still present in the thought structures of the present and thus shape our reception and thinking. While Derrida referred primarily to the theories of Karl Marx, which failed largely due to the end of the Cold War after 1989 and were considered to be no longer relevant, hauntology also includes the theory of 'haunted places', according to which certain events can be 'imprinted' on a place in a way that they are repeated over and over again. Such places are haunted by the past. Mark Fisher (2014) used the term to describe a musical aesthetic preoccupied with this temporal disjunction and the nostalgia for 'lost futures'. In another article, Fisher writes on hauntology: 'When the present has given up on the future, we must listen for the relics of the future in the unactivated potentials of the past.' (2013: 53)

It is remarkable that David Lynch chose the iconic city of Los Angeles as the location for his most intense 'haunted' thrillers. *Mulholland Drive* and *Inland Empire* as well as *Lost Highway* unfold the cityscape of the South-Western metropolis as a topography of mythical Hollywoodland – as a part of this area was called during the early studio years – and the life stream of this area is Mulholland Drive, winding its way through the Hollywood hills. The iconic presence of the Hollywood-sign is noted especially in *Lost Highway* where it looms in the background. The road of the *Lost Highway*/Fred Madison-house – which is owned by the director himself – is just off Mulholland Drive. Additionally, the car accident sequence from the beginning of the film *Mulholland Drive* clearly shows the road sign 'Mulholland Dr' as a stand in for the film's title – but shown in an unreal way, so it indicates more than just a location. David Lynch's topography of Los Angeles is all about the city and its own myth. The city appears as a hauntological mediated space.

As in his other films, Lynch establishes in *Lost Highway* and *Mulholland Drive* an easily identifiable location, characterised by two distinguishable faces: the day side and the night side – respectively the profane and the haunted and sometimes sacred spheres of LA. The two faces are similar, yet they seem different, as if the dimensions of space and time shift just a little bit during the transition of the twilight. Past, present and future sometimes fall together in Lynch's films. The night face becomes the city's own dark double with all kinds of uncanny elements and incidents. Here it has to be remembered how important doubles are to Lynch's imagination: *Lost Highway* has not only two male protagonists that resemble each other, but also all kinds of doppelgangers, especially Patricia Arquette's two characters of Renee and Alice (one brunette, the other blonde); *Mulholland Drive* tells two versions of the same story with all characters bearing different names in the end; and *Inland Empire* clearly plays on multiplied realities, which are partly identified as a cinematic imagination merged with different levels of time and consciousness. The permanent shifting of timelines evokes the melancholia of a place existing in face of its own lost potential – or as Fisher says: 'relics of the future in the unactivated potentials of the past' (2013: 53).

In this chapter, I would like to define David Lynch's use of the city of Los Angeles as the creation of a multifaceted 'hauntological' and mythical space – a world where realities overlap, where the sacred and the profane meet in performative realms, a mythical topography. In the first section I will define different categories and concepts of space in narrative cinema. The next section will specify the design and use of a mythical space within film mise-en-scène. Finally, I will show how this concept of the mythical space in film becomes one of the most significant elements in David Lynch's LA-trilogy.

Concepts of Space in Narrative Cinema

Although film and space are directly dependent – because without pre-filmic space there would be hardly any visible space in film – analytical reflections on this phenomenon are contradictory and often guided by specific interests (see Stiglegger 2006 and 2014). In his dissertation *L'Organisation de l'espace dans le FAUST de Murnau*, Eric Rohmer, filmmaker and critic of the *Cahiers du Cinéma*, differentiates between three types of space in cinema: the material architectural space as pre-filmic reality, the image space as two-dimensional spatial construction, and finally the film-space as a narrative or imaginative space that goes far beyond what is visible in the image or what is present in pre-filmic reality (Rohmer 1977: 10). The cinematically mediated space does not have its limits in the image frame but arises and unfolds in the imagination of the recipient. This phenomenon of an almost limitless space of imagination, which is only ever present as a significant section in the picture, benefits from another genuine characteristic of narrative feature films: its function as a modern carrier of myths. Beyond its realistic, metaphorical and symbolic function, the film space can become a mythical space, a hybrid space in which the profane linearity of time and space is annihilated. The mythical space itself becomes a statement in these films, and it is often the key to understanding a work – as we will see with David Lynch's films.

Eric Rohmer's idea of architectural space can only be seen in the context of film through the filmic image itself. It should be noted that the architectural space as a 'pre-filmic space' is in itself considerably larger than the section that the audience can see. The remaining space outside of the picture frame has to be imagined. According to Rohmer, this not only offers the possibilities of cinematic representation, but also the aesthetics of cinematic image composition, which is conveyed within the frame (Rohmer 1977: 10). The cinematic spatial aesthetics are also dependent on the spatial illusion, which is conveyed as the apparent depth of the visible space and transcends the fundamental two-dimensionality of the projected cinematic image on the screen. The use of different focal lengths can further promote this impression of depth. A long focal length isolates the central object from a rather blurred background, while a short focal length depicts the object from a sharp environment as part of it. The spatial dimensions of foreground, middle and background can be differentiated in this way. We will see that David Lynch makes use of extreme distance as well as the intended loss of distance to the point of distortion of the images representing specific spaces.

The image space can basically be expanded through movement within the image frame or the dynamics of the image recording technology. In this way, the movement of the figure in the architectural space (its proxemic coordinates) can be followed – by swivelling or travelling – and thus renders the space as a representation of the space of action. In addition, the figure can move out of the picture frame, which suggests the continuation of the image space. As the camera moves, the perspective changes, which brings about a change in the spatial relationship for the viewer, the change in the depth arrangement in the image ('mise-en-cadre'). This in turn has an impact on the 'mise-en-scène', because in the progression within the architectural space not only do the proportions change, but also it hints at new spaces outside the cinematic frame.

According to Rohmer, the third level is the film space, which can also be called narrative space or *diegesia*. The film space is also the imaginary space that the recipient can immerse themselves in given the fragments represented within the cinematic frame. Here, not only the camera's positions and movements come into play, but also the montage, in which different spatial fragments are combined from different shots and put in relation with each other.

Most film scholars assess a film's space on a phenomenological level, for example Ryad Khouloki in his volume *Der filmische Raum*, which helps to describe the represented space in its appearance. Most of these considerations are located on the level of the architectural space and the image space. According to Rohmer, film space can only be described on a semantic level, whose functions and meanings challenge mere phenomenological assumptions. In Khouloki's book, the deictic 'stage space' comes closest to such a 'film space' as it transcends the simulation of a supposedly real space of action – it emphasises the artificiality and staging of this space (Khouloki 2009: 118).

In comparison, the four spatial concepts of the geographer Ute Wardenga (2002: 47) may help to find access to a mythical dimension in film space, well aware that geographical spaces are not the same as mediated spaces. Firstly, spaces are understood in a realistic sense as containers in which certain phenomena of the material world are contained. These spaces are created in the process-like interaction between nature and people. Secondly, spaces are viewed as systems of positional relationships of material objects. This leads to questions about how these relationships contribute to the creation of a social reality. Thirdly, spaces are defined as a category of sensory perception and 'forms of perception'. Fourthly, this means that spaces must also be understood from the perspective of their social, technical and societal construction. Spaces are therefore determined by daily actions. The result is a completely constructed imaginary space, which is comparable to the constructed and meaningful mediated film space of Rohmer's and is thus an imaginary space (Wardenga 2002: 47).

In the medium of film, these spaces are not always linked to a naturalistic dogma – they can evoke very different world designs depending on the intention of those who create and represent this space. Especially because cinematic space is constructed as a symbolic form – referring to all the described material concepts of space as well as its symbolic meaning. A cinematic evocation of space may at the same time refer to an existing place as well as a completely symbolic topography of the mind. This is the perspective I would suggest for an analysis of David Lynch's film, depicting LA as an existing location and a mythical imaginary space at the same time, always shifting between those two concepts of space. This idea also underlies Richard Martin's exploration on *The Architecture of David Lynch*, where he already in the title alludes to the idea that the material architecture shown in Lynch's films is a mirror of the psychological architecture of his imagination. Here is also to be found the link between an imaginary space and an imaginary world, namely in myth and the representation of mythical worlds as the following section will show.

Mythic Space in Film

Narrative film has always been a carrier of myths because it can always be experienced in a relative present: by ritually viewing the film anew (think for example of the phenomenon of the cult film which applies to all films of the LA-trilogy), it becomes a genuine, contemporary experience for the audience. At the same time, the myth conveyed through film, like oral mythology, revolves around elementary and existential motifs: birth, life, death, sexuality, violence, fear, joy, hatred, happiness, etc. It turns out to be rather counterproductive to understand the mythical content of film as 'regression', as Hartmut Heuermann undertakes in his book *Medienkultur und Mythen*, or even to regard myth in general as opposed to enlightened thinking.

In any case – and especially in David Lynch's œuvre – film, popular culture, and myths are closely intertwined. The mythical quality of the medium of film is reflected in the cinematic space – in the cinematic architecture (Martin) – as David Lynch's films show. Because the medium of film only occurs at the moment of reception (as a play of light and shadow on the screen, an illusion of movement in time), it has similarities with

oral literature, which was also the primary medium of mythical mediation. Like the repeatedly retold oral literature, the narrative feature film
often revolves around elementary mythical themes. Whether it deals with
these topics affirmatively (that is, it cultivates a mythical way of meaning)
or strives for an open, ambivalent or ambiguous approach must be evaluated on a case-by-case basis. In the affirmative approach, there is at least
a suspicion of regression, as Heuermann notes (1995: 21). The following
examples demonstrate the cinematic possibilities of an open or even meta-
reflective approach to mythical topics and structures.

Mythical spaces in film can have a wide variety of functions and can be
constituted by a wide variety of stylistic devices. In the following section,
I would like to illustrate this different phenomenology – but also their
commonalities using specific examples. This will build a basis for my
argument that David Lynch uses the topography of Los Angeles in his
trilogy only as a vague reference to a diegetic 'reality' (a space of action),
that at the same time 'hauntologically' evokes the history of Hollywood
as well as its potential future. His films actively create a mythical topography of Los Angeles in different realities and evocations.

Case Studies of Mythical Spaces in Narrative Cinema

I would like to begin with an excursion into world cinema to show the
basic concept of how mythic spaces work within mise-en-scène. The
Japanese director Akira Kurosawa freely adapted Shakespeare's drama
Macbeth in 1957 in his jidai-geki (historical film) *Kumonosu-jō/ Throne
of Blood*. In contrast to his famous film *Shichinin no Samurai/ The Seven
Samurai* (Japan 1954), Kurosawa was not interested in a possible authentic
reconstruction of the past, but instead oriented himself along the strictly
stylised and abstract form of the Noh theatre in the architectural context
of the interiors. Kurosawa undoubtedly saw himself in the tradition of a
Japanese visual aesthetic and adopted several strategies for his own productions. In *The Seven Samurai* in particular, he had used telephoto lenses,
which, with their long focal length, made it possible to focus on details and
separated the actors from their surroundings, but also sacrificed the depth
of the images. The resulting two-dimensional, depthless image impression, which David Bordwell calls a *planimetric image* (Bordwell 2005:
60–63), corresponds in turn to the depthless image composition of the
Japanese visual arts. In addition, the veil of rain, present in many of his
films, obscures the view and further prevents any sense of depth. The fog
in *Throne of Blood* has a similar function. In his essay 'Models of spatial
staging in contemporary European cinema', David Bordwell refers to a

deliberately 'flat', 'deep' image staging in European auteur cinema, especially in connection with Jean-Luc Godard and Michelangelo Antonioni. He uses the concept of the planimetric image, coined by Heinrich Wölfflin, and applies it to film in this regard. This term describes the reduction of actual spatial depth through image-parallel planes, whereby the images lack any perspective and the impression of depth is greatly minimised. In addition, by using large focal lengths, the focus range can be reduced so that the depth of the room is reduced to an area and the actions appear to be playing in front of a tape. The figures are also reduced to their flatness due to the small focus area and the lack of spatial depth (Bordwell 2005: 20). David Lynch very early on in his work uses the simulation of deep spaces (even if they are completely constructed as in *Eraserhead*, 1977), but also introduces Kurosawa's technique of obscuring the image by fog to eliminate the idea of a physical space – juxtaposing the reality simulation of the mise-en-scène. In the early dream sequence of *The Elephant Man* (1980) this mysterious fog appears in similar way as it does later in Bill Pullman's home in *Lost Highway*. This technique underlines the stage-like appearance of his interiors, also obvious in Club Silencio in *Mulholland Drive*.

Sacrificial places and ritual places are magical places at the same time, where the natural laws seem to be overridden. All over the world there are places that are transfigured as places of spiritual power and that are sought out and appreciated in ritual passages. In Germany, the Externsteine are such a place, and Kenneth Anger staged them accordingly in his experimental film *Lucifer Rising* (USA/UK/FR 1972). In Australia, the Hanging Rock formation is one of them. Countless urban legends have developed around this towering place in the middle of the forest, and the most famous is based on the novel *Picnic at Hanging Rock* (1967) by Joan Lindsay, which was adapted for the screen in 1975 by Peter Weir. *Picnic at Hanging Rock* (AUS 1975) is about the mysterious disappearance of a group of schoolgirls on Valentine's Day in 1900. In the corresponding sequence, the film goes to great lengths to mystify the rock massif with references to paranormal phenomena. Thus, the time stops at noon, as you can see in a close-up on the watch of the teacher responsible for the group. The suspension of linear time establishes the presence of the mythical. Both *Throne of Blood* and *Picnic at Hanging Rock* are classic films from world cinema that create mythical film spaces using different stylistic approaches. Both films are embedded within a rich cultural tradition and refer to well-established concepts of the sacred and mythical. Recurring cinematographic elements include the use of specific camera angles and lenses to create an otherworldly impression, thus marking the spaces as 'different' from everyday experience. Here is a strong connection to the cinema of David Lynch's Los Angeles. Lynch establishes the hidden 'reverse' of the City of Angels in significant spaces like Club Silencio, an abandoned ranch, a lonely beach house, certain villas, as well as the film studio. The film maker in *Mulholland Drive* is urged to drive to a ranch outside town that is deserted at night and only lit by a flickering light above the door. From the *Twin Peaks* universe we know that, according to Lynch, demons travel through electric power lines and are the reasons for distortion noises and flickering. Whenever a person enters the twilight realm, where profane and supernatural space overlap, electric disturbances appear: when the protagonist (Kyle MacLachlan) in *Blue Velvet* is about to infiltrate the apartment of the woman in distress (Isabella Rossellini) – the light flickers. Even the strobe light show during Bill Pullman's saxophone solo in *Lost Highway* can be seen as a signum of the twilight area. The deserted ranch in *Mulholland Drive* is thus signified as the pathway to the other world and transforms the profane realm of a paddock into a mythical twilight realm, where the film maker meets a strange cowboy – himself a mythical figure of American frontier history who connects the past and the present.

David Lynch's Los Angeles is its own mythos while appearing as a realm of everyday activities. The idea of the city as its own double was mentioned above, and it has to be kept in mind that this is also the key to understanding Lynch's locations as haunted locations – and more: haunted by their 'own potential future', as the concept of hauntology implies.

Categories of Mythical Spaces in Cinema

From the previous considerations I come to the following central conclusions regarding mythical spaces in film (see Stiglegger 2015, "Mythische Räume im Film"):

1. The mythical space on screen is a semantically occupied space of imagination. It does not have to obey the laws of the realistically constructed architectural space but consists of intentional breaks in this illusionism (the fog out of nowhere, the flickering of the lights). Also, the sounds in this surrounding can be irritating as they might not be diegetic. In Lynch's films these sounds hint towards the layering of two or more different dimensions.
2. In mythical space, the boundaries between space and time are abolished. The dimensions can overlap. In Australian dreaming, for example, the ancestral sphere becomes accessible to the living within the ritual; here

the boundaries of space and time are completely removed, so that this dimension no longer exists in the profane sense. This will also be the case in mythical spaces in narrative cinema. In Lynch's films we see this overlapping coexistence of dimensions all the time – even the time has its double.

3. Although the mythical space has to be thought of as infinite in principle, it sometimes shows signs of dissolution due to fog in the distance – or in zones of ominous darkness (both elements appear in Fred Madison's house in *Lost Highway*) which are reflected by equally ominous sounds (like the typical dark drones in Lynch's films).

4. In mythological research it is established that the mythical space is not homogeneous, since places within mythical narrations differ in that they have not only a relative but also an absolute position (above, below, etc.). In narrative cinema, the abolition of spatial relationships to one another seems to be more essential. It is more likely that the situation is always meandering between potential worlds, from a space of physical action to a space of haunting, a merging of past, present, and future (*Inland Empire*).

5. Mythologically, a sacred space is distinguished from a profane space in the sense that Mircea Eliade elaborates in his *The Sacred and the Profane* (1961). The sacred is embedded in the secular space – for example in the form of a sacred building (Club Silencio in *Mulholland Drive*). Not all places of the sacred space can be embedded in the profane, they form singularities (so Olympus is both a profane mountain and a sacred seat of gods). In many of Lynch's works those sacred places are hidden from the profane world and materialise only under certain conditions like the Red Room in *Twin Peaks*. In most cases these sacred spaces are connected to a portal to the 'other world' like Club Silencio or the hotel room in the end of *Inland Empire*.

6. The mythical space is only accessible to the elect and only under certain conditions: In ritual, on the quest (for example, the search of the two women in *Mulholland Drive*), in stages of transition (for example, when dying – symbolically in Club Silencio, when Naomi Watts' character begins to shiver and lose control). Extraordinary incidents correspond to the sacred dimension of the specific space.

7. The mythical space on screen is ultimately a virtual 'non-space' (Augé), a radically stylised transition or passage space and thus a specific form of the cinematic imaginary space that eludes everyday (profane) laws. The construction of this non-space benefits from the fact that film images appear both flat and spatial, and yet remain an illusional projection of light on the screen.

In the sense of Marc Augé, who differentiates between anthropological spaces and temporary 'non-space' (non-lieux), the latter includes those
spaces that 'have no identity and cannot be described as relational or historical' (Augé 1994: 92). However, Augé also admits that the transition from
anthropological to 'non-places' is fluid and that one can become the other.

> Space and non-space are fleeing poles; the place never disappears completely, and
> the non-place never arises – they are palimpsests on which the confused play of
> identity and relation is constantly being reflected anew. (Augé 1994: 94)

A mythical space based on the film examples described above may be a
transit space (or 'space of passage'), a space that is passed through and
left again (such as the deserted ranch in *Mulholland Drive*) that eludes
clear topographical relations, but in some cases, it is culturally, anthropo-
logically and historically coded (like the Hollywood hills in *Lost Highway*,
or Hollywood Boulevard towards the end of *Inland Empire*). They are
charged by memories like the use of *Sunset Boulevard* in *Twin Peaks: The
Return* or the look into the mirror reflecting Laura Elena Harring as well
as the *Gilda* -poster in *Mulholland Drive*. Here is a connection to Fisher's
concept of hauntology at the same time conjuring up the past but denying
the nostalgia of retromania.

Mythical spaces can be described as hybrids in Augé's sense, which are
in permanent transformation or only take on temporary form. Mythical
spaces, however, are never arbitrary, but always symbolically charged and
have a specific function as imaginary spaces, even if this is only revealed
afterwards or can never be clarified with certainty (as in *Mulholland Drive*).

David Lynch's Los Angeles as a Mythical Urban Space

Finally, we should take a look at David Lynch's LA-trilogy. First, there is
an image of LA that is well known from uncountable other Hollywood productions. The light in LA is known to be unique, with an orange tinge to
it. Lynch covers this light in the oft-criticised postcard view of LA in *Lost
Highway*, framed by impressions from the car garage when the protagonist
waits for the return of the femme fatale. In this light, Lynch shows stereotypes of the American way of life: diners, car repair, film studios, suburban
villas, suburban bungalows, endless highways surrounded by the urbanity,
palm trees and the sunset itself. Lynch thus reproduces and invokes a pop
cultural image of LA, also seen in music videos and genre cinema and television. His protagonists are literally living in a world of Americana.

Secondly, Lynch creates the idea of LA as a mythical cityscape closely
connected to 'Hollywoodland' – as it was known in the earlier days of

cinema, during the much admired and influential studio era. It is the city of cinema legends from this Golden Era, and especially from the film noir as seen in *Mulholland Drive* with its various connections to Billy Wilder's *Sunset Boulevard* and Charles Vidor's *Gilda* with Rita Hayworth. There are many nods to Hollywood's past: the Grauman's Chinese Theatre, the Hollywood Walk of Fame in *Inland Empire*, and the ever-present Southern Gothic architecture of the old LA buildings.

Finally, in some places the dimensions seem to collide to channel haunted spaces. Lynch creates membranes through which the ghosts of the past enter the profane world: first on the drone soundtrack, and finally within the frame itself. One of such uncanny places is the backyard of the Winkie's Diner (in *Mulholland Drive* located on Sunset Boulevard), where a nervous man encounters the person with the burned face from his own nightmare, which he describes the moment before, in the parking lot. Subtly, Lynch's mise-en-scène creates a shift between dimensions: what had been a fantasy before slowly becomes reality, with the narrator and the listener taking the roles of the fantasy's actors. The soundscape changes via reverbs and echoes to muffled voices and culminates in a jump scare in image and sound when the black-faced creature appears. The well-known Americana world of the diner has become a mythical place of fear and nightmare, continually shifting out of our idea of reality. This scene – which seems somehow unconnected to the rest of the film due to its singular side characters – may well be the key to understanding how Lynch's cinematic universe works.

It seems no coincidence that the demonic lumberjacks from *Twin Peaks: The Return* (2017) also have blackened faces as they represent similar messengers from the other side: the universal dark side in Lynch's universe. It is also a carefully chosen theatre where the protagonists from *Mulholland Drive* find the key to understanding in which world they live ('Silencio'). Much like the protagonists, Lynch's LA is haunted by its own past, by the ghosts of Hollywoodland secretly taking over in certain places and moments. The 'City of Angels' seamlessly becomes the city of ghosts and demons, creating a topography of dreams and nightmares.

In connection to Francesco Casetti's concept of 'mediascapes' (2017: 71–90), David Lynch can be said to work hard to create a very specific mythical topography of Los Angeles as a stand in of his vision of the American dreamland. In our minds his films draw lines of a city between the life streams of Hollywood Boulevard (*Inland Empire*), Sunset Boulevard and Mulholland Drive (*Lost Highway, Mulholland Drive*), suggesting a somehow hermetic world similar to the real city, but more of a dark and haunted double with its own rules and characteristics – a hauntological parallel world 'behind the media mirror' of Los Angeles. As Casetti points out (2017: 75), mediascapes are established via a symbiotic interaction of several media, and it is highly important to notice how the locations from David Lynch's LA trilogy have developed a life of their own: on the internet, on websites collecting film locations to be visited by curious cinephiles, in books and videos. International tourists are not only familiar with classical Hollywoodland, but also with Lynch's dark variations of sunny California. In websites and guidebooks we find hints to the shooting locations of his films, we can explore the backyard of Winkie's as well as the car garage, or even drive by the *Lost Highway* house off Mulholland Drive. Reality and cinematic experience from past and present continually mingle in the perception of the film audience. This cross media-scaping of Lynch's Los Angeles creates a network of influences that I have defined earlier as a mythical topography in cinema: spaces that cannot be separated from the narrative that is so closely connected to them. You cannot un-see the cinematic double realities when driving along the streets of LA, and especially when passing a Mulholland Drive street sign. Los Angeles has become a Lynchian mediascape in our consciousness: The cinematic representation seems authentic in the end, while the real location seems somehow 'fake'.

Bibliography

Augé, Marc. *Orte und Nicht-Orte. Vorüberlegungen zu einer Ethnologie der Einsamkeit*. Translated by Michael Bischoff. Fischer, 1994.

Bordwell, David. *Figures Traced in Light. On Cinematic Staging*. Harvard University Press, 2005.

Casetti, Francesco. 'Mediascapes'. *Kinoerfahrungen*, Thomas Weber and Florian Mundhenke (eds). Avinus, 2017, pp. 71–90.

Derrida, Jacques. *Specters of Marx: The State of the Debt, the Work of Mourning and the New International*. Translated by Peggy Kamuf. Routledge, 1994.

Eliade, Mircea. *The Sacred and the Profane: The Nature of Religion*. Translated by Willard R. Trask. Harper Torchbooks, 1961.

Fisher, Mark. 'The Metaphysics of Crackle: Afrofuturism and Hauntology'. *Dancecult* vol. 5, no. 2, 2013, pp. 42–55.

Fisher, Mark. *Ghosts of My Life: Writings on Depression, Hauntology and Lost Futures*. Zero Books, 2014.

Fisher, Mark. *The Weird and the Eerie*. Repeater Books, 2017.

Heuermann, Hartmut. *Medienkultur und Mythen*. Rowohlt, 1994.

Khouloki, Rayd. *Der filmische Raum. Konstruktion, Wahrnehmung, Bedeutung*. Bertz + Fischer, 2009.

Martin, Richard: *The Architecture of David Lynch*. Bloomsbury, 2014.

Praz, Mario. *The Romantic Agony*. 2nd edition, translated by Angus Davidson. Oxford University Press, 1951.

Rohmer, Eric. *L'Organisation de l'espace dans le FAUST de Murnau*. Uniongénéral d'éditions, 1977.

Stiglegger, Marcus. *Ritual & Verführung. Schaulust, Spektakel und Sinnlichkeit im Film*. Bertz + Fischer, 2006.

Stiglegger, Marcus. *Verdichtungen. Zur Ikonologie und Mythologie populärer Kultur*. Hagen-Berchum, 2014.

Stiglegger, Marcus. 'Mythische Räume im Film'. *Orte. Nicht-Orte Ab-Orte. Mediale Verortungen des Dazwischen*, Silke Martin and Anke Steinborn (eds). Schüren, 2015, pp. 87–100.

Wardenga, Ute. 'Räume der Geographie: Zu Raumbegriffen im Geographieunterricht'. *Wirtschafts- und Sozialgeographie Wirtschaftsinformationen. Wissenschaftliche Nachrichten* no. 120, 2002, pp. 47–52.

Filmography

Gilda. Directed by Charles Vidor, performances by Rita Hayworth and Glenn Ford, Columbia Pictures, 1946.

Inland Empire. Directed by David Lynch, performances by Laura Dern and Grace Zabriskie, Studio Canal et al., 2006.

Kumonosu-jō/Throne of Blood. Directed by Akira Kurosawa, performances by Toshiro Mifune and Isuzu Yamada, Toho Company and Kurosawa Production Co., 1957.

Lost Highway. Directed by David Lynch, performances by Bill Pullman and Patricia Arquette, CiBi 2000, Asymmetrical Productions and Lost Highway Productions LCC, 1997.

Lucifer Rising. Directed by Kenneth Anger, Puck Film Production, British Film Finance, NDR, 1972.

Mulholland Drive. Directed by David Lynch, performances by Naomi Watts and Laura Harring, Les Films Alain Sarde et al., 2001.

Picnic at Hanging Rock. Directed by Peter Weir, performances by Anne-Louise Lambert and Rachel Roberts, The South Australian Film Corporation et al., 1975.

Shichinin no Samurai/The Seven Samurai. Directed by Akira Kurosawa, performances by Toshiro Mifune and Takashi Shimura, Toho Company, 1954.

Sunset Boulevard. Directed by Billy Wilder, performances by William Holden, Gloria Swanson and Erich von Stroheim, Paramount Pictures, 1950.

Twin Peaks. Directed by David Lynch et al., performances by Kyle MacLachlan and Mädchen Amick, Lynch/Frost Productions et al., 1990–1.

Twin Peaks: The Return [on DVD and BluRay *Twin Peaks: A Limited Event Series*]. Directed by David Lynch, performances by Sheryl Lee and Kyle MacLachlan, Showtime, 2017.

CHAPTER 10

Structures of Female Desire, Control and Withdrawal in Lynch's Cinematic Work

Lioba Schlösser

Female characters have a central role and function in Lynch's œuvre. Their sexual desire often carries an entire plot. In contrast to this, male characters often appear to be incidental elements that women use to express their physicality. In many of Lynch's films, women express their longing physically. They exhibit homosexual desire (*Mulholland Drive, Twin Peaks*), fetishes (*Blue Velvet*) or seductive behaviour towards men to get something they want. Moreover, Lynch's female characters are often defined by alienation, splitting of the ego, psychosis, fear or dissociative traits (*Blue Velvet, Mulholland Drive, Lost Highway*). Yet Lynch's characterisation of women draws directly from the film noir trope of the femme fatale. The pairing of mental illness as a weakness and the strength of a classical femme fatale might seem conflicting at first. Mental issues or weakness might be rather associated with the character of the femme fragile. Lynch, however, turns this concept on its head: he associates his female characters with strength and weakness at the same time. The weakness often derives from mental problems and therefore almost substantiates the strength that comes with it because these women endure so much suffering. Nevertheless, this combination leads to very specific character developments and therefore very powerful cinematic moments on screen, which this chapter is dedicated to exploring.

By analysing sequences and stylistic devices in the films *Blue Velvet, Lost Highway, Twin Peaks* and *Mulholland Drive*, I discuss how Lynch, in combining strength and weakness as well as control and withdrawal as central features of his female characters, represents their desire and sexuality in his films. I show how these contrasts become essential to characterisation and plot development. Moreover, I discuss how female sexuality functions as a projection of the spectator's own desire, wishes and needs. Female desire in this context often symbolises failure of normative structures, such as the nuclear family, patriarchal structures like monogamous marriage or masculinity as supremacy in family and career, and other normative values and standards. Making use of gender theory and psychoanalytic approaches, this chapter argues that Lynch creates a universe in which well-known narrative structures fall apart and where the ideals of patriarchal society face constant re-evaluation.

The Use of Lynch's Noir Aesthetics

First, I will take a brief look at noir aesthetics and motifs to evaluate the basic structure of Lynch's female characters in relation to their surroundings and male characters. Moreover, the relation between noir and gender perspectives needs to be explored. The settings of Lynch's films are largely informed by aesthetics of loneliness and darkness. Whether these are used to capture American cities, suburban and, with *Twin Peaks*, rural places, the colour palette and use of light evoke something scary, cold, unpredictable and mysterious in the atmosphere that adds to a sense of being lost. Similar aesthetics became well-established in the 1940s and 1950s with film noir. In the aftermath of World War II, the aesthetic conventions of the genre mirrored the fear and loneliness of post-war society. He does something similar in addressing the insecurities, fears and wishes of his audiences.

Lynch's characters become mirroring images for these fears. Their behaviour and appearance are stereotypically gendered according to noir conventions. Men often lose control, and are fearful and insecure, while women are portrayed as seductive, unpredictable, sneaky and self-assured. (Helmich 2010: 5) Thus, film noir aesthetics can offer interesting insights concerning feminist theory and gender perspectives:

> Feminist work on *film noir* and gender, such as that by Christine Gledhill and Janey Place, typify this focus. Gledhill argues that *noir* presents 'certain highly formalised inflections of plot, character and visual style', which 'offer[s] a world of action defined in male terms; the locations, situations, iconography, violence are conventions connoting the male sphere. (Hanson 2007: 3)

Film scholar Helen Hanson states moreover that women in film noir are divided into two categories: the femme fatales who act according to normative male behaviour in their manipulativeness and fearlessness, and women who seem to remain victims of male power, relegated to stereotypical roles where their only importance lies in their relation to men. What connects both is that they exist in a patriarchal society. Women in such a context are often defined by their appearance. The ideal is one of exaggerated femininity defined by the norms of the post-war era. The studio system of classical Hollywood provided expressionist influences within these character concepts and settings, especially in terms of the use of light and the staging of urban space. The naturalness of setting and characters receded in favour of idealised and stereotypical conceptions (Nochimson 2012: 33). This explains the non-naturalistic images of a normatively beautiful tough, criminal and extremely seductive woman in this film historical period.

All these aspects can also be found in Lynch's cinema. His films revolve around American metropolises, the explicit sexualisation of female characters, split personalities or characters who are doppelgangers. All of this is framed by an uncanny darkness or latent fear, stemming from both the setting and the characters, who often walk on the brink of death. Lynch uses noir aesthetics in his work but modifies their conventional use. The motif of the double or doppelganger is linked to German Expressionism and is a main characteristic of film noir. Lynch uses this aesthetic to create opposites or contrasts that are necessarily linked to each other but cannot occupy the same space at the same time. Their existence hangs by a thread and thus marks death as a central element. Although in film noir representations of death avoid the language of the gothic tradition – as in the divided self of a character – its film aesthetics constitute the characters and their interactions towards and away from each other as well. Here, the double mostly symbolises the dark, evil or hidden side of the protagonist, their negative character traits or fatal behaviours. Jean Baudrillard (1993: 113) connects this concept with Lacan's mirror stage as moment of self-awareness. The look in the mirror identifies the double, a version of the self, 'which haunts the subject as his "other", causing him to be himself while at the same time never seeming like himself' (ibid.) and often foreshadows death. He writes:

> Of all the prostheses that punctuate the history of the body, the double is doubtless the most ancient. The double, however, is not properly speaking a prosthesis at all. Rather, it is an imaginary figure, like the soul, the shadow or the mirror-image, which haunts the subject as his 'other', causing him to be himself while at the same time never seeming like himself. The double haunts the subject like a subtle death, but a death forever being conjured away. Things are not always like this, however – for when the double materializes, when it becomes visible, it signifies imminent death. (Baudrillard 1993: 131)

This death according to Baudrillard must occur because the double 'remains a phantasy' (ibid.). At the same time the onlooking subject is searching for continuity and procreation, which necessarily also leads to death. To prevent death, the fantasy of doubling comes to life. Lynch uses this exact motif to create many of his characters: Pete and Fred, Alice and Renee in *Lost Highway*, Rita and Camilla, Betty and Diane in *Mulholland*

Drive and Dale Cooper's doubles in 2017's *Twin Peaks: The Return* are just some examples. These doppelgangers almost always personify the dark and evil side of characters. Mr C, Cooper's doppelganger, who is obsessed with Bob, an evil spirit, murders many people throughout the third season. He is the classic antagonist and contrasts the real Cooper. Mr C haunts – through Bob – Cooper as a subject and signifies imminent danger as well as death for many characters of the series. A slightly different connection to death can be seen in Diane/Betty in *Lost Highway*. As Betty and Rita break into Diane's house, they find her dead in her bed. The camera perspective switches back and forth between Rita and Betty and the body of Diane, which lies putrescent on the bed. Only after Rita disappears can the body come back to life and Diane wake up – when the Cowboy tells her to. Strikingly, the whole atmosphere in the room changes. When she was dead it seemed dark, dirty and rotten, but after Diane's resurrection it is bright and cosy. The mise-en-scène mirrors the contrast between life and death, the known and unknown.

In contrast to *Twin Peaks,* the doppelgangers in *Lost Highway* and *Mulholland Drive* cannot exist at the same time as their original counterparts because they embody opposites, and one needs the death of the other to be alive. This resembles an idea that also can be found in the theoretical work of Baudrillard, who states that the double 'signifies imminent death.' (1993: 113) *Lost Highway* resembles this notion: Alice can be seen as Frank's fantasy of his dead wife Renee, while he dreams himself up as Pete. Alice is leading a double life, working as a porn actress for Mr Eddy while playing the victim for Pete. She seduces him to come to Andy's house to make the two men meet. Eventually, Andy dies in an accident and she puts the blame on Pete. As Pete strolls around in the house, confused and scared, he finds a framed picture of Alice with another woman, who looks like Renee while the audience is made aware that only Alice is in it. This moment is also emphasised by the camera work: The framed picture becomes clear in a close-up, followed by a reverse shot, which shows Pete's face in a close-up, too. The picture gets blurry, stressing Pete's confusion and transporting it onto the spectator, while drone sounds dominate the diegetic soundtrack. Alice, shown blurry in the background behind him, is wearing nothing but black lingerie, connecting the whole situation back to her body and sexuality. Stepping toward Pete, she comes closer to the camera, and explains that she can be seen on the right in the picture. The woman on the left who resembles Fred's wife is left mysteriously unidentified. This seems to suggest that the appearance of Alice requires Renee's physical death. Fred's existence, however, does not hinge on his death. He does not have to die in order to imagine himself as Pete. Instead, he goes to jail where he obviously suffers from serious mental health problems. This can also be seen as the death of his former self that gets lost in hallucinations and daydreams. In such instances, Lynch uses the concept of the fatal double following its tradition in film noir but adds something to it: that is the association of the opposition between life and death, imagination and reality, fear and comfort, past and present, mental health and illness.

Such a playful use of the tropes of film noir leads John Richardson to regard *Twin Peaks* as postmodern parody of the genre. As the most significant intertextual point of reference to noir, he names Otto Preminger's film *Laura* from 1944 (Richardson 2004: 78). *Twin Peaks* resembles film noir in several ways: the narrative, aspects of its visual style, the use of voice over and flashbacks and the representation of the femme fatale. In this context Richardson mentions the character of Laura Palmer. She is presented from several viewpoints, by other characters or in different moments in time (Richardson 2004: 79). He sees Laura Palmer as a parodic femme fatal and her absence as a parodic interpretation of the classic noir motif. Palmer shows some characteristics of a femme fatale. She is sexually active, manipulative, independent, intelligent and unpredictable. Yet she does not fit the classic noir image. She is an underage high-school girl, lost in life and drug addicted. Most importantly, she is absent due to her death and only becomes physically visible in the Black Lodge. Richardson states that the series is a puzzle that can be recognised as one, because the pieces do not fit. He calls Laura a paradoxical *femme fatale*, a family girl, who was abused as a child but nevertheless, or precisely because of this, acts in a highly sexual manner. This leads to her death and therefore makes her sexuality, unlike the original femme fatale's, a weakness. Laura is not at all strong or unrepressed by male power. Richardson concludes here 'a parodic, anti-narrative *about* such narratives' (Richardson 2004: 89, emphasis in original) A thesis that Lindsay Hallam elaborates on in her reading of Laura's death (2018: 75).

When Sexual Pleasure Becomes a Fetish

Another important aspect in Lynch's cinema is fetishism. Sexuality is linked to fetish, a theme that is apparent in *Blue Velvet*. The female protagonist of the film is Dorothy Vallens (Isabella Rossellini), a singer in a nightclub. She is married and mother to a son, who is kidnapped by the sadistic drug addict Frank. Meanwhile, Jeffrey and Sandy try to solve the crime after Jeffrey finds a severed human ear in the street. They sneak around Dorothy's house and Jeffrey eventually breaks into her apartment. There he finds himself hiding in her closet and witnesses her having brutal and ritualised sex with Frank, who suppresses and blackmails her. While trying to save her, Jeffrey starts a love affair with Dorothy. She leads him into an unknown world of desire and fetishism that ends up in violence and death. In her representation, Dorothy subverts established film noir notions of the femme fatale. This comes to light, for example, in a scene when Dorothy is on the phone with her son and the camera captures her removing her wig. In doing so, the camera hovers above her reducing Dorothy to a bald spot on the dirty red carpet. The contrast between her made-up face and her wigless head is strikingly grotesque. Such a mise-en-scène evokes an atmosphere of loss and solitude, which is not only mirrored in Jeffrey's pity for her. Dorothy's apartment is similarly dreary: sparsely furnished and with only one window, it seems more like a cellar than a home. The soundtrack comments accordingly: drone sounds constantly distort the non-diegetic music. The colours and use of light in the scene are reminiscent of the dark and grotesque nature of a Francis Bacon painting (Stiglegger and Wagner 2020: 185). In Lynch's films, Stiglegger and Wagner identify geometrical patters, cross-fades, long blurry shots and fuzziness reminiscent of Bacon's art (Stiglegger and Wagner 2020: 186). In a Baconian manner, spaces and individuals are shaped by loneliness and emptiness. Their representations are further informed by fear, lust, and 'hysteria'. Transformation also is a reoccurring leitmotif in both Bacon and Lynch's work (Stiglegger and Wagner 2020: 196). Lynch's characters transform into others. As a result, time, place and meaning become fluid. The resultant fragmentation of the story and its non-linear plot put the film's narrative discourse into the foreground. Consequently, the offered visual spectacle invites affective responses.

In this space, Dorothy's character may be read as a symbol for sexual pleasure as she becomes a key to new experiences for both Jeffrey and the audience. She is at once positioned as victim and manipulator in her relationship with Jeffrey, who is made to have sex with her, dominate, and hit her against his will. In making sense of Dorothy's complicated affair with Jeffrey, Sam Ishii-Gonzales notes a connection between psychoanalytic categories and Lynch's characterisation of Dorothy:

> Dorothy's triadic plea 'Hold Me – Hurt Me – Help Me' confers upon her a series of positionings which confuse and excite Jeffrey exactly because he does not know whether she is a helpless victim (castrated) or whether she is the aggressor (the castrator) whom he needs to revoke, whom he needs to flee in order to save himself. (Ishii-Gonzales 2004: 56)

Thus, Lynch creates in Dorothy an ambivalent character, who is torn between the role of seducer on the one hand, and helpless victim on the other. In his relationship to Dorothy, Jeffrey is similarly brought into an uncertain position. He lives a second life apart from the idyllic normalcy of his small-town existence in uncovering a mysterious criminal operation. Jeffrey's transformation is connected to Dorothy's physical appearance and especially her sexuality. His way of fetishising, protecting and desiring her initiates a change in his character. Being torn between two worlds in such a manner is a common motif of film noir. Due to the cultural context of classic film noir, character constellations such as the one in *Blue Velvet* were a well-established narrative device: during World War II, men were drafted for war and women stayed at home, thus occupying both the domestic sphere at the same time they took up professions previously held by men. As a result, women for the first time were emancipated professionally and became more open to notions of gender equality. During the so-called Second Wave feminism of the 1960s, the experiences during World War II translated into a struggle for women's liberation both from the domestic sphere and in their professional lives. The women's movement of the 1960s was a reaction to Eisenhower's domestic containment policy and the enforced notion of separate spheres. In the post-war years, returning soldiers were not able to fully reconnect with their families and to start living normal lives. While women's social position did change during the war years, men found themselves war-torn. Jeffrey's conflicting lives seem to follow suit with the conflicting emotions, morals and personal issues men had to endure after their experiences in the field.

As stated above, Helen Hanson distinguishes between manipulative femme fatales and female victims of male power. The two female protagonists in *Blue Velvet* are mirror images of these two types: on the one hand, there is Dorothy with her seductive and destructive sexuality. On the other hand, there is Sandy, the innocent girl. This duality stresses the self-destructive tendencies in Dorothy and eventually makes Sandy an uncorrupted sweetheart for Jeffrey. At the film's conclusion, patriarchal structures remain unchallenged. This is hinted at in the film's final montage: a robin first appears to Jeffrey in the garden and then lands on the windowsill of his home at the end of the film. It eats a bug and is believed to bring love to the freshly made couple. In the new household, Jeffrey remains the only man among the four women present in the house during the final sequence – his and Sandy's father are spatially separated in the garden. At the same time, the film reunites Dorothy with her son and puts an end to her role as seductress. Instead, the narrative restores her maternal character. The heterosexist patriarchal is re-established and the world can go back to normal, as it seems. In such a setting, the role of fetish seems to be obvious. It mirrors normative male phantasies of dominance and power and offers audiences – who become voyeurs – a possibility to project their own needs and dreams onto the fetishised object, while the actual object of desire is never really shown. Armand states that spectators as voyeurs appear to be more submissive to the cinematic image and its mise-en-scène than to the characters on screen. In their submission they themselves become exposed, naked and vulnerable.

> Like Isabella Rossellini/Dorothy Vallens's [sic] body in *Blue Velvet* – and the 'blue velvet' that acts as its metonym – we are never close to the nakedness it seems to present to us more than the moment our own seeing enters into the obsessive violent iteration of the *object coupled* to its negation: Dorothy's unnaturally red mouth juxtaposed, in Jeffery Beaumont's disturbed memory, with the distorted mask of Frank Booth's psychosis. Here we see the work the particular violence by which a radical *decoupage* evokes an equally visceral and intellectual sado-masochism; its alternation-effect *constituting* the spectator (the voyeur) as *subjection to* we might say – *the desire of the image*. (Armand 2010: 156, emphasis in the original)

In following Armand, the way the film constitutes its images in return makes them – and therefore the film itself – the actual fetish. Audiences are invited to watch select scenes or the whole film repeatedly, without attaining them. For the audience, Dorothy and her seductive behaviour become a surface on which to project their own issues and desires. If taken to the extreme, this is a potentially neverending activity the more often these images are revisited. In referring to Jean Baudrillard, Armand (2010: 156) writes:

> The medium itself is the fetish [. . .], 'an object which is not an object'. But this 'object which is not an object' continues, Baudrillard says, to obsess 'by its empty, immaterial presence', while threatening at the same time to materialize its very nothingness.

Film scholar Laura Mulvey in her later work finds a similar conclusion to Armand, while exploring the role new media technologies play in shaping our experiences of film. In *Death 24× a Second* (2006), Mulvey assesses the object relation between the visual appearance of the star and the film as one fetish:

> The star's visual apotheosis is no more material than the light and shadow that enhance it so that the human figure as fetish fuses with the cinema as fetish, the fusion of fetishism and aesthetics that characterizes *photogénie*. Here the symbolic quality of film aesthetics, even 'the more manageable temporality of contemplation', leads towards its eternal, unavoidable, shadow, the psychodynamics of visual pleasure. The extraordinary significance of the human figure in cinema, the star, its iconic sexuality, raises the question of how desire and pleasure are reconfigured in delayed cinema, as stillness both within the moving image and within a changed power relation of spectatorship. (Mulvey 2006: 164, emphasis in original)

The iconic representation of Dorothy Vallens, singing at the nightclub, renders her as a star in the plot of the film, and as a female sex symbol in the eyes of Jeffrey. As Mulvey (ibid.) explains, the fetishisation of the female star and her body in the eyes of another character fuses with the fetishisation of the film in the eyes of the audience. The fusion of cinema and fetish as well as the fusion of fetishism and aesthetics in this moment is pure *photogénie* and cinematic pleasure. In following Mulvey (ibid.), the resultant dimension of fetish can be understood as a stillness within the moving images and as ennui within Lynch's films since it is always present. This ionisation of the (female) main character seems to be one of the main characteristics and key features in Lynch's œuvre. It can be found in every single one of his films and seems to be one of the reasons why his films fascinate and confuse at the same time. Often, the projection surface offers sexual actions and, in the context of Mulvey's (2006) evaluations, fetishised motifs that remain without explicit explanation. The audience is invited to project their needs, wishes and ideals onto these sexualised surfaces on screen and at the same time to momentarily bracket out their nothingness only to make this element even more effective at the end.

The Power of the Male Gaze and Female Withdrawal

While discussing female sexuality and representations in Lynch's films, it is worthwhile to consider male characters, their traits and the male gaze of the camera. *Lost Highway*'s Pete and Fred can be seen as two embodiments of the same character, who desire Renee, the woman that Pete/Fred killed, because they could not fulfil their desire and could not satisfy her. Next to the common interpretation that Fred has a split personality and/or is a person with a dissociative identity disorder[1] it is to be noted that the projection of desire is mostly embodied through Fred's/Pete's imagination of Alice that even becomes a projection on screen. This is emphasised especially at the end of the film, when Pete and Alice have sex: 'You still want me, don't you, Pete? More than ever?' she asks, while seducing and drawing him towards her body. They start kissing and touching. Eventually he says: 'I want you' and she, who is on top of him, answers: 'You'll never have me!', and then leaves. The scene is rendered by an overexposure of key light on the naked bodies of the two actors. It is presented in slow motion, captured by American shots and close-ups to illustrate the details of the couple's intercourse. On the non-diegetic soundtrack, This Mortal Coil's 'The Song to the Siren' adds to the surreal atmosphere of this sexual encounter in the desert. Alice, who has a Monroe-like appearance, is the star of the scene and clearly dominates plot and frame at the same time. All movements seem extremely slow, soft and desiring, so the audience is invited to see her in full glam, as it becomes clear that she plays a cruel game. Nevertheless, it is interesting that the camera gaze all the while remains a male one. Mulvey describes gender representations in classic Hollywood cinema with the phrase 'women as image, men as bearer of the look' (Mulvey 2006: 837). Drawing from psychoanalysis, she defines men as the active bearer of the look and women as the passive object of the male gaze. The scopophilic audience identifies with the male look and objectifies female characters as well. Lynch also uses male gaze elements in the way he pictures women on screen, but in a slightly different way than in classic Hollywood cinema. He also sets the female body at the centre of attention. Lighting, editing and mise-en-scène support such a strategy, as seen in the above scene. The spatio-temporal dimension of the scene is completely occupied by a focus on Alice's body and Pete's pleasure, captured by close-up shots on his face during the intercourse. The high-pitched and angelic voice of This Mortal Coil's singer on the non-diegetic soundtrack together with the light, the slow sounds of the music and the images make Alice an object to be looked at by Pete and the audience. The camera fragments Alice's body into parts via close-ups rather than presenting her body as a whole, which is a clear sign of the male gaze. Even though Lynch's camera work seems to follow Mulvey's (1999 [1975]) descriptions of visual pleasure and narrative cinema by the book, he also strays from classic Hollywood cinema's male gaze, especially with regard to the elimination of the presence of the camera. Mulvey (1999 [1975]: 843) explains classic Hollywood's strategy here as follows:

> There are three different looks associated with cinema: That of the camera as it records the pro-filmic event, that of the audience as it watches the final product, and that of the characters at each other within the screen illusion. The conventions of narrative film deny the first two and subordinate them to the third, the conscious aim being always to eliminate intrusive camera presence and prevent a distancing awareness in the audience.

The elimination of the camera and an audience's awareness about their looking is not present in Lynch's cinema. If anything, he makes it clear that the audience can watch from an external perspective but can still be drawn directly into the scene, so perspective boundaries become fluid. His stories barely follow a linear plot so even these orientation marks are dissolved. Sometimes it seems as if the relationship between audience and characters on-screen is one of a discrepant awareness, thus their knowledge of both their own and the camera's position. After the sex scene between Alice and Pete, the burning house rebuilds by way of a rewind drawing an audience's awareness to the object status of the film itself. Also, the sudden change of locations and characters in *Lost Highway* add to this impression. Even if moments like these may irritate audiences, they also indicate the actual material existence of the film. 'In Hitchcock, by contrast, the male hero does see precisely what the audience sees,' Mulvey (1999 [1975]: 841) writes. In Lynch, this obviously is not the case. Neither the male nor the female characters have such an unrestricted view as the audience does. Uncanny characters such as *Lost Highway's* Mystery Man, *Mulholland Drive's* The Cowboy or the characters from the Black Lodge in *Twin Peaks* are an exception. None of these, however, seem to have answers to the questions audiences may have about what they see. Such strategies not only create a whole universe, called 'Lynchville' (Seeßlen 1994: 16) or 'Lynchtown' (Chion 1995: 83), but also a narrative perspective, that does not need linear structures but therefore doubles realities, dimensions, times and universes, thus dissolving both spatial and temporal linearity at the same time. Even though Lynch's cinema may invite audiences to occupy the position of voyeurs, while watching characters have sex on screen and murder each other, the audience remains locked out from the diegesis.

Film scholar Allister Mactaggart (2010: 117) sees a similar link in the narrative form and content of Lynch's cinema. He stresses the reminiscent use of cinematic styles such as long fades to black as segmentation to help this process:

> Lynch's film presents a short, oblique narrative which offers us a timely insight into the relationship of his work to early, 'primitive' cinema. The narrative, strangely realized in its form and content, echoes other Lynch films. In particular, the use of long 'fades' to black as segmentation is reminiscent of how this device is used, albeit by editing, in *Blue Velvet*, *Lost Highway* and *Mulholland Drive*.

Another difference between Lynch's films and classic Hollywood is the way the director stages men and their relationships with women. Lynch shows different types of men, sometimes even in the same storyline. In *Lost Highway*, the plot follows crucial moments in the relationships of two couples: That of Fred Madison (Bill Pullman) and his wife Renee (Patricia Arquette) as well as the one between Pete (Balthazar Getty) and his affair with Alice (Patricia Arquette). Fred and Renee's relationship seems dead. Even though she is presented as sexualised and normatively attractive with her short fringe and mostly red lips and he seems to desire her, their relationship evades any erotic union. They have nothing to say to each other, their life together seems more like an obligation, and Renee seizes every opportunity to find distraction in parties, and alcohol. Finally,

Fred kills Renee and the plot shifts to the affair between Pete and Alice. Alice embodies the perfect femme fatale: bleached blonde hair, hourglass shape, full lips and a promiscuous attitude, which captures Pete's attention right away. They begin a love affair in which Alice appears to take the part of the manipulator. Similar to the affairs in *Mulholland Drive* and *Blue Velvet*, the character constellation turns preconceived social expectations on their head. The women of both relationships are rather attractive in a heteronormative sense and appear as seductive to others. Even though the types of relationships differ, it is always women who play the more active and controlling part in the relationship. Men only follow their women and get rather frustrated over time. Even though this seems to follow the traditional gender roles Helen Hanson identified for women in film noir, Lynch's cinema creates a space for women's autonomy in their relationships to men.[2]

The Capabilities of Homosexual Desire

In *Mullholland Drive*, Lynch presents two types of women meeting and desiring each other: ingénue Betty/Diane (Naomi Watts) and femme fatale Rita/Camilla (Laura Harring). At Coco's house naive and light-hearted Betty meets Rita, who after an accident suffers from amnesia. While Rita's identity remains unknown until the end of the film, her persona adds mystery to her appearance, which resembles the way femme fatales are introduced in classic Hollywood cinema. Rita begins an affair with Betty, who does everything within her power to support and help her new friend. The film is divided into two parts. Rita's and Betty's narrative strand comes to an end when the plot introduces a mysterious blue box to which the two characters find a key. In the second half of the film, Diane resembles Betty and Camilla/Rita without her blonde wig. Camilla/Rita's male love interest Adam appears in both parts of the film and seems to be the male provider, who offers success, money and fame and therefore exercises control over Camilla/Rita. Due to his presence, Camilla in the second half of the movie seems to distance herself from her girlfriend Diane.

In both parts of the film, female homosexuality stands in contrast to heteronormative expectations about romantic love. In psychoanalytic terms, female sexuality is not made explicit, because it is missing a phallic symbol to mediate a sense of sexual arousal. As a result, female desire appears both inconceivable and mysterious. From a heteronormative perspective, Helmich (2010: 23) argues, women are thought to perform orgasms, lust and desire much more easily than men do, because female orgasms are not visual. She describes the vagina as a 'dark tunnel' and sexual experiences with a vulva as a 'way into the unknown' (Helmich 2010: 23). Therefore, female homosexuality, as seen in *Mulholland Drive*, can – in both a psychoanalytic and heteronormative sense – be read as ultimately inconceivable because no phallus or visible orgasm is involved. In return, this allows female homosexual intercourse to appear as very powerful. Still, a complete erotic union in a psychoanalytic sense remains impossible because it lacks the phallic signifier. This could also be the reason why Camilla ends her affair with Diane in and seeks a sexual union with Adam instead. He does not lack the phallic signifier and therefore can fulfil her need for an actual sexual reunion.

Nevertheless, female sexuality in Lynch's films not only symbolises power and the evasion of male dominance, but also the ability to play with and withdraw from male desire. Rita and Camilla are iconic images of femme fatales, who incorporate Mulvey's notion of a stillness within the moving image as the film's sex symbols. Despite its homoerotic content the camera films the female relationship by way of heteronormative visual standards. Body parts such as breasts, lips, eyes, the vagina and hips are captured as fragmented objects in focus. This stresses the female body as object of male desire and reduces the sense of female desire's autonomy in female homosexuality.

Taking into consideration the lack of a phallic signifier in the representation of homoerotic desire in Lynch's cinema, Judith Butler's concept of the lesbian phallus may help in illustrating how homoerotic pleasure becomes graspable in Lynch's cinema nevertheless. Butler describes the ontological difference between the phallus as an abstract symbol and the penis as a body part. In taking reference to Jacques Lacan, Butler illustrates that the phallus not only stands for an object the man believes he has, but also how the phallus symbolises body parts other than the penis, how by displacement it can signify the woman:

> And here it should be clear that the lesbian phallus crosses the orders of *having* and *being*, it both wields the threat of castration (which is in that sense a mode of 'being' the phallus, as women 'are') and suffers from castration anxiety (and so is said 'to have' the phallus, and to fear its loss). (Butler 1993: 84, emphasis in the original)

Due to an endless sliding of the signifiers beneath signifiers and thus the infinite displacement of the object referent for the phallus, it symbolises an object that does not exist. Thus, Butler (ibid.) proposes to conceive of the phallus as signifying something female: 'The question, of course, is why it is assumed that the phallus requires that particular body part to symbolise, and why it could not operate through symbolizing other body parts.' In tradition of psychoanalytic criticism, the point she makes is that the phallus is a signifier for something that the female body does not correspond to, so something else has to replace the penile object referent.

> On the one hand, the process of signification is always material; signs work by appearing (visibly, aurally), and appearing through material means, although what appears only signifies by virtue of those non-phenomenal relations, i.e., relations of differentiation, that tacitly structure and propel signification itself. (Butler 1993: 68)

If the phallus then only operates by performing a 'veiling' of its object referent, Butler suggests that the phallus's privilege shows by way of structural relations and their reification in the symbolic. If applied to the sexual relations represented in *Mulholland Drive* female homosexuality appears as a symbolic construction. On the one hand, lesbian sexuality can be understood as existing outside the economy of phallologocentrism and thus as a subversive form of sexuality. On the other hand, lesbian sexuality can be understood as a construct that exists within the symbolic of a society or system. Such an ambivalence is carried by both the stylistic elements of the film and the narrative itself. Lynch creates a world between illusion and facts, dreams and reality. He uses colours, sounds, settings, dialogues and other aesthetic elements to increase the spectators' desire to understand what is going on while at the same time encouraging them to forget about the narrative and become possessed by the cinematic images and atmosphere. Due to the ambivalence between lesbian sexuality as a subversive power and a bare construct, Butler (1993: 85) sees an importance in assessing how the phallus projects a structuring principle in the signification of lesbian sexuality and thus ponders how it is constructed or what happens to the 'privileged' status of that signifier in the displacement of its object referent in the context of the signifying practice of lesbian relationships. In other words, when the 'hegemonic symbolic of (hetero-sexist) sexual difference [. . .] and schemas for constituting sites of erotogenic pleasure' (Butler 1993: 91) are displaced. If the phallus thus can be understood as signifying the woman and thus becomes a structuring principle for signifying same sex relationships among women, this allows the discursive performance of contrasting notions to binary heterosexual erotogenic pleasure and desire.

> If the phallus is an imaginary effect (which is reified as the privileged signifier of the symbolic order), then its structural place is no longer determined by the logical relation of mutual exclusion entailed by heterosexist version of sexual difference in which men are said to 'have' and women to 'be' the phallus. (Butler 1993: 88)

By contrast the phallus can be understood as lesbian rather than a masculine signifier for power. Such a view would allow a lesbian phallus as a structuring principle in signifying the sexual relationship between Diane and Camilla in *Mulholland Drive*. Similarly, the lesbian phallic determination can be seen in *Lost Highway*'s Renee when she tells Fred/Pete that he could never have her. What Lynch creates here is a powerful signification of female sexuality that subverts the idea of being and having the phallus and counters established notions of power and the fear of castration. Both appear to be merely conceptual or abstract ideas of power and control, without being a structural principle to a specific gender.

Conclusion – Desire is Power

As these observations show, sexual agency in its different shapes and forms appears to be primarily attributed to women. Women, rather than men, have the capability to act in a sexual or even sexualizsd manner to produce the exact results they want. Sexuality therefore is rendered at the same time as a powerful tool and as a weakness. As the film narratives of this chapter suggest, as long as women are able to actively use this tool to satisfy their desire for others, they are successful characters. Lynch's fascination for film noir and the social norms of the late 1940s and 1950s has an obvious influence on his films, particularly in his representation of female sexuality and the recurrent figure of the double. The double or doppelganger signifies death as well as the fear of castration and phallic power in psychoanalytic terms. Moreover, Lynch's films, in following the conventions of film noir, render the stereotypical sexual banter of the femme fatale as more important than the criminal act of the story (such as kidnapping, blackmail or murder). In order to experience narrative pleasure in Lynchville, expectations about linear plot developments and the solutions of a crime or mystery need to be abandoned. In *Lost Highway*, for example, the police investigation is more interested in Pete's sex life than convicting him of his possible crime, as the following dialogue illustrates:

> Lou: 'Motherfuckin' job!'
> Hank: 'His or ours, Lou?'
> Lou: 'Ours, Hank!' [. . .] 'Fucker gets more pussy than a toilet seat!'

Sexual intercourse and seduction seem to be the plot's central point. When it comes to framing these moments, Laura Mulvey's concept of the male gaze aids in understanding the ways female bodies are fragmented in Lynch's cinema. Moreover, women embody what Mulvey described as a stillness within the moving image as they become iconic images of female sexuality. This reifies the female body and adds heteronormative notions about female homosexuality to the representation of women in Lynch's films, especially in *Mullholland Drive*. Female sexuality turns into something inconceivable and female pleasure's fulfilment remains mostly invisible as his films lack representations of the female orgasm. Butler's concept of the lesbian phallus allowed for terminology to describe how in Lynch's films notions about control and power are dodging heteronormative standards and expectations. In the resultant ambivalences, Lynch creates a place for subversion, as shown in *Mullholland Drive*. Further, his films follow postmodern patterns of storytelling and avoid offering solutions. Instead, his films manage to offer a field of projection where audiences can realise their own needs, wishes and desires and be in union with themselves. As a result, the medium of film in Lynch's cinema holds a different meaning as it becomes, in Ishii-Gonzales' terms, a fetish. In this context, female sexuality can be seen as removed from bourgeois ideals such as faith, loyalty and trust. David Lynch uses tropes of classic Hollywood cinema and at the same time employs them against their conventional use to create a unique universe: It invites audience participation, plays with the medium's affective powers, and can employ female sexuality as a powerful tool to liberate and encourage active pleasure and desire.

Note

1. Pietsch, Volker: *Persönlichkeitsspaltung in Literatur und Film. Zur Konstruktion dissoziierter Identitäten in den Werken E. T. A. Hoffmanns und David Lynchs*. Peter Lang 2008; Wedding, Danny/Boyd Mary Ann/Niemiec Ryan M.: *Movies and Mental Illness. Using Films to Understand Psychopathology*. Cambridge: Hogrefe Publishing 2014; Lim Dennis: *David Lynch. The Man from Another Place*. New Harvest: Houghton Mifflin Harcourt 2015.

Bibliography

Armand, Louis. 'The Medium is the Fetish'. *David Lynch in Theory*, François-Xavier Gleyzon (ed.). Litteraria Pragensia, 2010, pp. 147–56.

Baudrillard, Jean. *Transparency of Evil*. Version, 1993.

Butler, Judith. *Bodies that Matter*. Routledge, 1993.

Chion Michel. *David Lynch*. BFI, 1995.

Hanson, Helen. *Hollywood Heroines. Women in Film Noir and the Female Gothic Fiction*. I. B. Tauris, 2007.

Hallam, Lindsay. *Twin Peaks: Fire Walk with Me*. Auteur, 2018.

Helmich, Jenny. *David Lynchs Frauenfiguren*. AVM, 2010.

Ishii-Gonzales, Sam. 'Mysteries of Love: Lynch's *Blue Velvet/The Wolf-Man*'. *The Cinema of David Lynch*, Erica Sheen and Annette Davison (eds). Wallflower Press, 2004, pp. 48–60.

Kara, Sara. 'David Lynch – Ein postmoderner Regisseur'. *David Lynch: Der Film als Kunst*, Denis Pavlociv et al. (eds). Science Factory, 2014, pp. 8–45.

Mactaggart, Allister. *The Film Paintings of David Lynch Challenging Film Theory*. Intellect, 2010.

Mulvey, Laura. *Death 24× a Second. Stillness and the Moving Image*. Reaction Books, 2006.

Mulvey, Laura. 'Visual Pleasure and Narrative Cinema'. *Film Theory and Criticism: Introductory Readings*, Leo Braudy and Marshall Cohen (eds). Oxford University Press, 1999, pp. 833–44.

Nochimson, Martha P. *The Passion of David Lynch. Wild at Heart in Hollywood*. University of Texas Press, 2012.

Richardson, John. 'Laura and *Twin Peaks*: Postmodern Parody and the Musical reconstruction of the Absent Femme Fatale'. *The Cinema of David Lynch*, Erica Sheen and Annette Davison (eds). Wallflower Press, 2004, pp. 77–92.

Ryan, Scott and David Bushman. *The Women of David Lynch: A Collection of Essays*. Fayetteville Mafia Press, 2019.

Seeßlen, Georg. *David Lynch und seine Filme*. Schüren, 1994.

Stiglegger, Marcus. 'Distorsionen'. *Film| Bild | Emotion. Film und Kunstgeschichte im postkinematografischen Zeitalter*, Marcus Stiglegger and Christoph Wagner (eds). Gebrüder Mann Verlag, 2020, pp. 185–202.

Williams, David E. '*Twin Peaks*: Dreams, Doubles and Doppelgangers. Cinematographer', American Cinematographer, 11 July 2018, https://ascmag.com/articles/twin-peaks-dreams-doubles-and-dopplegangers (last accessed 17 September 2020).

Filmography

Blue Velvet. Directed by David Lynch, performances by Kyle MacLachlan, Isabella Rosselini, Dennis Hopper, and Laura Dern, De Laurentis Entertainment Group, 1986.

Lost Highway. Directed by David Lynch, performances by Bill Pullman and Patricia Arquette, CiBi 2000, Asymmetrical Productions and Lost Highway Productions LCC, 1997.

Mulholland Drive. Directed by David Lynch, performances by Naomi Watts and Laura Harring, Les Films Alain Sarde et al., 2001.

Twin Peaks. Directed by David Lynch et al., performances by Kyle MacLachlan and Mädchen Amick, Lynch/Frost Productions et al., 1990–1.

Twin Peaks: Fire Walk with Me. Directed by David Lynch, performances by Sheryl Lee and Ray Wise, CIBY Picture, 1992.

Twin Peaks: The Return [on DVD and BluRay *Twin Peaks: A Limited Event Series*]. Directed by David Lynch, performances by Sheryl Lee and Kyle MacLachlan, Showtime, 2017.

CHAPTER 11

Room to Meme: 'David Lynch' as Problematic and Self-evident Aesthetic Object in Digital Memes

Marcel Hartwig

This chapter will argue that the semiotic item 'David Lynch' has become a meme, and through memetic imitation in digital form is stripped of the very essence of David Lynch. It will assess the play that is at work in shaping transmedia aesthetics by way of media transpositions of elements from Lynch's œuvre into new media contexts and the role multimodality plays in this process. I understand digital memes as multimodal media that foster canonisation processes and turn David Lynch into an aesthetic signifier that normalises his shock aesthetics into a part of the everyday register. At the same time, the use and circulation of these digital memes evidence creative forms of polyvocal public participation. In collecting and discussing memes from social media platforms, closed and open online fan groups, discussion websites and popular online platforms such as 9gag or me.me that allow for the sharing of user-generated content, this chapter will ask about the function of David Lynch memes. In doing so it will reflect on the relationship between digital memes and networks of communities that operate by a logic of cultural (re-)appropriation, collectivism and the use of vernacular creativity.

Laura Dern Cries, the Internet Laughs

Sometimes ugly cries on screen can become long-lasting moments of comic relief. Among the internet community this might be the case in the memory work for David Lynch's *Blue Velvet* (1986). At one point in the movie, Dorothy Vallens (Isabella Rosselini) shows up at the door of her secret lover, Jeffrey Beaumont (Kyle MacLachlan). She is tattered, bruised and topless. Sandy Williams (Laura Dern), intended to be romantically involved with Jeffrey, is at Beaumont's place and, in an epiphany, understands what is going on between Dorothy and Jeffrey. She immediately bursts into a crying fit. In 2017, amidst the actress's very own career resurgence, Dern's crying face from *Blue Velvet* had a second life: cropped from the shot and photoshopped onto a fan-made rainbow the still of Dern's crying face was decontextualised from the movie and passed on as a digital meme. This meme was remixed and transformed in visual online conversations to comment on the actress's work: In one example the crying face from *Blue Velvet* is juxtaposed with Luke Skywalker's (Mark Hamill) bawling mien during his encounter with Darth Vader in *Star Wars: The Empire Strikes Back* (1980). In 2017, this was an apt comment on Dern's appearance as Vice Admiral Amilyn Holdo in *Star Wars: The Last Jedi* (2017). Much to the actress's surprise upon finding out about her digital alter ego, Dern posted the initial meme on her Instagram account stating 'Wait, I'm a meme? Uh, what's a meme?' (@lauradern, 6 July 2017).

Internet memes, digital snippets most often passed on as GIFs (graphics interchange format) with a relevant tagline, entertain, exist everywhere, and have become natives of our digital spaces. Originally coining the term in his book *The Selfish Gene* (1976) from the Greek word mīmēma (μίμημα), Richard Dawkins uses 'memes' as a descriptor for the way cultural information travels. Units of information replicate to such a great extent, not because of the messages they carry, but because they can. Like genes, their survival is ensured by fecundity, copying-fidelity and longevity (1976: 251). According to Dawkins, a meme is 'a cultural unit of convenience [. . .] with just enough copying fidelity to serve as a viable unit of cultural selection' (Dawkins 1976: 252). This can describe how a unit of Beethoven's Ninth may survive without the context of the whole symphony. In this sense, as memetics scholar Susan Blackmore holds, 'we don't think intelligence, we think replicators,' or, in other words, it is information rather than ideas that is copied. In Laura Dern's case, it is the image of her crying fit in *Blue Velvet* that gets copied as retrievable information, ready to be transformed into new sets of information by being photoshopped and shared.

Borrowing from Dawkins' discovery, a study of internet memes thus may present an opportunity to both recognise the presence of dominant and subcultural groups on the internet and to index specific cultural communities within and outside social networks due to their processes of cultural selection. Media scholar Ryan Milner would here point to Jean Burgess' concept of 'vernacular creativity' to illustrate how 'memetic media are employed for public expression' (Milner 2016: 110). Such 'netographic' work among digital communities has already been done and will not be the focus of this paper (see Cherry 2019; MacDonald 2021; Chen 2012). Also this chapter will not ponder in depth memes as 'a place where ideological practice takes place' (Wiggins 2019: iii). Rather, I argue that internet memes only work partially according to the logic of the 'unit[s] of cultural transmission' Dawkins (1976: 249) identified, as their whole context of transmission has changed. With internet memes deliberate acts of memetic alteration need to be taken into consideration (Solon). Wilful deliberation alters the blind and automatic replication by imitation that Dawkins sees in memes in analogy to genes. In recreating image macros as internet memes, already known units of convenience are repeated until their exhaustion. In return this influences the sources of culture the creators of internet memes poach from. This might also be the reason why Laura Dern's crying face has recently been replaced with a screengrab from *Big Little Lies* (2019). Together with her character's line 'I will NOT not be rich' from season 2, episode 2 this image macro is replicated with ever new items of added interior monologue captioning in the internet's blogosphere.

In 2012, Patrick Davison (2012: 122) could still argue that memes are 'a piece of culture [. . .] which gains influence through online transmission.' However, in 2023 this is too limited a view on internet memes. Today, memes provide a marketing aesthetic that is widely in use: *The Mandalorian* TV series was marketed by Baby Yoda memes on and offline, for example in the form of stickers, buttons and posters. The global creative team of Spotify, a music streaming provider, used the multimodal aesthetics for their memes in an image campaign in 2020 widely distributed on posters in urban environments (Nudd 2019). Additionally, digital memes appear offline on various kinds of apparel as an indication of a consumer's fashion choices. Similarly, a famous recurring subtitle for the hard of hearing from *Twin Peaks* season 3, 'intense ominous whooshing', not only became an important part of a series of digital memes, but also a success as a line on a series of t-shirts advertised to *Twin Peaks* fans offline (Welcome to Twin Peaks 2021). On a shirt, the mere appearance of the sound annotation becomes both an in-joke for the fan community as well as a wearable, tactile metameme for internet users familiar with a series of various internet memes featuring the same caption without any direct reference to the films or aesthetic work of David Lynch (for example, as an added text to Caspar David Friedrich's 'Wanderer above the Sea of Fog' (dopl3r.com)). Internet memes, no longer restricted to digital transmission, have thus travelled beyond the digital realm and fulfil both a phatic and a poetic function of everyday language. In a similar manner, Laura Dern responded to the wide resurgence of her crying face as a popular internet meme by sporting a T-shirt showing her copiously weeping countenance from HBO's short-lived dramedy series *Enlightened* (2011–13) on her Instagram (@lauradern, 7 July 2017). Thus, her post replicated and transformed the digital meme 'Laura Dern crying' at the same time into a performance, a wearable cultural in-joke, and a digital metameme.

Such transmedia transgressions between online and offline cultures have significance beyond a mere reading of digital culture – they have a lasting impact on cultural artefacts. Limor Shifman holds that memes 'shape and reflect general social mindsets' and thus are to be regarded as 'essential in contemporary digital culture' (Shifman 2014: 4). For her, memes no longer are single units of cultural information that get copied and imitated. Rather, internet memes are

> (a) a group of digital items sharing common characteristics of content, form, and/or stance, which (b) were created with an awareness of each other, and (c) were circulated, imitated, and/or transformed via the Internet by many users.' (Shifman 2014: 41)

Remixing and copying are here two operations that influence the production and circulation of internet memes. What's more, journalist and artist Xiao Mina contends that there is a synergy between grassroots activism and a digital native's oft-derided 'slacktivism' by having 'much larger groups of people acting in solidarity than might previously have been possible' (Mina 2019: 7), evidenced for example in the success of the 'pussy hats' during the Women's Marches of 2017. This is only another instance in which digital memes reach beyond the internet.

The idea of passing on images, collaboratively remixing and appropriating them to ever new contexts not only speaks to the aesthetic of an amateur culture. This process also affects the iconographic staples of the culture this mixed media's contents are poached from. 'Laura Dern crying' works as an in-joke among David Lynch fans at the same time as it works as an overacted crying face void of any context. As such, the image macro is ready to be remixed and transformed online, without its user being aware of the source it is coming from.

In this way, digital memes are haunted units of information. They operate by a mode of 'tele-technology' that Mark Fisher (2012: 19) defined in his work on hauntology:

> [W]e can distinguish two directions in hauntology. The first refers to that which is still effective as a virtuality (. . .) The second refers to that which (in actuality) has 'not yet' happened, but which is 'already' effective in the virtual.

As such, digital memes either emulate images 'poached' from the vast archives of past popular cultural works or they mimic an amateur aesthetic in image content drawn by hand on a computer with the help of simple raster graphics editors. In both cases, their aesthetic form at once creates a nostalgic sentiment for the pre-digital in the digital and prefigures the ways they will be further read, remixed and 'repartitioned'. Consequently, these tele-technological units of information erode both the dimension of space (their source) and time, in so far as memetic media make sure that the past keeps on repeating itself. This illustrates the ideological structure of digital memes: they operate by way of nostalgic iconoclasm. In *Reading Images: The Grammar of Visual Design*, Kress and van Leeuwen show that visual media are multimodal texts, that is, their 'meanings are realized through more than one semiotic code' (Kress and van Leeuwen 2020:177). These meanings are realised because of culturally habitualised ways of seeing. 'Laura Dern crying' takes a self-evident unit of information and shows this unit in its replication as something open for debate. In cropping Dern's character from *Blue Velvet*, users generating or remixing the digital meme remove the position of the character from the original frame and thus open possibilities for newly added information (image context, frames, added interior monologues). The digital meme instantiates a given element from an acknowledged cultural context (the canonisation of Lynch's *Blue Velvet*) and incorporates it into a commentary about that cultural context's values. At the same time, it deconstructs the status of the film by way of the image it uses to reference *Blue Velvet*. A moment of painful loss in the film's context is naturalised as an object of ridicule and is thus a lasting comment on both *Blue Velvet* and, above all, the actress, Laura Dern.

'Laura Dern crying' may work irrespective of her role in David Lynch's œuvre let alone her popularity as a Hollywood actress. Memes targeting the director's work directly, however, have existed before memes became a popular element on the internet. Cody Richeson (@Koko Ricky) uploaded a video edit of *A Goofy Movie* (1995) and turned it into *David Lynch's A Goofy Movie* in 2007. The edit features typical aesthetics from what Michel Chion coined the 'Lynch-Kit': a noir 'synesthesia of light and sound' (Chion 1995: 167), dream sequences, floating characters, and smoke. The clip sparked a whole range of "If David Lynch directed" clips on youtube.com, a series of 'performative memes' (Milner 2016: 18) that offered recut trailers for films such as *Dirty Dancing*, *Pretty Woman* or *Star Wars: Return of the Jedi*, all of them applying various elements from the 'Lynch-Kit'. These clips often work by way of mash-up and video remixing to establish a fake trailer for a film by David Lynch. In *Dirty Dancing* (Trae 2016) lines of dialogue from the film are distorted or played backwards, drone sounds are added and select scenes are presented in black and white. Further intertitles reading 'Beyond Real', 'Beyond Imagination', 'Beyond Words' are inserted to illustrate a dream state that is typical of David Lynch movies. To add another layer, the trailer ends with fake blurbs from magazines such as 'Meta magazine' ('Nasty, night-marish, and completely off the wall.') and 'Postmodern Weekly' ('A visual masterpiece.'). These intertextual elements are woven together in quick succession and offer the reader both a complex joke and a pastiche on David Lynch and connect his work with three distinct cues, recognisable for everyone who is not in on the specific references to Lynch's œuvre: dreamy, meta, and postmodern. In the memetic mode of nostalgic icon-oclasm, the remixed trailer revisits iconic moments from a mainstream film classic and it offers a series of aesthetic elements from David Lynch's movies without establishing a connection to their historical rootedness. It thus works merely on the commodification of Lynch's style by way of a sophisticated joke, blending highbrow and lowbrow entertainment with the auteur's quality pedigree.

Kramer Drinks, Larry David Goes Lynch

Digital memes then offer a critical conceit: Often discussed as example par excellence for participatory media (see Milner 2016, Shifman 2014, or Mina 2019) and the creative work of a polyvocal public, digital memes also stand for quantifiable user interactions. In this light, they are to be understood as creative currency in social media contexts and they are bound to the sta-tus of the users sharing these memes. Between 2014 and 2015, the Tumblr account @larrydavidlynch posted content that layered lines by comedian Larry David over screengrabs from *Eraserhead*, *Blue Velvet*, *Lost Highway*, *Mulholland Drive* and, mostly, *Twin Peaks*. The image macros aimed at out-bidding themselves by means of vulgarity and originality. The last post of January 21, 2015, for example, shows a screengrab of Carel Struycken as the Giant from *Twin Peaks* season 2, episode 22. There he appears when Annie (Heather Graham) announces to Agent Cooper (Kyle MacLachlan) that she is about to enter the Miss Twin Peaks pageant, only to warn Cooper by means of gesturing and mouthing a "No". On 'larrydavidlynch' the sub-titles to the screengrab read 'The problem didn't lie with his small penis, but rather with your big vagina,' a quote from season 5, episode 8 of *Curb Your Enthusiasm*. This does not add to the memory work of either of the two shows, but in a very aggressive manner works on deconstructing the iconic status both shows hold on American television. Rather than taking the con-tent of either of these two serious – Larry David's double-entendre on Lisa Thompson's (Mo Collins) emasculation of Jeff Greene (Jeff Garlin) due to the perceived miniscule size of his intimate parts and the warning gestures of the Giant in *Twin Peaks* – the digital meme strips both of their narrative contexts and turns the Giant's arm movement into a misogynist measuring gesture – thus allowing for the erasure of both TV moments by way of overcoming the iconic content with a retweetable vulgar joke.

In a similar manner, the social media account @seinpeaks, run by videographer and podcaster Jesse Brooks from Cumming, GA, to a greater extent collects screengrabs or clips from the sitcom *Seinfeld* merged with subtitles or sound cues from *Twin Peaks* and other David Lynch productions. His account has been active since 2018 and has since garnered a wider audience. In the same year Brooks opened an additional facebook group and invited users to share their own 'seinpeaks' memes. Brooks is also active on Twitter and runs the podcast 'The Other Side of Darkness: A Seinfeld Parody Podcast'. On the independent David Lynch Community website 'Welcome to Twin Peaks', Brooks gave a reason for starting 'seinpeaks': 'Both shows are iconic in their genre and era, they are well-written and well-performed, and I think it just gives me an excuse to dive into them every day.' Though in his approach Brooks may concede an iconic status to the shows, his digital memes work similarly to those of @larrydavidlynch minus the vulgarity. It is tempting to see much of Brooks' content as the work of Aby Warburg's 'Pathosformeln' (pathos formula), a concept derived from Warburg's visual cultural *Mnemosyne-Atlas*. Therein, Warburg (2020: 20) points to a repository of visual cultural gestures that offer potential for ever new interpretations and variations, which through their iconicity mediate social cultural evolution. Colleen Becker (2013: 11) puts emphasis on this collection's 'emotive force':

> Warburg discerned how ancient source materials demonstrated their resilience and relevance through time, but he also sought out examples of their altered states and corruption in wide-ranging contexts. Warburg's insistence on the emotive force of visual metaphor stands out as the most salient distinction between them.

Even though altered 'Pathosformeln' may completely invert their original meaning, these variations – highbrow or lowbrow – are produced by way of retaining 'comparable psychic or emotional dynamics' (Becker 2013: 11).

When, for example, @seinpeaks posts a screengrab from *Seinfeld* season 5, episode 4 showing Kramer (Michael Richards) smoking and drinking at the same time and merges this with the subtitle 'Drink full, and descend', a line spoken by the Woodsman (Robert Broski) during 'Part 8' of *Twin Peaks: The Return*, both iconic moments are neutralised of their emotive force. On the one hand, the unscripted performance of the eccentric Kramer was meant as a spontaneous act underlining this character's apathetic nature, the added subtitle creates a new context that makes him follow an order – thus contradicting Kramer's genuine indifference.

On the other hand, it reduces the cryptic and enigmatic moment from the much-lauded 'Part 8' of *Twin Peaks: The Return* to a punchline. The two moments are rendered as absurd and their meaning is destroyed. Again, the digital meme does not retain the theme of either of the two contexts and disbands them of their emotive force. Kramer's drinking screengrab with the new tagline invites further variations of the meme with either an ever-new tagline or restorations of the original context of the moment in episode 4 of season 5 of *Seinfeld* without changing the visual information itself and thus preserving the (tele)visual memory of the past in future reproductions. @seinpeaks thus operates like @larrydavidlynch by way of nostalgic iconoclasm and offers Lynch's aesthetics as a consumable unit of information. Furthermore, @seinpeaks by now has morphed into a podcast: This adds to the quantifiable flow of data created by this archive of memes that point further to the self-marketing of the platform's creator, Jesse Brooks. In today's form, the platform itself is a good example of the digital economy that invites free labour: it collects external user-generated content, reposts the work of other Lynch-meme platforms, and connects this archive to the internal cashflow of the podcast by inviting new streams and guests on the show who themselves are there to market their own productions. Most prominently the latter was the case in episode 8 with Alicia Witt (Gersten Hayward in *Twin Peaks*) who uses a greater share of the show to market both her new music album and forthcoming book. The examples of similar archives abound (see, for example, @sadpeaks, @dailydalecooper, or @wholseomepeaks to name but a few). All of them follow comparable strategies of content creation, that is to boost their own status in the web community by way of reblogging or mimicry and thus generate wider audiences for their own media creations.

HBO Forgot, Showtime Wins

While the above examples all deal with source material from David Lynch's film and television productions, there also exists a memetic discourse that uses the item 'David Lynch' as a meaning making unit in its set of information. As Cherry (2019: 72) holds,

> [p]rolific [. . .] memes are not limited to fan discourse, it is significant that they replicate popular culture in a milieu where 'we are all fans now' and may permit the demonstration of fannish behaviors including detailed knowledge of iconic moments from popular and cult texts.

In this way, the visual content of a digital meme can at the same time address (1) a specific 'discursive object' such as the auteur David Lynch,

(2) use a 'vernacular language' that communicates a code in-between fans while marking the lemma 'David Lynch' as a metalingual reference to both the 'Lynch-Kit' and the director's corpus, and (3) use these as a 'phatic expression' to make contact with other users on the platform these contents are shared on (see Cherry 2019: 72). Memes that carry the item 'David Lynch' in their interior monologue or overlayered levels of text cross the border that exists within message boards and online hubs of fan communities to carry a message to a more general audience. That is, these digital memes proliferate at the margins of fan communities and mediate a communication about David Lynch in a 'milieu where 'we are all fans now' (Cherry 2019: 72) so that the item 'David Lynch' is a popular unit of information that conveys a semiotics of its own.

For example, when in May 2019 the 'We kind of forgot'-meme became viral, it did not take long until it became about Lynch. The internet meme is a commentary on the quality of the screenwriting for the final season of *Game of Thrones*. The image macro captures one of the show's creators, David Benioff, who comments on episode 4 of season 8 in which Daenerys Targaryen supposedly forgets about an approaching enemy fleet. The irony here is: 'Dany' has repeatedly been warned and warned others about the fleet in previous episodes and the episode thus reveals flaws in the screenwriting. The added text from the subtitles repeats Benioff's comment that 'Dany kind of forgot about the Iron Fleet.' Meme creators took the image macro and added to it. The Facebook group 'Twin Peaks: Dwellers on the Threshold' circulated a variation of the 'We kind of forgot' meme when it went viral. Their version juxtaposes the original Benioff visual of the image macro with a photoshopped reappropriation of the same source. There David Lynch's countenance is overlaid onto Benioff's. The original visual's added text reads Benioff saying:

> We knew going into the final season [of *Game of Thrones*] that we needed to be respectful to the source material while trying to achieve everything we had to in just 6 episodes.

The reappropriated image macro below reads: 'I demanded 18 episodes [for *Twin Peaks: The Return*] based on an idea that I wouldn't elaborate on' (Huntington 2019) – an invented quote, here associated with David Lynch. This digital meme works solely with the annotated photoshop of David Lynch's portrait to add new meaning to the commentary on the writing quality of *Game of Thrones* mediated by the 'We kind of forgot' macro.

As such. the appropriated 'We kind of forgot' macro builds on the recognition of the two creators – David Benioff and David Lynch – and the identification with the referenced episodes and series – *Game of Thrones* and *Twin Peaks: The Return*. Shared in a group organised around *Twin Peaks* fandom, this meme may speak to what Milner (2016: 104) describes as a 'mark of collectivism': 'this ingroup identification comes with outgroup othering. Memetic logics, grammar, and vernacular are employed in subcultural conversations to differentiate insiders from outsiders, and to distinguish members of the collective from the uninitiated.' Huntington, in his post, however, credits another fan group: 'Bottom panel pic courtesy John Reynolds over on Logposting', whose image macro reads 'While Laura kind of forgot she was dead' juxtaposed with a screengrab from episode 18 of *Twin Peaks: The Return* showing Sheryl Lee as a screaming Laura Palmer (Reynolds 2019a). Huntington also shared his version of the 'We kind of forgot'-meme to the Facebook group 'Logposting', which offers all their postings to the public. There Huntington's post was privately shared by fifty more members (Huntington 2019b) and thus spawned a wider web of further shares. This compares mildly to the credited post by Reynolds, which garnered only one share in the same Facebook group. Such a miniature example illustrates the following: While Huntington by way of mimicry and reblogging is securing his status in the ingroup, Reynold's meme works in the mode of nostalgic iconoclasm. Reynold uses source material from a David Lynch production and creates both an ironic distancing effect from the TV show as well as an in-joke on the 'We kind of forgot' macro. Huntington's reappropriation, however, elevates the director's creative liberties, authority and implied artistic genius over the budget restrictions and regulated supervision that defines Benioff's work. He thus retains the emotive force that the director's countenance holds within the initiated collective and offers, by way of territorial demarcation, a dialogue with the uninitiated. The mitigating factor is the alienating effect that Lynch's portrait here is creating in the image overlay and thus invites fans of a different collective to explore the director's work. By the same token, it certifies a lower quality to *Game of Thrones* in comparison to *Twin Peaks: The Return* and thus confirms the ingroup in their more superior fandom. Lynch's iconic portrait superimposed over Benioff's face here stands for *Twin Peaks: The Return* and works as a semiotic item that shapes the imperative in Huntington's meme: consume better television. Even though Huntington's meme operates as 'Pathosformel' it rather inverts the iconic reproduction as a pastiche. That is, it connects a notion of Lynch's TV series with the well-known iconic appearance of the director himself as a response to the restrictive and marketing-oriented operations of HBO productions. At the same time, it invites the consumption of *Twin Peaks: The Return* in emphasising market demands in Lynch's work by way of his negotiation skills: 'I demanded 18 episodes based on an idea that I would not elaborate on'. Nevertheless, his eighteen episodes were produced and released by another Pay TV channel, Showtime, a CBS subsidiary, and HBO's premium cable rival. The visual conceit of Huntington's 'We kind of forgot' meme renders *Twin Peaks: The Return* not by its aesthetic merit or artistic design, but rather as the result of a creative impulse predefined by market demands and thus the socioeconomic climate in which it was produced and circulated.

Displacing Lynch, Reinstating 'Lynch'

Apart from specific fan pages, internet memes that carry the lemma 'David Lynch' as meaning making item sprawl on popular platforms such as AhSeeIt.com, me.me or 9gag.com and are open to an even wider audience. There the memetic discourse can more effectively shape the units of information that are to be copied and passed on. Digital memes using 'David Lynch' as a semiotic item can shape the more general and thus future memory work about the director's corpus. The abstractions there are less specific and avoid poaching from any source material linked to David Lynch but aim at making more universal claims about the director and his work. Memes here reach from liking the director's hair to Hokusai's 'The Great Wave off Kanagawa' (Me.me) or similar artworks – a polemic on the director's art house status – to making affective statements about the experience of watching films by David Lynch. To illustrate affect, "When you're watching a David Lynch movie"-macros use screengrabs from any source but a David Lynch film as reaction shots. In one version, it is a still from Christopher Nolan's *Following* showing Cobb (Alex Haw) and the Young Man (Jeremy Theobald) of the movie with the added subtitle 'What the fuck is going on?'. Other versions emulate a similar stance by taking striking media images and add interactive dialogue by way of overlayed text. For example, a popular paparazzi shot of Kirsten Dunst and Jake Gyllenhaal at a London restaurant in 2003 is turned into a visual meditation on the affective dimension of the figurative ingestion of David Lynch. The photo shows Gyllenhaal spoon-feeding Dunst some soup, the actor's mien is stern while he holds the spoon to the actress's open mouth. The added text labels items in the visual frame of the photo: Gyllenhaal is tagged as 'David Lynch', Dunst is 'me', and the soup becomes 'weird shit' (@nitehawkcinema). Variations of this meme repeatedly show characters from popular culture – SpongeBob (@ShaneMP01), the Simpsons (awwmemes), Kanye West (reddit) – labelled as 'David Lynch' feeding, digesting or showing 'weird shit' to the person posting the Internet meme, self-identifying as 'me'. These oppositional readings reject meaningful descriptors from film discourses to apply an alternative code to the reading of the semiotic item 'David Lynch'. In this way these Internet memes open a channel to communities of readers unfamiliar with the work of David Lynch and allow them to participate in memetic conversations about Lynch by appropriating the code these oppositional readings offer. The memes' awareness of each other is marked by their similar stance and use of labels, together they mark the existence of a communication between subcultural groups. All of them use popular cultural items and connect them with information units from their ingroup. Posted on mainstream platforms such as 9gag, Reddit or Twitter they can generate global attention and invite further contributions by way of competitive 'one-upmanship' (see Jahn-Sudmann and Kelleter 2012 for one-upmanship, or serial outbidding in contemporary television). In all these affective digital memes, 'David Lynch', on the one hand, is subsumed with the notion of the 'weird' – a term that in film criticism is used synonymously with artistic innovation by way of affect (see Christiansen 2021). On the other hand, his work is likened to the language signifier for excrements that in the modern jargon both has an elevating as well as deprecating meaning.

Taken together these memetic conversations offer an abstracted understanding of the aesthetics of David Lynch's cinema. In their use of visual contents and cues from different media, memes emulate an idea of self-sufficient items of information to which David Lynch's cinema is not the origin, but rather a transmedia framing device. As such it extends an affective idea of 'David Lynch' across multiple sources or platforms and offers a unified experience of 'David Lynch' as entertainment (for transmedia storytelling see Jenkins 2006: 293). Accordingly, it suffices to add the lemma 'David Lynch' to visual items outside the director's œuvre to explore the range of affective responses his work has to offer. For example, an image taken during the '2014 London Destination Star Trek Convention' showing a staff member vacuum cleaning the carpet of the Enterprise D bridge (Krammer 2014) was apt material for a popular image macro among *Star Trek* fans. In revisiting 'Part 7' of *Twin Peaks: The Return*, the Star Trek macro became popular again, this time around in a different fan community and with a new added commentary: 'If David Lynch directed *Star Trek*' (@HarryPottahIsDead). As this image macro illustrates, 'David Lynch' as a semiotic item has become a meme and through memetic imitation is transmitted as culturally relevant unit of information. At the same time, it exposes 'David Lynch' to both variation and modulation.

Conclusion

As the above examples have shown, the miniscule unit of meaning 'David Lynch' is stripped of the cinematic essence of David Lynch. This works either by way of nostalgic iconoclasm or bricolage using the information unit 'David Lynch' as transmedia framing device. Digital memes through image cropping and decontextualisation foster canonisation processes of affective readings of David Lynch's cultural work. By the same turn, Lynch is turned into an aesthetic signifier as added written content or added interior monologue in image macros that normalise his artistic expressions into a phatic part of the everyday register in Internet communities. Thus, the use and circulation of these digital memes evidence forms of polyvocal public participation that offer oppositional inferences about 'David Lynch'. David Lynch memes point to existing networks of communities that operate by a logic of cultural reappropriation, collectivism, and the use of vernacular creativity. These processes allow the decontextualisation, reframing and displacement of David Lynch to the outer margins of their subcultural discourses that co-exist with high culture's celebration of Lynch as an auteur. Thus, they evidence a dynamic connection between the subaltern and the common, that is the porous relationships that exist between high and low cultural media collectives and illustrate the neutralising power of memetic media. Classic memetics holds that arguments and ideas must be out there before they can become structures of knowledge that shape and inform a community. In short, Lynch memes do not suddenly become popular out of nowhere, but rather emulate preformulated ideas as new image macros. In the reception history of David Lynch, he was often referenced as 'Czar of Bizarre' (Corliss 1990), Mel Brooks called him 'Jimmy Stewart from Mars' (Conterio 2017), and one of the early appreciations of 'the obsessive universe of David Lynch' was called 'Weirdsville, USA' (Woods 1997). In internet memes, such a reception is amplified, imitated and widely circulated. Here, human users, not film are the medium of these visual jokes.

As the above discussion has shown, these Internet memes surpass the actual search for meaning and the aesthetic fragmentation often conducted in the high cultural experience of 'David Lynch'. This recalls a more recent statement by David Lynch, who, in remembering his 1950s childhood experiences, states: 'Television did what the Internet is doing more of now: It homogenized everything' (Lynch and McKenna 2019: 22). Internet memes add to this in their modulations of David Lynch. In this way, the 'madman in sheep's clothing', as Sting once called David Lynch (Woods 1997: 64), has lost his offensive character in becoming the internet's laughingstock. These retrospective revisitations either by way of nostalgic iconoclasm or prospective modulation neutralise the semiotic item 'David Lynch'. This is reminiscent of Adorno's (1997: 311–12) thoughts on the objectification of art:

> More often, reception wears away what constitutes the work's determinate negation of society. Works are usually critical in the era in which they appear, later they are neutralized, not least because of changed social relations. Neutralization is the social price of aesthetic autonomy.

Likewise, Internet memes are to be understood as affective forms and results of reception. They either poach from or reinstate 'David Lynch' as a semiotic item in their image macros. Thereby they actively empty out the cultural work of David Lynch.[1] In this way, he is homogenised with everything, reduced to a simple and faddish visual statement.

Note

1. Indeed, it could also be argued that Lynch's artistic cultural practice aims for this effect. Lynch's character of Gordon Cole in *Twin Peaks* turns Lynch into an agent within his own pop cultural network. Such a strategy is reminiscent of the personas created by other pop artists from Andy Warhol to Tim Burton. I am indebted to Andreas Rauscher for this valuable observation.

Bibliography

Adorno, Theodor Wiesengrund. *Aesthetic Theory*. Bloomsbury, 1997.

Becker, Colleen. 'Aby Warburg's "Pathosformel" as Methodological Paradigm'. *Journal of Art Historiography*, no. 9, 2013, pp. 1–25.

Blackmore, Susan. 'Memes and 'temes''. *TED2008*, February 2008, https://www.ted.com/talks/susan_blackmore_memes_and_temes (last accessed 14 November 2021).

Chen, Carl. 'The Creation and Meaning of Internet Memes in *4chan*: Popular Internet Culture in the Age of Online Digital Reproduction'. *Habitus*, spring, 2012, pp. 6–19.

Cherry, Brigid. '"The Owls Are Not What They Meme": Making Sense of *Twin Peaks* with Internet Memes'. *Critical Essays on* Twin Peaks: The Return, Antonio Sanna (ed.). Springer, 2019, 69–84.

Chion, Michel. *David Lynch*. Translated by Robert Julian. BFI, 1995.

Christiansen, Steen Ledet. *The New Cinematic Weird: Atmospheres and Worldings*. Rowman & Littlefield, 2021.

Conterio, Martyn. 'Five things we learned about David Lynch from *The Art Life*'., BFI, 27 July 2017, https://www2.bfi.org.uk/news-opinion/news-bfi/interviews/david-lynch-art-of-life (last accessed 14 November 2021).

Corliss, Richard. 'Czar of Bizarre'. *Time*, 1 October 1990, p. 84.

Davison, Patrick. 'The Language of Internet Memes'. *The Social Media Reader*, Michael Mandiberg (ed.). New York University Press, 2012, pp. 120–34.

Dawkins, Richard. *The Selfish Gene*. Oxford University Press, 2016.

Fisher, Mark. 'What Is Hauntology?' *Film Quarterly*, fall, 2012, pp. 16–24. Jenkins, Henry. *Convergence Culture: Where Old and New Media Collide*. New York University Press, 2006.

Jahn-Sudmann, A. and Kelleter, F. 'Die Dynamik serieller Überbietung: Zeitgenössische amerikanische Fernsehserien und das Konzept des Quality TV'. *Populäre Serialität: Narration – Evolution – Distinktion. Zum seriellen Erzählen seit dem 19. Jahrhundert*, Frank Kelleter (ed.). Transcript, pp. 205–24.

Krammer, Victor. 'Cleaning the Bridge in the 24th Century'. *Viki Secrets*, 20 March 2014, https://vikisecrets.com/news/cleaning-the-bridge-in-the-24th-century (last accessed 14 November 2021).

Kress, Gunther and Theo van Leeuwen. *Reading Images: The Grammar of Visual Design*. 3rd edition. Routledge, 2020.

Lynch, David and Kristine McKenna. *Room to Dream*. Canongate Books, 2019

MacDonald, Shana. 'What Do You (Really) Meme? Pandemic Memes as Social Political Repositories'. *Leisure Sciences*, 43.1–2, 2021, pp. 143–51.

Mina, Xia. *Memes to Movements: How the World's Most Viral Media Is Changing Social Protest and Power*. Beacon Press, 2019.

Milner, Ryan A. *The World Made Meme: Public Conversations and Participatory Media*. MIT P, 2016.

Nudd, Tim. 'Spotify Riffs on Meme Culture in a New Global Brand Campaign'. *Muse by Clio*, 30 April 2019, https://musebycl.io/music/spotify-riffs-meme-culture-new-global-brand-campaign (last accessed 14 November 2021).

Shifman, Limor. *Memes in Digital Culture*. MIT Press, 2014.

Warburg, Aby. *Bilderatlas Mnemosyne – The Original*. Haus der Kulturen der Welt, 2020.

Welcome to Twin Peaks. 'The Convenience Store'. *Welcome to Twin Peaks*, 11 March 2021, https://welcometotwinpeaks.com/store/apparel/intense-ominous-whooshing-t-shirt/ (last accessed 14 November 2021).

Wiggins, Bradley E. *The Discursive Power of Memes in Digital Culture: Ideology, Semiotics, and Intertextuality*. Routledge, 2019.

Woods, Paul A. *Weirdsville USA: The Obsessive Universe of David Lynch*. Plexus, 1997.

Filmography

A Goofy Movie. Directed by Kevin Lima, performances by Bill Farmer and Jason Marsden, Walt Disney, 1995.

Big Little Lies. Directed by David E. Kelley et al., performances by Reese witherspoon and Nicole Kidman, HBO, 2017–19.

Blue Velvet. Directed by David Lynch, performances by Kyle MacLachlan, Isabella Rosselini, Dennis Hopper, and Laura Dern, Dino De Laurentiis Entertainment Group, 1986.

Curb Your Enthusiasm. Directed by Larry David et al., performances by Larry David and Jeff Garlin, HBO, 2000–.

Dirty Dancing. Directed by Emile Ardolino, performances by Jennifer Grey and Patrick Swayze, Vestron, Lionsgate, 1987.

Enlightened. Directed by Mike White et al., performances by Laura Dern and Luke Wilson, HBO, 2011–13.

Eraserhead. Directed by David Lynch, performances by Jack Nance and Charlotte Stewart, American Film Institute, Libra Films, 1977.

Game of Thrones. Directed by David Benioff and D.B. Weiss et al., performances by Sean Bean and Emilia Clarke, HBO, 2011–19.

Lost Highway. Directed by David Lynch, performances by Bill Pullman and Patricia Arquette, CiBi 2000, Asymmetrical Productions and Lost Highway Productions LCC, 1997.

Mulholland Drive. Directed by David Lynch, performances by Naomi Watts and Laura Harring, Les Films Alain Sarde et al., 2001.

Pretty Woman. Directed by Gary Marshall, performances by Richard Gere and Julia Roberts, Buena Vista, 1990.

Seinfeld. Directed by Art Wolff et al., performances by Jerry Seinfeld and Michael Richards, NBC, 1989–98.

Star Trek. Directed by Donald R. Beck et al., performances by William Shatner and Leonard Nimoy, NBC, 1966–9.

Star Wars Episode VI – Return of the Jedi. Directed by Richard Marquand, performances by Mark Hamill, Carrie Fisher, Harrison Ford, and Billy Dee Williams, Lucasfilm Productions, 1983.

Star Wars Episode VIII – The Last Jedi. Directed by Rian Johnson, performances by Daisy Ridley, Mark Hamill, Carrie Fisher, John Boyega, and Adam Driver, Lucasfilm/Disney, 2017.

The Mandalorian. Directed by Jon Favreau et al., performances by Pedro Pascal and Carl Weathers, Walt Disney, 2019–.

Twin Peaks. Directed by David Lynch et al., performances by Kyle MacLachlan and Mädchen Amick, Lynch/Frost Productions et al., 1990–1.

Twin Peaks: The Return [on DVD and BluRay *Twin Peaks: A Limited Event Series*]. Directed by David Lynch, performances by Sheryl Lee and Kyle MacLachlan, Showtime, 2017.

Other Media and Sources Cited

AwwMemes. 'David Lynch.' *AwwMemes* n.d., https://awwmemes.com/i/david-lynch-bme-none-815ac780e569411cbf5339af28e0e8fc (last accessed 14 November 2021).

Dern, Laura [@lauradern]. 'Wait. I'm a meme? Uh, what's a meme?' *Instagram*, 6 July 2017, https://www.instagram.com/p/BWLrbusAR5b/ (last accessed 14 November 2021).

Dopl3r.com. 'Dank Memes and Gifs: intense ethereal whooshing' *dopl3r*, 21 October 2017, https://en.dopl3r.com/memes/dank/intense-ethereal-whooshing/107799 (last accessed 14 November 2021).

Huntington, Marc. 'We knew going into the final season' *Facebook*, 15 May 2019a, https://www.facebook.com/photo/?fbid=10156237601218093&set=gm. 801309526906862 (last accessed 14 November 2021).

Huntington, Marc. 'we knew going into the final season' *Facebook*, 15 May 2019b, https://www.facebook.com/photo/?fbid=10156237948198093&set=gm. 2050062861969377 (last accessed 14 November 2021).

@HarryPottahIsDead. 'Laughed so hard' *Reddit*, 18 January 2020, https://www.reddit.com/r/twinpeaks/comments/eqm230/laughed_so_hard/ (last accessed 14 November 2021).

@Koko Ricky. 'David Lynch's A Goofy Movie.' *YouTube*, 08 August 2007, https://www.youtube.com/watch?v=z7baCckh-XE (last accessed 14 November 2021.

Reddit. 'It's David [No Spoilers].' *Reddit*, 10 March 2019, https://www.reddit.com/r/twinpeaks/comments/aziqds/its_david_no_spoilers/ (last accessed 14 November 2021).

Reynolds, John. 'While Laura kind of forgot she was dead.' *Facebook*, 14 May 2019, https://www.facebook.com/photo/?fbid=2575493885817379&set=gm. 2049471168695213 (last accessed 14 November 2021).

@ShaneMP01. 'We love some weird shit.' *Reddit*, 26 June 2020, https://www.reddit.com/r/davidlynch/comments/hg06ne/we_love_some_weird_shit/ (last accessed 14 November 2021).

Me.me. 'David Lynch's Hair vs. The Great Wave off Kanagawa.' *Me.me*, 16 April 2019, https://me.me/i/david-lynchs-hair-vs-the-great-wave-off-kanagawa-5c12aa88675641d19bdd74cc41406865 (last accessed 14 November 2021).

@nitehawkcinema. 'old meme, still true – A month's worth of weird David Lynch shit begins this weekend with BLUE VELVET on 35mm.' *Twitter*, 3 May 2018, https://twitter.com/nitehawkcinema/status/992101697710379023/photo/1 (last accessed 14 November 2021).

Trae, Dozier. 'If David Lynch directed *Dirty Dancing . . .*' *dailymotion* November 2016, https://www.dailymotion.com/video/x2ot4gw (last accessed 14 November 2021).

Part IV

Videographic Criticism of David Lynch's Cinematic Work

Researching Audiovisually: Experiments in Videographic Criticism in David Lynch's *The Elephant Man* and *Blue Velvet*[1]

Liz Greene

In '*La Caméra-stylo*: Notes on Video Criticism and Cinephilia', Christian Keathley draws out the tension between the explanatory and poetic mode in the production of digital film scholarship. Keathley (2011: 181) writes 'it is language in that mode (spoken and written) that guides it. Images and sounds – even when carefully and creatively manipulated in support of an argument – are subordinated to explanatory language'. This definition of the explanatory register aligns somewhat with what Bill Nichols describes as the expository mode in documentary film, that which 'emphasizes verbal commentary and an argumentative logic' (ibid.: 31). However, as Keathley asserts, the explanatory mode also incorporates written text on–screen. Keathley suggests that works in the poetic register 'resist a commitment to the explanatory mode, allowing it to surface only intermittently, and they employ language sparingly, and even then as only one, unprivileged component' (ibid.: 181). Keathley, an early advocate for videographic criticism, has highlighted the unruly tendency of audiovisual material to 'not willingly subordinate themselves' to critical authority, instead posing further questions for the digital film critic (ibid.: 190). In this chapter, I will illustrate where some of the tensions lie between the poetic and explanatory modes and will extend this to include a discussion of the 'exploratory' mode in videographic criticism when considering five audiovisual essays I made about *The Elephant Man* (1980) and *Blue Velvet* (1986).

By the exploratory mode I am referring to 'research that is not explicitly intended to test hypotheses (as in basic research) nor to solve practical problems (as in applied research) but is used to make initial forays into unfamiliar territory when studying new or poorly understood phenomena' (Oxford Reference, n.p.). I am adopting the term exploratory broadly to encompass speculative research which describes some of the audiovisual essays I have created. The combination of images, sounds and text in the audiovisual essay allows a researcher to 're-imagine the very relationship between a cinematic object of study and critical commentary about it'

(Keathley 2011: 190). Catherine Grant later labelled this a form of 'material thinking' (Grant 2014: 49–62). Developing on the work of Keathley and Grant, I will explore how videographic criticism offers a more rigorous audiovisual process for research than traditional scholarly methods and will also argue that this form of research production offers a broader opportunity for the dissemination of research.

All five of the audiovisual essays I will discuss are the result of experiments in form: form that follows content, and form that follows process. *The Elephant Man: an audiovisual essay* (2015, 3 minutes) is in the explanatory mode and documents some of the gaps in film history around the post-production process for the film. This audiovisual essay uses archival sound effects recordings and interview material to highlight a tension when the English film crew potentially cut an alternative soundtrack for the film, believing that David Lynch would be later fired from the project. This early audiovisual essay would subsequently be developed into the later work, *The Elephant Man's Sound, Tracked* (2020, 25 minutes). *Velvet Elephant* (2015, 3 minutes) presents a comparison of the opening sequences of *The Elephant Man* and *Blue Velvet* exploring the asynchronous approach to the film that illustrates Lynch's rhythmic technique in his filmmaking practice. This audiovisual essay poetically uses split-screen technology to make its argument. *Do it for Van Gogh* (2018, 10 minutes) questions Dorothy's (Isabella Rossellini) subjectivity in *Blue Velvet*, unpicking both point of view and point of audition, this audiovisual essay reframes the gaze with two moments when Dorothy's look back to camera threatens the patriarchal order. *Do it for Van Gogh* is in the explanatory mode, but not firmly so, as its conclusion is speculative and more in keeping with the exploratory mode. Using the poetic mode, *Dorothy, Isabella, Dorothy* (2018, 4 minutes), an accompanying audiovisual essay to *Do it for Van Gogh*, uses slipped sound, archival sound effects recordings, archival film footage, and stargazing software to offer a speculative position of Isabella Rossellini as star performer, a star in a relationship with the director of the film, and a star who is problematised by her on- and off-screen presence, through the manipulation of sound and image. My most recent audiovisual essay, *The Elephant Man's Sound, Tracked*, offers a speculative reason for the omission of a gasp of breath in *The Elephant Man* drawing on interviews, archival research and audiovisual analysis. This audiovisual essay is in the exploratory mode.

The production of these five audiovisual essays was prompted by two distinct research phases. Firstly, my PhD research (2004–8) into *Sound Mountain*, a sound effects library housing the work of Alan Splet and Ann Kroeber, key collaborators of Lynch. Secondly, my attendance at a two-week videographic essay workshop at Middlebury College, Vermont,

USA in June 2015, which led to the development of my research practice in this medium and the production of these audiovisual essays over the subsequent five years.

Research Background – First Phase

I began my research into the *Sound Mountain* sound effects library after contacting Kroeber in 2004. She is the curator of this archive of sounds which contains her and her husband Splet's sound effects recordings. He worked with her until his premature death in 1994 after a long battle with cancer. She has continued to work as a sound designer and sound effects recordist. Splet worked closely with several filmmakers but is most celebrated for his collaborations with Lynch. He worked on *The Grandmother* (1970) and *Eraserhead* (1977), and he and Kroeber worked on *The Elephant Man*, *Dune* (1984) and *Blue Velvet*, although she only received a film credit on *Blue Velvet*.

On a week-long visit to the *Sound Mountain* archive in Berkeley, California, USA, in March 2005, I got an overview of what was contained within the library. When I visited the archive for a month in June 2006 the whole library had not yet been digitised. Kroeber reckoned about 75% had been converted from ¼-inch reels to digital sound files. I had access to only the digitised version of the library, so my research was restricted to what was available at that time. I spent the month accessing the Pro Tools files (Digital Audio Workstation), listening to all the sounds for *The Elephant Man*, *Blue Velvet*, *Dune*, and films by other filmmakers, *The Black Stallion* (1979), *Never Cry Wolf* (1983), *The Mosquito Coast* (1986), and *The Unbearable Lightness of Being* (1988). I cross-checked these sound effects files with the written catalogues where they were available and with the Excel sheets from the library. I made notes of particularly interesting sounds, repetitions of sounds, and miking and processing techniques highlighted in the recordings, noting what I could of Splet's methodology.

As I was about to leave Berkeley, Kroeber offered me a copy of the entire digitised sound library. I signed a contract with her to use the sound library for research purposes only. Getting a copy of the library changed my PhD focus, as now I had access to the original sounds created for the films that Splet and Kroeber had worked on. I no longer had to rely entirely on the finished films but could access the sound effect recordings and edited, processed, and manipulated sounds to ascertain Splet's techniques and his contribution to the overall soundtrack. Since getting a copy of the archive I have continued to research the individual sounds that went into creating the overall sound design for many films that Splet worked on. The ability to access the archive has guided the choice of films I examined for my PhD, as some films are better represented than others in the library, while some soundtracks are completely absent. For example, Lynch's *The Grandmother* and *Eraserhead* are absent from the catalogue and sound archive.

In my PhD thesis, I considered Splet's working methods with four filmmakers– Lynch, Carroll Ballard, Peter Weir and Philip Kaufman – as these were the more significant collaborations in his career. I wrote about two films made by each of these directors. For the purposes of this chapter, I will draw on my research into Lynch and briefly outline what were the key themes to emerge from my archival research on *The Elephant Man* and *Blue Velvet*. In the thesis I wrote about what was contained within the archive for *The Elephant Man*, detailing Splet's approach to recording organic sounds, voice, music, noise, silence and the limitations of terminology for film sound. For the *Blue Velvet* section, I wrote about Splet's approach to recording atmos sounds whilst Kroeber was recording the location sound. I discussed the more conventional sound design for the film, location sound recording, ADR (automated dialogue replacement), what was in the archive, noise, and voyeurism and eavesdropping. As can be seen from what is outlined here there is an overlap in my focus and attention to specific sounds and approaches. The most sustained sections of writing on both films were to do with Lynch's asynchronous approach to these films. Asynchrony refers to image and sound that are out of time with each other. I will come back to discuss this in detail later when outlining the outcomes of the videographic workshop and what this earlier research later prompted me to create.

Research Background – Second Phase

In 2015, I was fortunate to participate in a two-week 'Scholarship in Sound and Moving Image: Workshop in Videographic Criticism' at Middlebury College, funded by the National Endowment for the Humanities. This workshop was led by Christian Keathley, Jason Mittell and joined by Catherine Grant for the second week. In preparation for the workshop, the participants were asked to bring along two media texts to work on, I brought *The Elephant Man* and *Blue Velvet*. The workshop is structured around a series of exercises each day of the first week and then in the second week the participants work towards a draft of a project that they continue to work on after the workshop. In the first week I worked solely on *The Elephant Man* and created homework exercises for each assignment. The voice-over homework became my first piece, *The Elephant*

Man: an audiovisual essay. As mentioned above, I would later significantly rework and expand upon this material to make *The Elephant Man's Sound, Tracked*.

In the second week of the workshop, I turned my attention to *Blue Velvet* and, in trying to refamiliarise myself with the material, I decided to rework an earlier assignment, called the videographic epigraph (inspired by the work of Grant), which uses text dynamically on-screen with audio-visual material. This exercise would later prompt my audiovisual essay, *Do it for Van Gogh*. During the workshop I also re-read my PhD thesis chapter on Lynch and decided to look at the opening of the two films in split-screen. This became my audiovisual essay, *Velvet Elephant*. As is clear from what I produced during the workshop and what I was to make subsequently, this was an enormously generative process for me. The productive and creative time spent at the workshop led to discoveries within my own research, which I will detail below. I will discuss each of these audiovisual essays to unpick what this methodological approach brings to the study of Lynch, the archive and, more broadly, film studies.

The Elephant Man: an audiovisual essay

The second assignment set during the first week of the workshop was a voice-over exercise. Each assignment had strict parameters attached, and for this exercise we were to use one continuous film sequence (no longer than 3 minutes duration) and audio from the film, and then record, edit and mix a voice-over to accompany it. I chose a sequence from the film where there was limited dialogue which I knew would support the addition of voice-over. The sequence I chose was the scene when Treves (Anthony Hopkins) walks through the streets of London in search of Merrick (John Hurt), which culminates in him meeting Bytes (Freddie Jones) for the first time. I was prompted to tell a story of Splet's difficult post-production process for this exercise, as I thought this would make for a compelling story for the assignment. Thankfully, alongside the two films I was working on I had also brought my external drive with the sound effects archive and other research materials I had gathered during my PhD.

Each day at the workshop we worked in crit groups and together looked at the previous day's assignment. In my small group I received feedback on this piece, which was illuminating to me. One member of the group said that they did not know what the different sound effects were in my audio-visual essay and wondered whether I should attach some visual information to make this more explicit. This surprised me as I had taken for granted my background in sound recording, and I had mistakenly assumed that everyone would understand how recordings are idented with a reference tone. At the time, I remember thinking that what was being suggested was not how I wanted to present my work. I was leaning more towards the poetic mode and felt a more explanatory piece would undermine the story-telling capacity of the work. However, I subsequently shifted my position on this and five years later would create an expanded piece that does use an exploratory approach to the visualisation of the sonic elements in *The Elephant Man's Sound, Tracked* in order to underline the argument being set out. This initial peer feedback session was an important part of the process when it came to developing the project later on.

The Elephant Man's Sound, Tracked

Over time I returned to this project with a view to extending the argument and subsequently created *The Elephant Man's Sound, Tracked.* This audiovisual essay sets out to investigate the clean-up of a line of dialogue, 'I am not an animal, I am a human being, a man, a man', in *The Elephant Man*, and explores the possibility of an alternate soundtrack or even picture edit being cut for the film, which was the central point of the earlier audiovisual essay. Through archival research, interviews, close textual analysis and videographic criticism, I proposed that the relationship between Lynch, Splet and the local English crew on *The Elephant Man* offers a significant case study in critical post-production studies. This audiovisual essay concludes with a reflection on a moment in 1980 when the role and title 'sound designer' was just coming into use – prior to *The Elephant Man* it had been used on *Apocalypse Now* (1979) – and posits that there were significant tensions during post-production on *The Elephant Man* due to the workflow encompassing both unionised and non-unionised personnel.

In the *Sound Mountain* archive, I discovered location/production sound that was atypical for a sound effects library. This led me to consider what it was doing there and prompted me to pursue a line of enquiry that revealed an unexplored post-production history. For several reasons (which are explored in the audiovisual essay) I was unable to track this alternate cut of the film and in 2008, when I was writing up my PhD thesis, it meant that at that point of my research I had to drop this line of investigation. As mentioned previously, I began thinking about these issues again in 2015, when I attended the workshop at Middlebury College. What emerged from the short voice-over assignment prompted me to reconsider my earlier research and I began to slowly investigate this abandoned story, whilst getting on with other research projects.

As my ideas for a critical post-production study of *The Elephant Man* germinated, I began to teach and write about *The Elephant Man*. In 2016, I published 'The Labour of Breath: Performing and Designing Breath in Cinema' in a special issue of *Music, Sound, and the Moving Image* (*MSMI*) entitled *Breath and the Body of the Voice in Cinema* (which I co-edited with Ian Garwood). Here, alongside an analysis of Philip Kaufman's *Rising Sun* (1993), I considered the breathing performance of John Hurt as Merrick in *The Elephant Man*. In my article I touch upon the clean-up of the line of dialogue, 'I am not an animal. . .' but, I do not go into detail about the absence of a gasp for breath from that line of dialogue, which subsequently became the starting point for this audiovisual essay. The absence of a discussion of this gasp for breath is a consequence of the limitations of writing about sound, it is particularly difficult to write about the absence of a sound when there is no point of comparison. The inherent strength of the audiovisual essay is to be able to focus on a singular object of study and, through repetition, draw attention to that detail or its absence.

Following on from my *MSMI* article, I wrote a short pedagogical piece, '(Not) Teaching *The Elephant Man*', which was published in *The Cine-Files* in 2017. This article was based on a class I taught in 2015/16 where I asked postgraduate students to replace the soundtrack for a scene from *The Elephant Man* with two new soundtracks, a traditional period soundtrack and one that would represent the sonic style of an auteur. I was interested in teaching production history through practice, but I was also seeking out a hypothetical alternate cut of the soundtrack that I could not access. This teaching exercise nudged me to pursue this post-production story and to see what components of *The Elephant Man* soundtrack I could track down.

Further prompts came when I was invited by Eric Dienstfrey and Katherine Quanz to join them and Julie Hubbert at the 2019 Society for Cinema and Media Studies (SCMS) annual conference on a panel entitled 'Disquieting Labor: The Battles of New Hollywood Audio Workers'. There, I presented the paper '(Re)placing Sound: Postproduction tensions during the making of *The Elephant Man*'. The panel's focus on labour issues and the transition to New Hollywood workflows helped me to further formulate some of the issues I was working through within this project. My research raised questions about the nature of studio structures in England, Hollywood and the Bay Area, and the tensions that were present when the (new) sound designer credit was introduced within a unionised post-production workflow. In early 2020, I presented a revised version of that paper at the University of St Andrews, and I realised, through the process of putting audiovisual materials together for that presentation, that this research should be presented as a lengthier audiovisual essay.

I took my research back to the classroom and began to make this audiovisual essay whilst teaching an undergraduate class in 2020. On this audiovisual essay module, I choose an object of study to work on alongside the students. This facilitates sharing and creates an opportunity to carry out structured research while teaching. I received feedback on a weekly basis from the class as we presented our audiovisual essay homework to each other. Whilst considering a structure for this audiovisual essay I was inspired by the approach taken in the seven-chapter podcast series, *S-Town* (2017), with its use of non-linear temporal jumps. I wanted to present my research in a similar vein, one where the narration weaves between different times to tell a story, this structure reflected my research journey. After I completed a rough draft of the audiovisual essay for my class, I reached out to fellow scholars to get their feedback. This feedback process has been the most extensive I have received to date, and I am indebted to my students and peers for their careful audioviewing of the work, as they each helped to shape and inform further drafts of the audiovisual essay.

I am detailing this 'slow' research process here not to suggest that my audiovisual essay is a translation of the sum of research undertaken and written about in these spaces, but rather to suggest that it is a working through of these ideas afresh or, as Eric Faden posits, to 'suggest possibilities' with the research presented. In 'A Manifesto for Critical Media', Faden (2008: 3) asserts:

> The traditional essay is argumentative – thesis, evidence, conclusion. Traditional scholarship aspires to exhaustion, to be the definitive, end-all-be-all, last word on a particular subject. The media stylo, by contrast, suggests possibilities – it is not the end of scholarly inquiry; it is the beginning. It explores and experiments and is designed just as much to inspire as to convince. (Faden 2008: 3)

The Elephant Man's Sound, Tracked in many ways feels close to what Faden labelled the media stylo, in that it lays bare all the gaps in audiovisual evidence, archival documentation, and in film personnel's recall and willingness to disclose information in order to construct a post-production history that challenges traditional truth claims. It presents the research in the spirit of a beginning, and not just a beginning to this research but as beginning into what John T. Caldwell describes as the "slippery territory" of critical production studies (Caldwell 2009: 172). The audiovisual essay is in the exploratory mode, a mode of research and presentation of research that looks to discover through argument the extent of the known, the unknown and the unknowable.

Velvet Elephant

During the second week of the workshop, I turned my attention to Lynch's asynchronous approach to filmmaking. In my thesis, I had considered Lynch's films as separate entities and had written different passages on the asynchronous approach taken in *The Elephant Man* and *Blue Velvet*, my conclusions drew from these films in isolation from each other. My approach was traditional within Film Studies, using close textual analysis when analysing the films, and this was supported by discussing writing about sound and Lynch from authors such as Michel Chion, Gustavo Costantini, Todd McGowan, Kenneth C. Kaleta, Chris Rodley, Lisa Vincenzi and Paul A. Woods. I detailed the specific sounds and images in both films and much of my attention was placed on how sound and image deviated from each other.

The use of asynchronous sound is one of the key methods Splet and Lynch used to create a surrealist world in their film collaborations. This approach imbued the films with affect and meaning. I interviewed Lynch in 2007 and it is important to stress that he disagrees with my use of the term asynchrony. Rather he contends:

> It has to feel correct, if it's wrong it breaks it, and you go out of the picture, you go out of the world. If it's right, you feel it, and you feel it, not just a feeling but it is intellectually satisfying and it says something bigger than what's there in the picture. It's real, real important. I say sometimes it's more than 50% of the thing, but sometimes it's 40%. But sound and picture go together and that's cinema. . .For sure, it can make seventeen new meanings, abstractions, you know the world is filled with abstractions, cinema can say those things and so what you can conjure with the language of cinema is something that can't be said except by poets maybe with words. And yet people feel it and understand it intuitively. But how did it get there, it is a combo of all these elements going together. (Greene 2007)

For Lynch, the sound must feel right for the picture, and vice versa, he does not consider that a sound would work asynchronously or against an image. This is interesting, as this leaves Lynch with a completely open sound palette. If there is no sound that automatically would go with an image, then there is also no sound that would not go with an image. He does not consider, for example, the sound of elephants roaring accompanying the image of a woman's face as a use of asynchrony, rather that these sounds go with the picture. Conceptually Lynch is in fact using an asynchronous approach to the soundtrack, but because he does not conceive of it in that way, he becomes free to use whatever sound feels right for the picture. Lynch more freely uses asynchrony because the very premise of the idea is one that he does not accept. For Lynch, any sound, if it feels right, should work with the picture. However, so many directors take a literal approach to the soundtrack and would find it inconceivable to have the sound of elephants roaring with the image of a woman's face. The freedom Lynch possesses in not considering image and sound that are bound together is what allows him to be such a creative director.

When I was initially researching *The Elephant Man* I heard and saw how the opening and dream/nightmare sequences spoke to and answered each other, what opens as asynchronous becomes synchronous within the nightmare world of Merrick. Following the logic of the film, it made sense to analyse these scenes together. In my thesis, I included screenshots of the two scenes, the numbering here indicates that there were earlier images in the thesis, but these are all the screenshots for these two scenes that I created (see Figures 12.1 and 12.2). I have included the screenshots from the thesis so that I can illustrate what my process was then and what has changed through my engagement with videographic criticism.

Opening Sequence

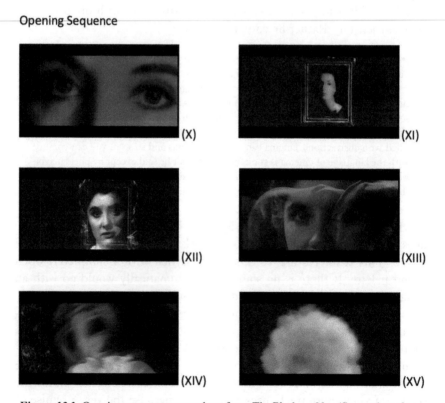

Figure 12.1 Opening sequence screenshots from *The Elephant Man* (Screenshots from *The Elephant Man*, Blu-ray, © StudioCanal)

Nightmare Sequence

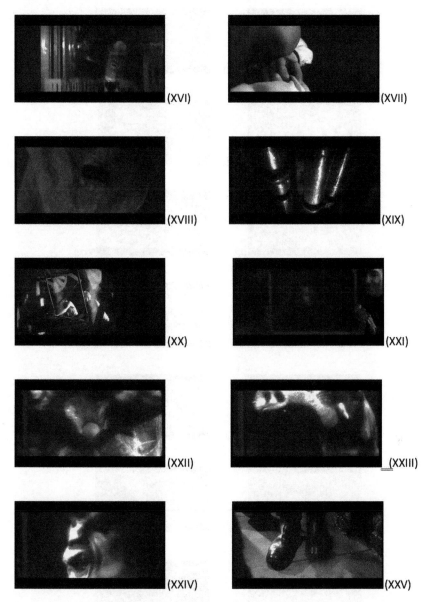

Figure 12.2 Nightmare sequence screenshots from *The Elephant Man* (Screenshots from *The Elephant Man*, Blu-ray, © StudioCanal)

The screen shots helped me to describe these scenes and illustrate what is going on in terms of sound and image. I followed this approach with opening sequence of *Blue Velvet* to enhance my argument (see Figure 12.3).

Opening Sequence of *Blue Velvet*

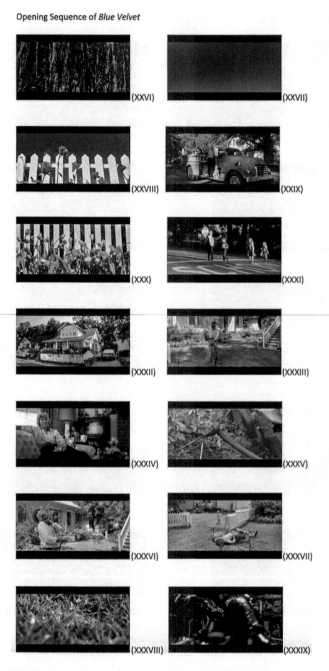

Figure 12.3 Opening sequence screenshots from *Blue Velvet* (Screenshots from *Blue Velvet*, Blu-ray, © MGM)

When I was working with *Blue Velvet* during the second week of the workshop, I had an idea: I would cut the opening sequence for the film and the opening of *The Elephant Man* to see what I might discover. I was immediately excited as I noticed there was just a one second difference in the duration of both openings. It was at that point that I thought I should experiment with the material and put them into split-screen in my timeline in Adobe Premiere Pro to see what they looked and sounded like. I scaled the images to fit both screens in the display and hit play. I was amazed by how well the sound and music played out together, John Morris's score with Bobby Vinton's song seemed to work seamlessly, although stylistically they were very different. Splet's sound design also worked alongside the music, and it was possible to differentiate the sonic nuances of both opening sequences.

What was most unexpected were the moments of synchrony in an experiment to explore asynchrony. When Bobby Vinton sings 'Bluer than velvet were her eyes' we see both Merrick's mother (Phoebe Nicholls) and Jeffrey's mother, Mrs Beaumont (Priscilla Pointer) onscreen, Merrick's mother's eyes are seen in close-up as we also see a superimposed image of elephants pass in front of her at 54 seconds (see Figure 12.4).

At 1 minute 21 seconds an elephant's trunk is seen sweeping in the air as Jeffrey's father, Mr Beaumont (Jack Harvey) reaches for his neck whilst he is watering the garden. The movement of the elephant and Mr Beaumont and Mr Beaumont's gesture to his neck and the water hose are a loose graphic match to the image of the elephant (see Figure 12.5).

Figure 12.4 Screenshot from *Velvet Elephant* at 54 seconds (Screenshots from *The Elephant Man*, Blu-ray, © StudioCanal and *Blue Velvet*, Blu-ray, © MGM)

Figure 12.5 Screenshot from *Velvet Elephant* at 1 minute 21 seconds (Screenshots from *The Elephant Man*, Blu-ray, © StudioCanal and *Blue Velvet*, Blu-ray, © MGM)

At 1 minute 24 seconds both Merrick's mother and Mr Beaumont collapse on the ground, writhing in pain. The look of these two visual images is powerful and striking. At this moment I realised there was a profound rhythmic and narrative correlation between the two opening sequences (see Figure 12.6).

At 1 minute 35 seconds an elephant can be seen and through shot-reverse shot we perceive that the elephant is looming over Merrick's mother. At the same time a dog is drinking water and barking on top of Mr Beaumont (see Figure 12.7).

At 2 minutes 6 seconds we can see a cloud of smoke on *The Elephant Man* screen and close details of ants scurrying underground in *Blue Velvet*. The images diverge from each other here, but I consider them a moment of synchrony as they are both abstract images that lead us out from the opening sequence/overture into the film proper (see Figure 12.8).

The final image on-screen is textual information outlining my approach to the audiovisual essay at 2 minutes 30 seconds (see Figure 12.9).

In this final screenshot I indicate that I placed the films in split-screen and did not alter anything else in relation to the sound or image. I allowed the two opening sequences to play out, the only adjustment I made was to the scale of both images, setting them both at 50% for a side-by-side comparison. The final sentence from the text on-screen, 'What was discovered through this simple act of placing both films together was rather revealing', illustrated my approach at that time which was in the poetic mode. It appears to me now that I was reluctant to write anything substantial here, instead wanting the audience to make up their own minds about what they have audioviewed.

Figure 12.6 Screenshot from *Velvet Elephant* at 1 minute 24 seconds (Screenshots from *The Elephant Man*, Blu-ray, © StudioCanal and *Blue Velvet*, Blu-ray, © MGM)

Figure 12.7 Screenshot from *Velvet Elephant* at 1 minute 35 seconds (Screenshots from *The Elephant Man*, Blu-ray, © StudioCanal and *Blue Velvet*, Blu-ray, © MGM)

Figure 12.8 Screenshot from *Velvet Elephant* at 2 minutes 06 seconds (Screenshots from *The Elephant Man*, Blu-ray, © StudioCanal and *Blue Velvet*, Blu-ray, © MGM)

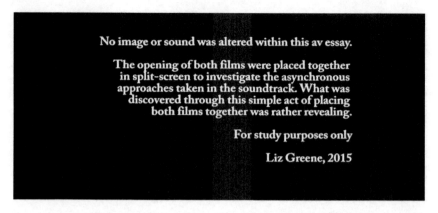

No image or sound was altered within this av essay.

The opening of both films were placed together
in split-screen to investigate the asynchronous
approaches taken in the soundtrack. What was
discovered through this simple act of placing
both films together was rather revealing.

For study purposes only

Liz Greene, 2015

Figure 12.9 Screenshot from *Velvet Elephant* at 2 minutes 30 seconds

Through videographic criticism I was able to learn more about my object of study than was previously possible through close textual analysis. The placement of both films into the timeline opened the films up to me in ways I could never have anticipated, although my instinct from my earlier research was pushing me in this direction. When I first audioviewed this piece within Adobe Premiere Pro, I began to cry. These were tears of release, with a profound sense of discovery which was unlike any other academic discoveries I have made about my work. I was overjoyed to see and hear how these films aligned. Lynch and Splet were working on me and I felt overwhelmed on my first audioviewing. I went into this research with a concept of how asynchrony was operating in each individual film and came away with a discovery of synchrony between the films that spoke to Lynch (and Splet's) audiovisual aesthetic. It is important to point out that I looked at the rest of the openings of Lynch's films whilst at the workshop and none of them chime like these two films do. However, I subsequently discovered that two films that Splet worked on with the director Carroll Ballard, *The Black Stallion* and *Never Cry Wolf*, also have sequences that synch up in similar ways, I have included this moment of synchrony in *Looking Across the Abyss: Human/non-human animal* (2019). Splet was the only common denominator on all four of these films and there are specific approaches in his soundtracks that lend themselves to this type of synchronised listening.

Velvet Elephant was uploaded to Vimeo on my return from the workshop at Middlebury College. I didn't feel that there was much to say about the piece, believing instead that the audiovisual material made the argument for me, so I chose to release the piece without a written accompaniment. Soon afterwards I was contacted by Max Winter at *IndieWire* who wanted to embed the piece on their website. I agreed to this and Winter (2015) wrote the following commentary on *Velvet Elephant*:

> If I were to say that David Lynch's *Blue Velvet* was a pillar movie of my adolescence, and remains something of a gold standard against which I measure other films, that wouldn't speak very well of me, in some senses. But in other senses, it might. The film is indelible for a number of reasons, chief among them being its opening: there are few films I can think of that start in such a settled way, as if the strange universe we are entering at the story's start has always been there, waiting for us. So, I was delighted to discover this short piece by Liz Greene focusing on *Blue Velvet*'s opening, honing in on its similarity to the opening of *The Elephant Man*, another great Lynch film but one which has not, perhaps, lodged itself in the public consciousness to such a great extent as the later work. Viewed this way, side by side and simultaneously, all sorts of correlations arise: the movements, the visual cadences, even the music . . . Take a look.

This feature in *IndieWire* drew an audience for the audiovisual essay, in fact, this is the most watched audiovisual essay I have made to date. If I were to write a piece about *Velvet Elephant* at the time of making it, I imagine it would have been closer to what is presented in this chapter than to what Winter wrote, but in some ways, Winter's reading of the audiovisual essay indicates that he understood the ambition and revelation of these openings that I wanted to share with an online community. However, my not writing an accompanying text for *Velvet Elephant* leaves this audiovisual essay open to being considered too opaque to be readily accepted as scholarship. Both Jason Mittell and Miklós Kiss reference *Velvet Elephant* when discussing what is videographic scholarship. Mittell (2019) wrote:

> While manipulating footage in Premiere, she discovered uncanny similarities between the timing of sounds and images in the opening sequences of *The Elephant Man* and *Blue Velvet*. The result was *Velvet Elephant*, a juxtaposition of these two sequences that experientially conveys her discovery and enables viewers to watch and hear the parallels between the otherwise quite different films. I would not call the resulting video 'scholarship' per se, as it lacks analysis, argumentation, or context; however, it is most certainly 'research', sharing a discovery that could only be realized through Greene's computational transformation of the two films.

Kiss (2020) argues:

> Liz Greene's 2015 *Velvet Elephant* is among the most powerful examples of the power of videographic tinkering. Even while knowing David Lynch's 1980 *The Elephant Man* and 1986 *Blue Velvet* inside out, Greene probably wouldn't have spotted the bizarre audiovisual overlaps between the opening scenes of the two films– a kind of recurrence that might contribute to the definition of Lynch

as an auteur director – without some playful tinkering with editing software. Her communication of this realization – through a split-screen and superimposed audiovisual juxtaposition of the two opening scenes, published online with the title *Velvet Elephant* – has a clear *intention:* to be an audiovisual essay . . . Although *Velvet Elephant* is, no doubt, a brilliant audiovisual essay, I fully agree with Jason Mittell.

I too would agree with Mittell and Kiss, *Velvet Elephant* is an audiovisual essay based on research and the results are felt and understood, however, as a work firmly in the poetic mode it would need to be accompanied by a written text if it was to be put forward for a peer-reviewed publication as scholarship. I never intended *Velvet Elephant* to be published in this way. Like other short pieces I have made, *Eyebrows* (2020), *The Raging Man – Elephant Bull* (2019), *The Shipping Forecast: the audiovisual poetics of Ken Loach* (2018), *Harry Dean Stanton – The Straight Story* (2017), *Walton Peaks* (2017) and *Atmospheres* (2016), I have released the work on Vimeo and shared the links on social media without presenting them as scholarship. The need for the written or spoken word to accompany poetic works suggests that scholars are not quite ready for this type of approach, or at least not within the gatekeeping process of peer-reviewed publications. I have made a number of other pieces that remain in the poetic mode, but the next piece I had published on Lynch was within the peer-reviewed online journal *NECSUS* and was firmly in the explanatory mode, although with a speculative and an explorative ending.

Do It for Van Gogh: Detecting and Perverting the Audience Position in David Lynch's *Blue Velvet* (1986)

During the second week of the workshop, I chose to work on a videographic epigraph as I was struck by a quotation from Elisabeth Weis, in her chapter 'Eavesdropping: An Aural Analogue of Voyeurism' which outlines the role of eavesdropping in the cinema:

> Movie eavesdropping raises issues having to do with the nature of the medium itself. For one thing, it can foreground, as does voyeurism, the way in which cinema seems to invade privacy – the way all of film drama feels overheard and spied on. Like voyeurism, eavesdropping can reflexively question our prying relationship to film, our love of listening in, our complicity with the eavesdropper. When we find the eavesdropping to be central to the diegesis, as in Coppola's *The Conversation*, the device thematises these issues. Eavesdropping is inherently cinematic; as I will argue, the situation requires both audio and visual information and therefore perhaps can be most fully exploited on film. (Weis 1999: 80)

In my thesis I discussed this quote from Weis in relation to Frank (Denis Hopper) as he watches Dorothy at the Slow Club. But when cutting up

Blue Velvet in Adobe Premiere Pro I became interested in the three scenes where we see Jeffrey (Kyle MacLachlan) in Dorothy's closet. I cut all the shots from these three scenes together of Jeffrey in the closet and attached the soundtrack of Dorothy singing at the Slow Club with the text from Weis. Collapsing the audiovisual space between the club and the closet brought Jeffrey, Frank and (our) the audience's eavesdropping into the one space.

I was happy with the results from this exercise but knew there was scope to expand upon it. After the workshop I continued to experiment with the audiovisual material from the closet, layering all the shots from the closet space on top of each other and then expanding the duration of them to the length of the film (2 hours). For teaching purposes, I was editing with Final Cut Pro X (FCPX) at my home institution, and I used FCPX for this process of expanding the footage until the software was unable to handle the time stretching (it produced an inverted video image that took up a small portion of the top right-hand side of the screen). I then moved back to Adobe Premiere Pro for this expansion process. Adobe Premiere Pro was able to handle this task, however, it was unable to handle the stretching of audio, so I took the film into Avid Pro Tools and stretched the audio there. This process, of 'deformative criticism' (McGann and Samuels 1999: 25–56; Mittell 2015) tested the software I was using but finally created some interesting results. The soundtrack created for this feature length version was haunting and terrifying, much in the vein of Lynch and Splet, (see Greene 2012 and 2016b; Hainge 2020) and I thought this could work well within a gallery space.

I was invited back to Middlebury College in 2017 to act as a mentor for graduate students, and it was during this time that I presented my updated work and discussed my approach with my peers. I was prompted by Mittell to look at some software that Kevin L. Ferguson was using in his research (Image-J), and StarStax, both of which are open-source software programmes. I continued to experiment with the form and the deformation process whilst at Middlebury College. However, it was also during this visit that I recut the *Blue Velvet* closet scene as I had obtained a new Blu-ray disc of the film and, thus, wanted the better-quality image and sound from the film. It was with this re-cutting of the scene that I made an accidental new discovery about the closet space in the film (I had been previously cutting the film with my focus on the visual image). Listening to this new cut I could hear hard audio cuts in the closet that allowed the audio to cut from inside and outside the closet with equal clarity. I realised that Lynch and Splet were doing something very interesting here with both point of view and point of audition that was not obvious from other forms of researching the material and that would make for a compelling investigation.

On returning home from the workshop, I received an invitation from Kiss to produce a close analysis of a scene for a special edition of *NECSUS* that he was editing. Kiss's parameters were strict, and they appealed to me, I felt this might be a good fit for my project on *Blue Velvet*. Kiss described what he was looking for in his editorial:

> My aim was to inspire the creation of videographic works that provide straight-forward close analyses of specific scenes of movies – not entire films, not entire œuvres, not poetic associational montages but focused, analytical, exploratory, and explanatory analyses that take advantage of the novel affordances of the audiovisual medium to clearly present, prove, and argue for their observations on a particular – perhaps key – moment of a film. (Kiss 2018)

I created *Do it for Van Gogh* over a period of a few months using some of the deformative experiments that I had worked on at Middlebury College, alongside a more conventional scene analysis coupled with a voice-over that was both explanatory and exploratory. What I discovered during this edit was that, outside of the closet space, in Dorothy's apartment, there were a couple of moments when Dorothy looks at the closet, towards Jeffrey, the camera and us and I realised that there was potential to offer a specula-tive position for Dorothy at the conclusion of the audiovisual essay. This appealed to me as it gave Dorothy agency in a film that I find uncomfort-able and difficult to watch. These discoveries were made in the timeline, whilst cutting the film up, although I had seen the film many, many times before engaging in this editing process.

Laura Rascaroli, in *How the Essay Film Thinks*, has stated, 'Essay films are performative texts that explicitly display the process of thinking; their reflexive and self-reflexive stance implies that issues of textual and contextual framing are at the center of their critical practice' (Rascaroli 2017: 20). Rascaroli's definition, although pertaining more to the essay film than the audiovisual essay per se, is useful here in considering how the explanatory and exploratory modes can collapse within the audiovi-sual essay. *Do it for Van Gogh* sets out to explain the use of point of view and point of audition and does so, but through the journey of the audio-visual essay arrives somewhere else, the patriarchal order is up ended. The transition from explanatory to exploratory modes is critical in this rethinking in *Do it for Van Gogh*.

Dorothy, Isabella, Dorothy

I was delighted to discover these looks from Dorothy in *Do it for Van Gogh*, as I had been working on a companion piece centred on Dorothy, between attending the first workshop and second workshop at Middlebury College.

I presented early versions of *Dorothy, Isabella, Dorothy* at the University of Reading and during my second visit to Middlebury College. This audio-visual essay used the *Sound Mountain* archive and specifically the sounds from the Walla recordings from the Slow Club. Walla is the US term for the sound that extras or background actors make in film. Whilst listening to sound recordings in the archive I felt very close to the production of the film, listening in to what almost sounded like outtakes. At one point you can hear Rossellini ask for another take after she has mimed a singing performance and in this recording we can hear her being denied this request. I found this fascinating, as she is a star, and was a star who was at that time in a romantic relationship with the film's director. It was the discovery of this sound recording in the archive that led me to pursue this project.

Dorothy, Isabella, Dorothy has a feminist perspective. I started the audiovisual essay in the Slow Club using the StarStax software to provide a deformed image of her performance. I then layered the soundtrack of Dorothy's singing voice, slipping the audio by a very small amount towards the end of the song to illustrate that all is not right. The visual imagery then cuts to footage from Peter Braatz's 1988 film *No Frank in Lumberton*. I attached the sound of Walla to this footage, which should appear as if this is synch sound we are listening to, but these are two very distinct and discrete sources. I cut up *No Frank in Lumberton* into very short shots, making Rossellini's vulnerability backstage explicit. The audiovisual essay shifts perspective to consider Dorothy as a character, Rossellini as an actor and then returns to focus on both Dorothy and Rossellini by the end. *Dorothy, Isabella, Dorothy* is clearly in the poetic mode although it uses the archive and behind the scenes footage in its construction, which is more typical within the explanatory mode.

Although I was working on *Dorothy, Isabella, Dorothy* before I started *Do it for Van Gogh*, it feels as if *Dorothy, Isabella, Dorothy* picks up where *Do it for Van Gogh* left off. *Do it for Van Gogh* was published in *NECSUS* in 2018 and I released *Dorothy, Isabella, Dorothy* on Vimeo on the date of publication, packaging them up together. However, *Do it for Van Gogh* has been viewed significantly many more times than *Dorothy, Isabella, Dorothy*.

Conclusion

What can be learnt about Lynch, the archive or film studies more generally through the application of videographic criticism? I made new discoveries about the archive and the films I was studying through the process of bringing the audiovisual material into the editing software. I saw patterns emerge that were not visible to me through close textual analysis. I was able to discover synchrony across Lynch's films from materials that seemed very different from each other. Recognising the filmic approach taken by Lynch seen in the opening of *The Elephant Man* and *Blue Velvet* was not possible until my methodological approach encompassed videographic criticism. As mentioned above, I found similar patterns in Ballard's work, and I would contend that film scholars will make many more discoveries by placing their object of study into an editing timeline, cutting up the material and experimenting with form.

Using videographic criticism as a method of research allows for a new space to make discoveries about an object of study. This approach is highly generative and offers new ways to interrogate audiovisual material. This can lead to increased productivity and further knowledge production. I would argue that this can also be a distraction for a researcher, especially if they already had a clear idea of what they would like to argue. As Keathley has suggested, the audiovisual material does 'not willingly subordinate themselves' to the researcher's agenda (2011: 190). The audiovisual material does not always relent in the ways that we may wish. Certainly, I would never have thought that I would make a piece like *Do it for Van Gogh*. The process of editing the film using the editing software brought up new findings that were not present in my PhD thesis and I felt compelled to follow through with these. As I made discoveries while making *Do it for Van Gogh* it felt like research I had to go through with and make before I was ready to move on to what was closer to my original intentions. Doing videographic criticism revealed new details of Lynch's filmmaking that I was not aware of. It also offered a way for me to think differently about my object of study. Without the material thinking of videographic criticism, I would not have felt it possible to speculate about an actor and character as I do in *Dorothy, Isabella, Dorothy*. Such thinking certainly did not fit with my focus on sound and the archive, it felt liberating to be able to try out different arguments and take different approaches with the audiovisual material.

Although close textual analysis and videographic criticism may seem very similar and are, indeed, natural methodological allies, the significant strength of videographic criticism is its ability to cut up and rearrange audiovisual material allowing shots, clips and sequences to be audioviewed alongside other material that they were never conceived to be arranged with. In some cases bringing a synchronicity to what are asynchronous components. Many audiovisual essayists even do their audioviewing within their editing programmes, marking up and editing material 'on the fly' as they consume screen media. I do not adopt this approach, but I do re-watch screen media within the editing software and make decisions with these later viewings within the editing programme.

For my research into *Sound Mountain*, I found new ways to present the archive allowing me to share my archival research with a broader audience. Facilitating other scholars to see my evidence first-hand is in line with a turn to more open-access approaches within research practice. The dissemination of research also allows for my work to reach a non-academic audience. I imagine many more people have watched my research as audiovisual essays than have read my work as academic journal articles or book chapters. Knowing that my academic labour is not going to be confined or constrained behind paywalls is a compelling reason to engage in this type of research. Even if my research is published in an online peer-reviewed academic journal, it is possible for people to discover this research outside of these spaces, by directly accessing Vimeo content or coming across the work via social media.

Publishing research material about Lynch online can lead to a sizeable audience, Lynch has a ready-made audience and fan base who are keen to consume a range of material about him. This has led me to have online conversations with niche audiences and fans who have knowledge of materials I was previously unaware of. Disseminating videographic criticism online allows the scholar to be reachable and in contact with fan communities. If the object of study already has a lot of interest, then there is great potential for a wide audience.

I have found that the mode of presentation, be that explanatory, exploratory or poetic, has been determined by the material itself. Form follows content and form follows process. I have not yet approached an audiovisual essay with a sense of how I would like to make an argument. The argument gets teased out in the editing software. This may then lead me back to a Word document to write a voice-over or sketch out a plan, but the major decisions are made within the editing programme, often trying out a scratch voice-over 'on the fly' with the audiovisual material in the timeline. I feel led by the audiovisual material in many respects, and feel duty bound to honour the questions the material poses.

I have learned that people tend to have greater capacity to watch short audiovisual essays compared with longer projects. In an online environment there is so much material vying for our attention. My shortest work, *Velvet Elephant* has been the most successful online and I believe its duration is part of the reason for its success. Although *Velvet Elephant* is in the poetic mode, it managed to resonate with a broad audience and, to date, has the most plays and likes on Vimeo of all my audiovisual essays.

That said, my sense, particularly when considering my own output of audiovisual essays, is that work in the explanatory or exploratory modes are generally better received as scholarship within the academy than works in the poetic mode. This, however, does not necessarily translate to a broader audience for the material. A general audience is not as caught up with the definitions of 'scholarship' and is more readily open to poetic approaches. When teaching the audiovisual essay to students I set assignments that allow them this freedom to be poetic, which allows stand-alone work to be uploaded online if they wish to do so. However, within the university context I also require students to present their work as scholarship. For this reason, when I set assignments for my students, they write accompanying papers to make explicit the scholarly intervention their work is producing. I have previously published on my approach to teaching the audiovisual essay in *The Cine-Files* in 2021.

Actively researching audiovisually allows the researcher to experiment with form and make new discoveries about their object of study. Film and media studies will be all the richer if we allow ourselves to research, experiment and play with this emerging form of scholarship. I look forward to learning more about Lynch, and screen media, and from other researchers as this form takes hold within the academy.

Note

1. Earlier sections of writing within this chapter appeared in my PhD thesis 'Alan Splet and Sound Design: An Archival Study' (2008), 'The Labour of Breath: Performing and Designing Breath in Cinema', *Music Sound and the Moving Image* 10:2 (autumn, 2016): 109–33, and '*The Elephant Man*'s Sound, Tracked', *NECSUS: European Journal of Media Studies* (autumn, 2020).

Bibliography

Caldwell, John T. 'Screen studies and industrial "theorizing"'. *Screen*, spring, 50:1, 2009, pp. 167–79.

Chion, Michel. *David Lynch*. 2nd edition, translated by Robert Julian. BFI, 2006.

Costantini, Gustavo. 'David Lynch: Cinema Beyond Time and Space'. *Filmwaves: the Magazine for Low/No Budget Filmmakers and Audiences* vol. 19, 2002, pp. 46–51

Faden, Eric. 'A Manifesto for Critical Media'. *Mediascape: UCLA's Journal of Cinema and Media Studies*, spring, 2008, https://scalar.usc.edu/works/film-studies-in-motion/media/FADEN%20Manifesto%20for%20Critical%20Media_Spring08.pdf (last accessed 2 May 2021).

Grant, Catherine. 'The shudder of a cinephiliac idea? Videographic film studies practice as material thinking'. *ANIKI: Portuguese Journal of the Moving Image*, 1 (1), 2014 pp. 49–62.

Greene, Liz. 'Interview with David Lynch'. Europa Hotel, Belfast, Northern Ireland, 22 October 2007.

Greene, Liz. 'Bringing vinyl into the digital domain: Aesthetics in David Lynch's *Inland Empire*'. *The New Soundtrack*, Edinburgh University Press, 2.2, 2012, pp. 97–111.

Greene, Liz. 'The Labour of Breath: Performing and Designing Breath in the Cinema'. *Music, Sound and the Moving Image*, 10.2, 2016a, pp. 109–34.

Greene, Liz. 'From Noise: Blurring the Boundaries of the Soundtrack', *Palgrave Handbook of Sound Design and Music in Screen Media: Integrated Soundtracks*, Liz Greene and Danijela Kulezic-Wilson (eds). Palgrave Macmillan, 2016b, pp. 17–32.

Greene, Liz. '(Not) Teaching *The Elephant Man*'. *The Cine-Files*, Issue 13, 2017, http://www.thecine-files.com/not-teaching-the-elephant-man/ (last accessed 2 May 2021).

Greene, Liz. 'Looking Across the Abyss: Human/Non-Human Animal'. *The Cine-Files*, Issue 14, spring, 2019, www.thecine-files.com/lizgreene/ (last accessed 2 May 2021).

Greene, Liz. 'Sound and the audiovisual essay, part 1: Dialogue, music, and effects'. *NECSUS: European Journal of Media Studies*, autumn, 2020. https://necsus-ejms.org/sound-and-the-audiovisual-essay-part-1-dialogue-music-and-effects/ (last accessed 2 May 2021).

Greene, Liz. '*The Elephant Man*'s Sound, Tracked'. *NECSUS: European Journal of Media Studies*, autumn, 2020, https://necsus-ejms.org/the-elephant-mans-sound-tracked/ (last accessed 2 May 2021).

Greene, Liz. 'Teaching the student, not the subject'. *The Cine-Files*, Issue 15, 2021. http://www.thecine-files.com/teaching-the-student-not-the-subject/ (last accessed 18 March 2022).

Hainge, Greg. 'When a Door is not a Door? Transmedia to the *n*th Degree in David Lynch's Multiverse'. *Transmedia Directors. Artistry, Industry and New Audiovisual Aesthetics*, Carol Vernallis, Holly Rogers and Lisa Perrott (eds). Bloomsbury Academic, 2020, pp. 271–84.

Kaleta, Kenneth C. *David Lynch*. Twayne Publishers, 1993.

Keathley, Christian. '*La Caméra-stylo*: Notes on Video Criticism and Cinephilia', *The Language and Style of Film Criticism*, Andrew Klevan and Alex Clayton (eds). Routledge, 2011, pp. 176–91.

Kiss, Miklós. 'Videographic scene analyses, part 1'. *NECSUS: European Journal of Media Studies*, spring, 2018, https://necsus-ejms.org/videographic-scene-analyses-part-1/ (last accessed 2 May 2021).

Kiss, Miklós. 'Videographic criticism in the classroom: *Research Method* and *Communication Mode* in scholarly practice'. *The Cine-Files*, Issue 15, fall, 2020, http://www.thecine-files.com/videographic-criticism-in-the-classroom/ (last accessed 2 May 2021).

McGann, Jerome and Lisa Samuels. 'Deformance and Interpretation'. *New Literary History*, 30, no. 1, 1999, pp. 25–56.

McGowan, Todd. *The Impossible David Lynch*. Columbia University Press, 2007.

Mittell, Jason. 'Videographic Criticism as a Digital Humanities Method'. *Debates in Digital Humanities* 2019, dhdebates.gc.cuny.edu/read/4805e692-0823-4073-b431-5a684250a82d/section/b6dea70a-9940-497e-b7c5-930126fbd180 (last accessed 2 May 2021).

Nichols, Bill. *Introduction to Documentary*. 2nd edition. Indiana University Press, 2010.

Rascaroli, Laura. *How the Essay Film Thinks*. Oxford University Press, 2017.

Rodley, Chris (ed.). *Lynch on Lynch*. Faber & Faber, 1997.

Vincenzi, Lisa. 'The Sound of *Blue Velvet*: Director David Lynch, Sound Designer Alan Splet, Composer Angelo Badalamenti, and Sound Crew Tell an "Ear-ie Tale"'. *Millimeter*, November 1986, pp. 121–30.

Weis, Elisabeth. 'Eavesdropping: An Aural Analogue of Voyeurism'. *Cinesonic: The World of Sound in Film*, Philip Brophy (ed.). Australian Film Television and Radio School, 1999, pp. 79–106.

Winter, Max. 'Watch: David Lynch's *Blue Velvet* and *The Elephant Man* have eerie similarities'. *IndieWire*, 27 July 2015, http://web.archive.org/web/20150729025757/http://blogs.indiewire.com/pressplay/watch-david-lynchs-blue-velvet-and-the-elephant-man-have-eerie-similarities-20150727 (last accessed 2 May 2021).

Woods, Paul A. *Weirdsville USA: The Obsessive Universe of David Lynch*. Plexus Publishing Ltd, 2000.

Filmography

Apocalypse Now. Directed by Francis Ford Coppola, performances by Martin Sheen and Marlon Brando, American Zoetrope, 1979.

Blue Velvet. Directed by David Lynch, performances by Kyle MacLachlan, Isabella Rosselini, Dennis Hopper, and Laura Dern, Dino De Laurentiis Entertainment Group, 1986.

Dune. Directed by David Lynch, performances by Kyle MacLachlan and Sean Young, Dino De Laurentiis Company, Estudios Churucusco Azteca, 1984.

Eraserhead. Directed by David Lynch, performances by Jack Nance and Charlotte Stewart, American Film Institute, Libra Films, 1977.

Never Cry Wolf. Directed by Carroll Ballard, performances by Charles Martin Smith and Brian Dennehy, Walt Disney Pictures, Amarok Pictures,1983.

No Frank in Lumberton. Directed by Peter Braatz, 1988.

Rising Sun. Directed by Philip Kaufman, performances by Wesley Snipes and Sean Connery, Twentieth Century Fox, Walrus & Associates, 1993.

The Black Stallion. Directed by Carroll Ballard, performances by Kelly Reno and Mickey Rooney, Omni Zoetrope, 1979.

The Elephant Man. Directed by David Lynch, performances by John Hurt and Anthony Hopkins, Brooksfilm, 1980.

The Grandmother. Directed by David Lynch, American Film Institute, 1970.

The Mosquito Coast. Directed by Peter Weir, performances by Harrison Ford, Helen Mirren and River Phoenix, The Saul Zaentz Company, Jerome Hellman Productions, 1986.

The Unbearable Lightness of Being. Directed by Philip Kaufman, performances by Daniel Day-Lewis, Juliette Binoche and Lena Olin, The Saul Zaentz Company, 1988.

Audiovisual Essays

Greene, Liz (2015) *The Elephant Man: an audiovisual essay*, https://vimeo.com/165701313 (last accessed 2 May 2021).

Greene, Liz (2015) *Velvet Elephant*, vimeo.com/131802926 (last accessed 2 May 2021).

Greene, Liz (2016) *Atmospheres*, vimeo.com/150434511 (last accessed 2 May 2021).

Greene, Liz (2017) *Harry Dean Stanton – The Straight Story* vimeo.com/234111488. Accessed on 2 May 2021).

Greene, Liz (2017) *Walton Peaks*, vimeo.com/232537946 (last accessed 2 May 2021).

Greene, Liz (2018) *Do it for Van Gogh: Detecting and Perverting the audience position in David Lynch's Blue Velvet*, vimeo.com/245270432 (last accessed 2 May 2021).

Greene, Liz (2018) *Dorothy, Isabella, Dorothy*, vimeo.com/256476029 (last accessed on 2 May 2021).

Greene, Liz (2018) *The Shipping Forecast: the audiovisual poetics of Ken Loach*, vimeo.com/258107902 (last accessed 2 May 2021).

Greene, Liz (2019) *The Raging Man – Elephant Bull*, vimeo.com/325461777 (last accessed 2 May 2021).

Greene, Liz (2019) *Looking Across the Abyss: Human/Non-Human Animal*, vimeo.com/316386769 (last accessed 2 May 2021).

Greene, Liz (2020) *Eyebrows*, vimeo.com/480817334 (last accessed 2 May 2021).

Greene, Liz (2020) *The Elephant Man's Sound, Tracked*, vimeo.com/413827977 (last accessed 2 May 2021).

Other Media and Sources Cited

Behnke, Frank and Peter Braatz. 'Alan Splet interview on the set of *Blue Velvet*.' 12 October 1985, CD.

'Exploratory Research' *Oxford Reference* https://www.oxfordreference.com/view/10.1093/oi/authority.20110803095805461 (last accessed 18 March 2022).

Sound Mountain sound effects library www.soundmountain.com/ (last accessed 2 May 2021).

Reed, Brian and Julie Snyder (2017) *S-Town* (Serial &This American Life) stownpodcast.org/ Accessed on 2 May 2021.

CHAPTER 13

A Form that Keeps Unravelling: On David Lynch, Spontaneity and Organic Fluidity in Videographic Essay Production and Academia

Chris Aarnes Bakkane

'We are like the dreamer who dreams, and then lives inside the dream. But who is the dreamer?'

Monica Bellucci, *Twin Peaks: The Return* (Lynch, Frost 2017)

Introduction

It was autumn 2017: the dawn of a new semester, riddled with new challenges. Fresh from my undergraduate studies, I was thrown into a new role as a masters student, and I was reeling with anticipation for the years to come. The academic expectations were higher, and the workload hit me like a brick wall. Although I felt ashamed to admit it, I had never been an academic at heart. I was, and always would be, a Bohemian soul that thrived on creativity and emotions rather than science and logic. But I was pleasantly surprised during a course called 'Outreach and Communication', which served to 'equip the students with the tools to express and share their knowledge and expertise beyond the bounds of academia, and through different forms and genres.' (Norwegian University of Science and Technology 2017). As the course description further elaborates, the aim was to teach students about the various forms of communication in online environments, which included blogs, academic articles, op-eds, and so on. The compulsory assignment consisted of an oral presentation of a project that would form the basis for the exam. When I realised that the exam was quite open for experimentation, I decided to explore the still vastly uncharted territory of the videographic essay with a focus on the aesthetics and filmography of David Lynch.

I had recently watched the television series *Twin Peaks* (1990–1) for the first time and have since been exposed to Lynch's earlier works; his art, his short films and the surreal *Eraserhead* (1977). Lynch appeared to me a visionary postmodern genius who confronted and reconstructed the familiar commercial traditions of filmmaking into something new and exciting. There is no doubt that his films are a direct extension of his art. Film allowed Lynch to add movement and sound to the muteness and static nature of his paintings as well as 'an opportunity to extend beyond their frame.' (Mactaggart 2010: 12). Lynch's particular style of filmmaking, the themes and interpretations of the physical and spiritual world his films presented were intriguing to me, and I soon discovered the sheer extent of academic literature that existed concerning these elements of his filmography.

My aim for this chapter will therefore be twofold: to explore Lynch's aesthetics and themes by way of a personal creative and academic endeavour in producing my videographic essay *In Dreams* (2017), and to touch on the more technical aspects of creating such a project, from its initial conception to its realisation. In Section 1, I attempt to contextualise the thought-process that went into creating my videographic essay. By reflecting on my choices, I intend to delve deeper into the academic discourse and give a brief introduction to various interpretations of David Lynch's filmography. In Section 2, I will go into more detail about the technical aspects of my videographic essay and the editing process. Some questions I consider in this section are: how does videographic essay editing work? Does one need expensive editing software to create an interesting and captivating videographic essay? I also provide a rather detailed description of the elements that make a videographic essay impactful. In Section 3, I will briefly discuss the subject of copyright and fair use, and how these laws may set certain standards (and restrictions) for the future of the videographic essay on platforms such as YouTube. I further discuss false ID content claims and show how YouTube's own guidelines may be weaponised against their creators. I will also show why it is important to be up to date on fair use and copyright law. Finally, I aim to give tribute to the growing and existing academic discourse concerning the videographic essay and how it can be utilised in academic spaces. I recommend available sources one can access to find more detailed information about the videographic essay, both in creating and viewing them. In doing so, I hope to prompt the reader to further explore the various approaches, creative and critical, to understanding audiovisual and videographic criticism.

In Dreams (2017): An Experimental, Poetic Approach to Lynch's Cinematic Dreamscape

There are many ways to construct a videographic essay, and such a wide range of choices makes the digital landscape truly diverse. While many strategies make use of an academic approach, such as structural analysis or comparative analysis of scenes, there is also room for artistic experimentation and exploration. It is possible to present convincing arguments without being well-versed in editing software such as Adobe Premiere Pro or Final Cut Pro. I firmly believe that the aesthetic of a videographic essay can be just as effective in furthering its argument. A strong aesthetic was very important for my own videographic essay, since my aim was to re-create a similar sense of uncanniness and visual disorientation, which Lynch's work can excite in its viewers. While I did not aim for a pure imitation of Lynch's style of filmmaking, it was important that the viewer could recognise certain Lynchian tropes and stylistic choices from each individual film.[1] While the videographic essay has its roots in academia, the development of Internet platforms such as Vimeo and YouTube, and the advances in technology and accessibility of editing software, has made it possible for any artist to 'shoot and edit video, compelling video, on a cell phone'(Bresland 2010).

The thought process in creating *In Dreams* was quite visceral and creative. There was no preliminary written sketch or storyboard, nor was it initially planned. The starting point was my keen interest in Lynch's aesthetic, the narrative themes in his films, and the existential horror the images can produce in its audience. These subjects are not unknown in written academic discourse. Thus, it seemed appropriate to utilise the medium to its full capacity; to show, rather than tell. Neither format, however, seems adequate to fully grasp the various layers of Lynch's works. Lynch rarely explains his intentions behind certain artistic choices. This often leads to discussions and interpretations about authorial intentions. This is addressed in the introduction of *The Cinema of David Lynch: American Dreams, Nightmare Visions* (2004). There Erica Sheen and Annette Davison argue that questions about authorial intention are 'a clichéd address to, perhaps even an accusation of, artistic impenetrability. It implies that any difficulties experienced in understanding an artwork derive from the formal struggle between artist and medium' (Sheen and Davison 2004: 2). As with film itself, the videographic essay can suffer the same difficulties. Interpretations of my own videographic essay have taken on a life of their own outside my preliminary intentions. For me there was nothing inherently academic about my videographic essay. But as fellow students, lecturers and academics viewed and enjoyed the editing and stylistic choices, the videographic essay transformed into an academic exploration of the complex mind of Lynch. The struggle became less between artist and medium, and more about the difficulties between the medium and the viewer: my own artistic intentions were altered into academic discourse, whether it was my intention or not. With this is mind, going back to Lynch's indecisiveness about his work, it becomes clear that interpretations of his films are of particular interest and distress for many of his fans, just like myself. But this is also what fans of Lynch enjoy the most, as memes and video clips of the filmmaker in interviews constantly adorn social media sites like Facebook, Twitter and Reddit. One of the most famous moments is Lynch's reluctance to elaborate on a statement which he made on his film *Eraserhead* that occurred during a 2007 interview in collaboration with the BFI in London:

> LYNCH: [Believe or not] *Eraserhead* is my most spiritual film.
> INTERVIEWER: Elaborate on that.
> LYNCH: No, I – No one sees it that way. Maybe somebody out there does, but . . .
>   It is. (Fernandes 2015)

Many might have grievances with Lynch's reluctance to comment on his dreamlike and often strange worlds and narratives, but this should not deter scholars or audiences from seeking answers. The artist hands us the tools to interpret their work, and it is up to the viewer to utilise said tools and attempt to make meaning of the images on screen. For is it not this that makes Lynch's films and art so compelling in the first place? Sheen and Davison concur that Lynch's work is 'a continuing, unfixed, fluctuating experience' (2004: 4). It is exactly these considerations that became the basis for my own videographic essay.

Initially, I did not have a specific template for my essay. After a short brainstorming I understood that including the entirety of Lynch's filmography would be a fruitless exercise. Instead, I wanted to focus on specific films I had a personal connection to. The list of films was now clear: *Eraserhead* (1977), *Blue Velvet* (1986), *Twin Peaks: Fire Walk with Me* (1992), *Lost Highway* (1997) and *Mulholland Drive* (2001) were the films that would represent Lynch's pantheon in my videographic essay. The document also included a small section dedicated to the various approaches that could be of interest. While not that interesting, I found that phenomenology in relation to film and media studies became an important aspect in my creative choices. Phenomenology is a vast and interesting field, but according to Christian Ferencz-Flatz and Julian Hanich (2016) 'in its contemporary guise, [film phenomenology] has limitations'. The field of film phenomenology felt highly relevant for my project, as it questions the way we experience films not only through our eyes, but also how we 'comprehend and feel films with our entire bodily being, informed by the full history and carnal knowledge of our acculturated sensorium' as theorist and critic Vivian Sobchack (2004: 63) observes. The impact cinema has on its viewers' sensory responses, both in a measurable sense (like eye tracking and other tools, for example) and in the way it touches us metaphorically and on an experiential level, are all important factors that should be taken into consideration. This insight aided me in understanding the language of affect I wanted to incorporate into my work. But I realised that an explanatory or exegetical approach would work against the aesthetic and narrative work of Lynch's films. Also, such an approach would have limited my own design in presenting the intrinsic values Lynch's films incorporate: the enigmatic nature of the sublime and humanity's encounter with it.

There are many other Lynchian themes and keywords that influenced my work: parallel worlds that exist beyond the physical realm, split characters or doubles, sexuality, electricity and what I labelled 'decaying suburbia' or 'decaying Americana'. This specific term derives from the ways Lynch represents American society in his art, the superficial façade that often conceals a deteriorating nature beneath. In his films, this is not only addressed on an aesthetic level, but also by way of a narrative theme: *Eraserhead* presents a desolate and unnerving world, where a previously normed and hegemonic perception of the nuclear family is recontextualised from something covetable into something constrictive. *Blue Velvet* portrays the seemingly joyful small town of Lumberton, NC, that hides dark secrets: here the American idyll of the middle class collides with the American nightmare of the apartment dwellers (see Odell and LeBlanc 2007: 59). *Twin Peaks: Fire Walk with Me* tells the heart-breaking story of a seemingly normal teenage girl who leads a double life. She is driven to madness by nightmares and drug abuse, and eventually dies by her own father's hand. *Lost Highway* recounts the narrative of the jazz musician Fred Madison, whose life is torn asunder by VHS tapes and a mysterious man, who drives him to seemingly murder his wife. *Mulholland Drive* tells the story of an aspiring actress chasing the American Dream, but who is drawn into a strange and dreamlike venture with another woman, trying to navigate the toxic landscape of Hollywood and its double-natured culture. Lynch's attempt to recontextualise and criticise the coveted American Dream and its ideals adds interesting perspectives to the subject of dreams, doubles, and alternative realities, which is often uncannily yet beautifully portrayed in Lynch's cinematic aesthetic. Therefore, my awareness of 'decaying suburbia' or 'decaying Americana' in Lynch's work became a focal point in my project.

The title of my videographic essay is a reference to the track 'In Dreams' by Roy Orbison, which was released in 1963 by the label Monument. This track bears a significant role in Lynch's filmography, despite only being used in the film *Blue Velvet* in the 1980s. Lynch did not obtain authorisation from Orbison to use the song in the film, but Lynch felt the song evoked a specific feeling, that the lyrics

> meant something to him [Orbison]. And it just so happened that a song in a certain situation could mean something else. And the way that Frank Booth used that song in two different places, it is just kind of unbelievable. But I can see why Roy was upset because for him it meant a third thing. (Lehman 2010: 63–4)

But what were Orbison's feelings regarding the use of 'In Dreams'? According to writer and critic Nick Kent (2007: 322) Orbison seems to have been 'initially shocked by David Lynch's interpretation of "In Dreams"'. In an interview conducted by Kent himself in 1988, Orbison agrees to this notion, and elaborates further on his initial feelings:

> Oh God! I was aghast, truly shocked! I remember sneaking into a little cinema in Malibu, where I live, to see it. Some people behind me evidently recognised me because they started laughing when the 'In Dreams' sequence came on. But I was shocked, almost mortified, because they were talking about 'the candy-coloured clown' in relation to doing a dope deal. Then Dean Stockwell did that weird miming thing with that lamp. Then they were beating up that young kid. I thought, 'What in the world?' (Kent 2007: 323–4)

Despite Orbison's initial shock however, Kent surmised that Lynch's usage of the track in 1986 contributed to a regeneration in Orbison's career, and suddenly the 'shy, remarkably wistful man' (Kent 2007: 315–16) was snapped back into the contemporary pop-cultural sphere. In Kent's interview, Orbison seems grateful to Lynch's creativity and cinematic imagination, agreeingly stating that he

> appreciate not only what David gave to the song and what the song in turn gave the film, but how innovative the movie was, how it really achieved this otherworldly quality that added a whole new dimension to 'In Dreams'. I find it hard to verbalise why, but *Blue Velvet* really succeeded in making my music contemporary again. (Kent 2007: 323–4)

While it might be reasonable to empathise with Orbison in regard to loss of creative control of his intellectual property, there is no doubt that *Blue Velvet* reawakened Orbison's career, which had lain dormant since the 1970s. As well as an interesting deep-dive into the life and career of the legendary musician, Kent's interview also invites the reader into the mind of Orbison and his creative process while writing and composing his music. Orbison describes his first experience with 'In Dreams' as a song that was 'given to him' while he was falling asleep. (Kent 2007: 321–2) This would seem a fitting narrative, as the song reflects the sombre and calming effect of being asleep: it is reminiscent of a lullaby. However, the lyrics are pain stricken and heart breaking, and they describe a man whose only way of spending time with the ones he loves is by dreaming of them. I had no intention of using the song in my own videographic essay, since I knew it would be considered copyright infringement. While it is an iconic song, I felt it would be counterproductive as it has already been utilised so appropriately in *Blue Velvet*. Upon taking into consideration the statement by Monica Bellucci from episode 14 of *Twin Peaks: The Return*, the various connotations of Orbison's song, and Lynch's continual use of dreamlike themes and imagery, the title *In Dreams* felt like an appropriate working title for my venture.

My initial idea was leaning towards a more explanatory videographic essay, where the combination of narration and juxtaposition of scenes and sequences would create a cohesive whole. I deemed this somewhat counterproductive in this context. Lynch's narratives and images need to be experienced rather than explained, which would make text and narration excessive. It is not an impossible task, but my visceral reaction and sense of aesthetic could not bring me to be so critical and analytical in this process. This in and of itself could be conceived as unconventional, since a videographic essay is usually quite academic in nature. At the same time this is also why the videographic essay and other audiovisual ways of presenting academic material are so interesting: it is a multimedia form that is still in development, by engaging both scholars and private individuals via the Internet. It is a mixed medium that is influenced by academia and conventional film and editing styles.

The Technicalities

My editing software was Adobe Premiere Pro (version CS3), which is a non-destructive and timeline-based video editing software first launched in 2003. It is a proprietary software, but a free trial to explore the software is available on Adobe's website. The main save file is .prproj for projects, and it is possible to export files and projects in formats such as H.264 AVC, MOV (QuickTime format), WMV (Windows Media, Windows Only), AVI (DV-AVI) and MP4 (QuickTime Movie, XDCAM EX) (see Adobe 2020). Adobe Premiere Pro is a versatile software, and it is very easy to learn basic editing techniques with various media objects. As Keathley and Mittell write in *The Videographic Essay: Criticism in Sound & Image*

(2016), the ways in which Ethan Murphy taught the tools of video production in a 2015 workshop to the participants made all the difference. By creating small assignments to be completed, the participants via practice and consultation were able to manage the first step in videographic essay production: this way 'one learns by doing' (Keathley and Mittell 2016: 5). This autodidactic approach was precisely what I was also following at the time.

This section is not supposed to be a tutorial on how to edit in Premiere Pro. The main goal is to explain my idea and the experience with creating *In Dreams* and videographic essays in general. Since there are various ways of editing, I want to encourage readers to explore and navigate video editing software for themselves. There was no specific reason for choosing Adobe Premiere Pro, this simply was the software I had the most experience with at that time. Other video editing software, such as Final Cut Pro, DaVinci Resolve or iMovie, are also good alternatives to Premiere Pro (although iMovie and Final Cut Pro are exclusively for Apple Mac operating systems). Premiere Pro places a variety of tools at one's disposal. It is possible to customise the interface of the workspace to make it more organised and to fit the user's needs. Other possibilities can be to create bins or other types of assets inside the Project panel in the programme. Having quite limited practical experience in Premiere Pro meant that I had to start navigating and understand the workspace again after many years.

My video editing process began with viewing and studying the material. During my viewings I occasionally took notes of memorable moments or recurring themes I found particularly interesting. At first, the connection between the scenes that I superimposed over each other in the final essay did not matter. It was pure creative experimentation that led to what became the main theme and narrative of my videographic essay. After choosing the main films that would be lain out for analysis and discussion, I imported the content to my computer and into Premiere Pro. There are several ways of acquiring clips or films for a videographic essay: some are legal, but most are illegal. One can get clips from YouTube or other websites, or one can rip DVDs of the films they wish to discuss. Once the films were imported into Premiere Pro, the editing process started fully. Initially, I had to refer to my time stamps so I could edit the parts I wanted to include in my project. This can be an arduous phase of the video editing process, and it is the most time consuming. If you are accurate and alert during this phase of your project, it will prove to be very helpful later in the process. It will cut down editing time and it will be easier to navigate the timeline, which can become quite crowded as you add effects, new sequences, or captions. Even though selecting the scenes and clips can be a tiresome procedure, the 'real' editing starts when you begin to compose the videographic essay by juxtaposing the scenes and clips of your selection. In my case, this was the most creative and experimental phase of the project. This process of the composition depends on the approach each individual feels comfortable with: is it, for example, a scholarly approach that might be viable for publication in a digital journal, or is the approach more reliant on the entertainment value of the medium? In my planning stage, I chose to create an explanatory essay, since it seemed to be the most academic form at the time. As I researched and continually gained more knowledge about the various forms of scholarly and artistic essays, I opted to create something that could bring together the best aspects of the medium, to be academic, creative and entertaining at the same time.

When the first part of the editing process came to a close, the timeline in Premiere Pro was still quite bare, but the scenes from Lynch's films were now superimposed onto each other, with some added transitions to conjoin the scenes. This was the main editing I did of the raw material, as I was still unsure in many ways how the videographic essay would manifest itself in the end. The superimposed scenes and images were suddenly transformed as I put them together, and I was quite surprised by the result. The scenes I used from Lynch's films merged into an almost cohesive narrative: starting as a dream that slowly turns into a nightmare, resulting in an awakening. I assumed this formalistic structure was a part of my subconscious trying to rebel against Lynch's dreamlike and surreal ways of presenting his stories on-screen. Being acclimated to commercial Hollywood filmmaking and storytelling, my mind struggled to construct the videographic essay in the style and tone of a Lynch film that I originally had in mind. Intentional or not, however, the narrative of my videographic essay can be more easily consumed. This may invite and perhaps tempt the viewer to subject themselves to his work in more detail, and to give the viewer a sense of the complex veil of emotions that envelops Lynch's films. This was one of the reasons why I made use of Lynch's own voice. I believed his eccentric way of describing and communicating his creative thought-process would add further context to the dreamlike visuals from his various films. Even though Lynch is famously known for evading questions concerning meaning and interpretation in his films, his perspectives and philosophy on film and art are an intriguing and important addition to the visuals I chose for the videographic essay. The audio is from a discussion Lynch hosted via the American Film Institute in 2001, where he talks about how 'abstract thoughts and intuition can be communicated through filmmaking' (American Film Institute 2009). The first time I listened to this talk, I felt captivated by the way he described abstractions and dreams in such an organic and improvised way. His way of speaking flows naturally, and he is very engaging with his enthusiasm regarding his art. This talk became a crucial part of my project, since it was now the blueprint that would shape my final version of the videographic essay.

Admittedly, the subject of audio and sound editing in videographic essays can vary in complexity. This depends on whether one utilises a voice-over narration or uses a variety of royalty-free sound effects and music. The opening sequence of *In Dreams* is an example of how intricate sound editing can be in certain videographic essays. It consisted entirely of sounds and audio that was intentionally placed to create an ethereal atmosphere, akin to what Lynch experiments with in his own work. The sound consisted of flickering candles, electric lights, heavy breathing and ghostly melodies. Later, I set my focus on electric and organic sounds; of fire, wind and insects, establishing a creepy and lulling sensation that underlines the juxtaposed images on screen. The sound effects and ambient music tracks are all from Epidemic Sound: a digital library consisting of over 32,000 tracks and 64,000 sound effects, including stems, according to their website (Epidemic Sound 2020). While this is a varied and very professional library, Epidemic Sound requires a fee, depending on what kind of licence you choose, ranging from payment each month or per year. It does offer a 30-day free trial, which one can cancel any time, and gives one full access to the various sound effects and original music in any genre. This does, however, present a problem, or at least it did for me. I created my videographic essay during my 30-day free trial and published it to YouTube soon after. I then believed I could cancel the trial and keep the licence to the sound effects and music. Unfortunately, that was not the case. I received a Content ID claim from Epidemic Sound, advising me to put my videographic essay on the private setting or buy a licence for unlimited usage. If I bought a licence, I would still be able to keep the videographic essay on YouTube. My economic situation at that time would not allow me to buy a personal licence, so I had to put my video on private mode. This was very unfortunate, as YouTube is one of the biggest audiovisual platforms with high traction and views. If I had read the terms on Epidemic Sound more carefully or used other royalty-free or Creative Commons libraries, like Free Music Archive, Stock Music Site and Incompetech, *In Dreams* would still be publicly searchable on YouTube and thus much easier to access.

Copyright and Fair Use

There are many considerations to make when creating and publishing videographic criticism. On their website, *Learning on Screen* highlights a section that directly concerns copyright duration, exceptions and licensing schemes. Said section provides a comprehensive guide on 'what you can do with other people's works' and lays out the basic principles for copyright law (Learning On Screen 2020). As the British Universities and Colleges Film and Video Council [BUCFVC] running the website describes, there are a number of exceptions in copyright law that 'allows teachers and students to reuse protected works without permission for educational, research and private study purposes' (Learning On Screen 2020). This topic is also considered in Mittell's essay 'But Is Any of this Legal? Some Notes about Copyright and Fair Use', where Mittell notes that 'there comes a time in any discussion about videographic criticism when the question of copyright comes up' (Keathley and Mittell 2016: 53). Mittell could not be any more correct, especially when stressing that he and other scholars are not lawyers and should not be hailed as the authority on copyright laws . I agree with that notion, as I have neither the experience nor the knowledge to be a figure of authority in this specific field. I will, however, attempt to share good sources for further reading and expand upon my own experiences while making my own videographic essay.

As I understood fair use at the time, within the context of United States copyright law, my videographic essay would fall under the conditions of fair use. As Mittell surmises, fair use is vague by design. Whether videographic criticism violates copyright law or not is based on 'four interrelated factors: the nature of the use (it should be transformative), the nature of the copyrighted work, the extent of the original being used, and the impact the use might have on the market value of the original'(Keathley and Mittell 2016: 54). Mittell further writes that none of these factors overrides the other, and that rather than a simple 'yes or no' answer, they are all evaluated on a spectrum of degrees. Mittell has the same assertion as many other creators of videographic and audiovisual content; that a videographic essay is 'by definition a transformative use of original material, aimed at providing commentary, criticism, and/or parody that fulfils the spirit of fair use' (Keathley and Mittell 2016: 55). Furthermore, Mittell continues, despite the videographic essay being non-commercial and educational, 'some videographic essays have been distributed commercially, as with supplements to DVD releases, so there is no single mandate that fair use must be non-commercial' (Keathley and Mittell 2016: 55). While there are no formalities required for copyright to be granted, there may be instances of false copyright claims on certain online forums or video sharing websites. Having been a passionate consumer of various YouTube content myself since 2008, I have witnessed many cases of false copyright claims against individual creators. Most of the cases end with the removal of videos that violate copyright without further consequences since most of these false copyright claims have no bearing on YouTube's guidelines. Although these types of cases do not cause international debate, nor change YouTube's copyright guidelines, the discussion of the good, the bad and the ugly concerning copyright and fair use still thrives between YouTube creators and consumers. Often, creators on such platforms can experience a false DMCA takedown, and sites such as YouTube have implemented certain systems that enable a copyright owner to use Content ID to make it easy to identify and manage their content. According to YouTube Help, 'copyright owners get to decide what happens when content in a video on YouTube matches a work they own' (Google 2020).

There is no question that companies and artists need to have their works protected in our digital millennium. There are many instances of art theft, plagiarism and blatant illegal reproduction and redistribution of various visual and audiovisual content. Being a visual artist myself I have first-hand experience of plagiarism and art theft by private individuals via various social media platforms. Small cases like mine often get settled privately outside the courtroom, but in other instances there are those who intend to take a case to court in order to bring justice to artists and awareness to the public on the issues of copyright infringement. While some of these issues do not fully extend themselves to the same aspects as creating videographic essays, I feel it is still important to broaden the discussion about why these laws and regulations can be a saving grace for small, independent visual and audiovisual artists, but also how these laws can be abused by companies or infamous Internet trolls. Mittell later warns in his chapter that 'just because legal proceedings are rare does not mean that infringement accusations do not occur in the videographic realm' (Keathley and Mittell 2016: 58). This may naturally deter creators from producing their own audiovisual content. Mittell also asserts that the risks and repercussions for posting a video 'using unauthorised copyrighted material are quite low' (ibid. 58). The most common outcome in these types of cases is that a video is deleted from the platform where it was first published. If this is the case, there are ways to repurpose or re-edit the copyrighted material to make it more transformative for republishing. Still, as a content creator, it is sometimes difficult to navigate the laws and their legal interpretation. In both UK and US copyright law (particularly in relation to the DMCA) there are exemptions, which make it legal for critics, scholars and students to 'override DVD protections to edit clips for scholarly and educational purposes, including videographic criticism' (ibid. 59). There are other exceptions, as described on *Learning on Screen*, where UK copyright law allows one to use copyright-protected material without permission from the copyright owner. However, this does not extend itself to videographic criticism that is published for commercial purposes; 'you could rely on the exception for non-commercial research and private study' (Learning on Screen 2020). Other exceptions include criticism or review, quotation, caricature, parody or pastiche, which is the most common content one would find on an audiovisual video sharing platform.

As previously stated, I did not have many initial thoughts regarding copyright when I created my videographic essay. My reasoning for this is that I did not intend to publish my work on any online platform: I did not think my videographic experiment was worthy of sharing outside my university classes. In the end, I was fortunate that the clips from each film I made use of seemed transformative enough for publication. The commentary provided by Lynch could be of some concern in relation to copyright since I did not ask the American Film Institute for permission for the usage. As I described in Section 2, I received a Content ID notice from YouTube by Epidemic Sound, for not upholding my part of the licensing deal. To reiterate, it is important as a creator to understand licensing agreements, guidelines which a service provides and the according copyright laws.

Further Reading

While the format of a videographic essay is more commonplace in the digital landscape today, the scholarly landscape of the videographic essay is still in its genesis. Academic literature on this field is expanding every year, following the progress and change in both culture and technology. Despite this growth, it was initially a daunting task trying to navigate the academic papers and publications online. In 2017, even though I was producing a videographic essay for a university course, I did not consider the academic aspect of videographic criticism and the audiovisual essay until later. Admittedly, I did not deem it necessary to commit myself to the various papers and writings on the subject. How complicated could it be to create a videographic essay? Are papers, blog posts, books and other writings an essential part of the process? While I will contend that the creative process of producing a videographic essay does not necessarily warrant an academic mindset, it is still important to recognise the scholarly possibilities in producing such content. Creative processes such as storyboarding and editing can be an experimental phase to immerse oneself with film aesthetics and themes. Despite holding that belief, I also recognised that to convey filmic ideas and criticism there had to be a certain academic framework. Although there are a variety of academic sources available online, I found myself struggling to find a comprehensive source oriented around the history and origin of the videographic essay as a form of audiovisual criticism. Reasons for this may differ, but there seems to be no agreed consensus on the origin of the videographic essay. So, during my initial research, I contacted Catherine Grant, a leading audiovisual essayist and author in Film and Moving Image Studies, for some guidance on where to begin my research. She quickly recommended some useful sources that I advise the reader to explore for themselves.

Christian Keathley's chapter 'La caméra-stylo: Notes on video criticism and cinephilia' in Andrew Klevan and Alex Clayton's edited volume *The Language and Style of Film Criticism* (2011) discusses the audiovisual manifestation of criticism and cinephilia. Keathly points to how the love for certain images may lead to a point of fixation, where viewers 'wished to find ways of celebrating them by holding on to them, extending their power, recontextualising and refiguring them' (Klevan and Clayton 2011: 24). With the introduction of the DVD in the mid-1990s, the media carrier made rewatchability more possible, and transformed film criticism. As Keathley writes: 'with new technologies of film viewing and digital manipulation, the cinephilic impulse is revitalised and the 'desire to write' is both facilitated and transformed' (Keathley 2011: 189). Furthermore, the advancements in digital media and technology creates new ways of experiencing older films, like the replayability of a DVD or the freeze-frame, slow-motion and delay. Laura Mulvey (2006: 144) concurs:

> [. . .] with the spread of digital technologies, this kind of fragmentation of film has become easier to put into practice. In this context, textual analysis ceases to be a restricted academic practice and returns, perhaps to its origins as a work of cinephilia, of love of the cinema.

The videographic essay, therefore, can be seen to challenge the written discourse of film studies by inviting the reader or viewer not just to 'move critical discussion into a new presentational context, but to re-imagine the very relationship between a cinematic object of study and critical commentary about it.' (Keathley 2011: 190). Keathley's intriguing argument about the cinephilic nature of the videographic essay is vital to consider when studying or writing critically and academically about audiovisual criticism. The inherent challenges that videographic essays present to literary discourse can change how one perceives and engages in film criticism and reshapes the way in which scholars approach their object of study and analysis.

There is also Peter Monaghan's online survey 'Has the Video Essay Arrived?' (2017) from the website *Moving Image Archive News*. In this survey, Monaghan describes the increased interest in video production and audiovisual film essays. He continues by asserting that fan-created and commentary videos have become a very common 'reflection on feature films, television programming, and other moving-image works' (Monaghan 2017). His approach to the subject is highly educational and clearly conveyed, and Monaghan describes the developments and the various ways in which the audiovisual essay can be portrayed and explored in academic research. The main advantage of the videographic essay, according to Monaghan, is that it engages the creator and the viewer to analyse and 'discover striking aspects of moving-image form and technique'. While the numerous ways of producing a videographic essay are usually contained in specific methods or forms, that does not mean that the approach is set in stone: it is evolving and taking various shapes that give freedom to its creators. As a comprehensive set of templates emerged during the first wave of the videographic essay, there also emerged certain risks of videographic essays being imitations or being closer to illustrated lectures rather than being an experimental way of analysing moving images. Jason Mittell would second this point in his contribution to *The Videographic Essay* (2016).

Mittell's chapter in *The Videographic Essay: Criticism in Sound & Image*, which is a wonderfully informative explanation on how copyright and fair use functions in practice. Mittell cites resources at the end of the chapter that provide a comprehensive view on copyright and fair use. I, along with other scholars, would advise future content creators to be up to date on copyright exemptions in both US and their own national laws. Participating in legal updates encourages content creators, scholars, critics and students to be more aware of the risks involved, while also educating creators on how exceptions can be used as a defence if one's content is challenged by the copyright owners (Learning On Screen 2020). In addition, the website *Learning On Screen's Introductory Guide to Video Essays*'s section on copyright considerations is a helpful tool for understanding the basic principles of copyright law and the stages of video production: from ideas to distribution. Further reading can include a PDF document of the Digital Millennium Copyright Act (which is readily available via Wikipedia), and an article from Stanford

University Libraries called *What Is Fair Use?*, where US Attorney at Law Rich Stim explains the basics of fair use in a very intelligible and comprehensive manner (Stim 2021). In conclusion, I want to convey some parting words from Mittell on the importance of fair use for videographic criticism that resonate deeply with me: 'Fair use has been compared to a muscle that will atrophy if not exercised – and videographic criticism is some of the most vigorous exercise that scholars can offer their fair use muscles' (Keathley and Mittell 2016: 60). With contributions from Catherine Grant, Eric Faden and Kevin B. Lee, *The Videographic Essay: Criticism in Sound & Image* has been an immensely important piece of scholarly work regarding the videographic and audiovisual criticism.

Lastly, I want to bring swift attention to Tiago Baptista's doctoral thesis *Lessons In Looking: The Digital Audiovisual Essay* (2016). As Baptista describes in his abstract, his thesis

> examines the contemporary practice of the digital audiovisual essay, which is defined as a material form of thinking at the crossroads of academic textual analysis, personal cinephilia, and popular online fandom practices, to suggest that it allows rich epistemological discoveries not only about individual films and viewing experiences, but also about how cinema is perceived in the context of digitally mediated audiovisual culture. (Baptista 2016: 3)

His chapters include in depth discussions concerning cinephilia, performative research methodology, ideological implications of the audiovisual essay, and four case studies on David Bordwell ('the absent lecturer' (Baptista 2016: 130)), Catherine Grant ('continuous experimentation' (ibid.: 142)), [sic] ::kogonada ('tautological supercuts' (ibid.: 170)), and Kevin B. Lee ('desktop cinema' (ibid.: 189)). It is important for me to honour this thesis, since Baptista has supplemented intriguing and valuable analyses to the discourse of videographic and audiovisual criticism. It is an important piece of scholarly work, which has found its place in the ever-growing academic and digital landscape of the videographic essay.

Conclusion

Film criticism as a genre has through years of experimentation and innovation increasingly found its footing in academia. While written film criticism is regarded as the genre's founding father, its audiovisual heir has gradually rooted itself in poetic criticism, which touches upon the phenomenological aspect of film more closely than perhaps any other genre may be capable of. The videographic essay can invite us into the object of analysis and envelop us in the narrative, themes and aesthetics of the subject. It aids us in breaking through the cinematic artifice, uncovering the verisimilitude that may exist beneath the surface. I discovered this for myself when creating *In Dreams*, as it made me view and experience Lynch's approach to filmmaking in new ways. Recontextualising Lynch's works and deconstructing their narratives became an almost therapeutic affair, banishing rationality in favour of abstractions and creativity. In an interview with film director and critic Mark Cousins in 1999, Lynch describes his open-minded thinking during the production of the first episode of *Twin Peaks* in 1989, which led to a major change in lore and narrative structure for the series' future. While filming a shot in the bedroom of Laura Palmer (Sheryl Lee), Lynch had a vision of set decorator Frank Silva locked in the room while he was moving furniture. After asking Silva if he was an actor, Lynch urged Silva to take part in the panning shot they were planning to film. At the time, Lynch had no idea what he was going to do with this particular shot, but as he was filming another scene in the Palmer household with actress Grace Zabriskie (Sarah Palmer), they discovered that someone was reflected in a mirror in the scene. Discovering that it was Silva, Lynch knew he discovered something special and took it as a big sign. The frightening figure of Bob was born. These two events, as Lynch surmised, kept unravelling (TaggleElgate 2015). This interview and Lynch's spontaneity in both his direction and creative thinking feel like an almost perfect allegory for my own creative process in creating my videographic essay. Keeping an open mind and being willing to accept outside influences was in my case essential, despite the sometimes stringent disciplines and attitudes present in academic discourse. In the end, my aim for this text, and in turn my videographic essay, was perhaps not only to contextualise my personal creative and academic process in creating audiovisual content. It was also about me realising the academic ability of it and embracing both facets of the digital audiovisual essay: the artistic and the academic. By interweaving the two, I came to understand the deeper epistemological aspects as well as the organic fluidity of the genre of criticism, which led me to understand more of Lynch's way of projecting his inner life and imagination on-screen. If the reader has found anything of academic or creative value in this text, my hope is that whoever is reading it will not be afraid of taking a risk in search of understanding film by utilising videographic and audiovisual resources at their disposal. Perhaps delving deeper into the technical aspects of creating something by themselves will enrich their perspectives on film-making as an art form.

Note

1. It was important to structure and edit my videographic essay in such a way that the viewer could recognise certain tropes from some of Lynch's films. Some important tropes include, but are not limited to: existential horror, suburbia, 1950s aesthetics, Americana, cryptic phrases, eroticism, deformities of the human body, meta narratives, surrealism, doppelgangers, dreamworlds, organic vs. industrial material and electricity.

Bibliography

American Film Institute. 'David Lynch: On Communicating with Film'. *YouTube*, 13 August 2009, www.youtube.com/watch?v=nVE8dDOpiPw (last accessed 7 November 2021).

Baptista, Tiago. *Lessons In Looking: The Digital Audiovisual Essay*. Online Repository of Birkbeck Institutional Theses, University of London, 2016, bbktheses.da.ulcc.ac.uk/215/ (last accessed 7 November 2021).

Bresland, J. 'On the Origin of the Video Essay'. *Blackbird: an online journal of literature and the arts*, vol. 9, no. 1, 2010, http://blackbird.vcu.edu/v9n1/gallery/ve-bresland_j/ve-origin_page.shtml (last accessed 7 November 2021).

Elsaesser, Thomas and Malte Hagener. *Film Theory: An Introduction through the Senses*. Routledge, 2010.

Ferencz-Flatz, Christian and Julian Hanich. 'Editor's Introduction: What is Film Phenomenology?' *Studia Phaenomenologica*, vol. 16, 2016, pp.11–61.

Gonçalo Fernandes. 'The 2007 David Lean Lecture Given by David Lynch'. *YouTube*, 23 December 2015, www.youtube.com/watch?v=0eN4rpDDg1M (last accessed 7 November 2021).

Keathley, Christian and Jason Mittell. *The Videographic Essay: Criticism in Sound & Image*, Caboose, 2016.

Keathley, Christian. 'La Caméra-Stylo: Notes on Video Criticism and Cinephilia'. *The Language and Style of Film Criticism*, Andrew Klevan and Alex Clayton (eds). Routledge, 2011, pp. 176–91.

Kent, Nick. *The Dark Stuff. Selected Writings on Rock Music, New and Updated Edition*. Faber and Faber, 2007.

Klevan, Andrew and Alex Clayton. 'Introduction: The Language and Style of Film Criticism'. *The Language and Style of Film Criticism*, Andrew Klevan and Alex Clayton (eds). Routledge, 2011, pp. 1–26.

Learning On Screen. 'Copyright Considerations For Video Essay'. *learningonscreen*, 2020, https://learningonscreen.ac.uk/guidance/introductory-guide-to-video-essays/copyright-considerations-for-video-essays/ (last accessed 7 November 2021).

Lehman, Peter. *Roy Orbison: Invention of An Alternative Rock Masculinity*. 3rd edition. Temple University Press, 2010.

Mactaggart, Allister. *The Film Paintings of David Lynch: Challenging Film Theory*. Intellect Books, 2010.

Monaghan, P. 'Has the Video Essay Arrived?' *Moving Image Archive News*, 15 March 2017, http://www.movingimagearchivenews.org/has-the-video-essay-arrived/ (last accessed 7 November 2021).

Mulvey, Laura. *Death 24× a Second: Stillness and the Moving Image*. Reaktion Books, 2006.

Norwegian University of Science and Technology. FM3001 – Outreach and Communication, 2017. https://www.ntnu.edu/studies/courses/FM3001/2017#tab=omEmnet (last accessed 7 November 2021).

Odell, Colin and Michelle Le Blanc. *David Lynch*. Oldcastle Books, 2007.

Sheen, Erica. and Annette Davison. *The Cinema of David Lynch: American Dreams, Nightmare Visions*. Wallflower Press, 2004.

Sobchack, Vivian. *Carnal Thoughts: Embodiment and Moving Image Culture*. University of California Press, 2004.

Stim, Rich. 'What Is Fair Use?' *Stanford University Libraries*. https://fairuse.stanford.edu/overview/fair-use/what-is-fair-use/ (last accessed 7 November 2021).

Filmography

Blue Velvet. Directed by David Lynch, performances by Kyle MacLachlan, Isabella Rosselini, Dennis Hopper, and Laura Dern, Dino De Laurentiis Entertainment Group, 1986.

Eraserhead. Directed by David Lynch, performances by Jack Nance and Charlotte Stewart, American Film Institute, Libra Films, 1977.

Lost Highway. Directed by David Lynch, performances by Bill Pullman and Patricia Arquette, CiBi 2000, Asymmetrical Productions and Lost Highway Productions LCC, 1997.

Mulholland Drive. Directed by David Lynch, performances by Naomi Watts and Laura Harring, Les Films Alain Sarde et al., 2001.

The Elephant Man. Directed by David Lynch, performances by John Hurt and Anthony Hopkins, Brooksfilm, 1980.

Twin Peaks. Directed by David Lynch et al., performances by Kyle MacLachlan and Mädchen Amick, Lynch/Frost Productions et al., 1990–1.

Twin Peaks: Fire Walk with Me. Directed by David Lynch, performances by Sheryl Lee and Ray Wise, CIBY Picture, 1992.

Twin Peaks: The Return [on DVD and BluRay *Twin Peaks: A Limited Event Series*]. Directed by David Lynch, performances by Sheryl Lee and Kyle MacLachlan, Showtime, 2017.

Other Media and Sources Cited

Adobe. 'Adobe Help Center.' *Adobe.com*, http://helpx.adobe.com/no/premiere-pro/using/supported-file-formats.html (last accessed 5 November 2021).

TaggleElgate. 'David Lynch 1999 SCENE BY SCENE Interview.' *YouTube*, 30 August 2015. https://www.youtube.com/watch?v=MIlmdLPUdpg (last accessed 7 November 2021).

Bakkane, Chris Aarnes. 'In Dreams.' *YouTube*, 16 November 2017, https://www.youtube.com/watch?v=IyEcagv_o58&feature=youtu.be (last accessed 14 November 2021).

Google. 'How Content ID works – YouTube Help.' n.d., *Google Help*. https://support.google.com/youtube/answer/2797370?hl=en (last accessed 7 November 2021).

Epidemic Sound. 'Pricing & licensing – Royalty free music | Epidemic Sound.' *Premium Music for Content Creators | Epidemic Sound*, 2020, www.epidemicsound.com/pricing/ (last accessed 14 November 2021).

Conclusion: Leaving Lynchtown

Andreas Rauscher, Marcel Hartwig and Peter Niedermüller

The various contributions in *Networked David Lynch* illustrate a more open structure to Lynch's body of work and debunk notions about a 'Gesamtkunstwerk' as something imaginary rather than something graspable by way of transmediality. While TV and media scholars such as Henry Jenkins and Jason Mittell (2015) argue for the importance of world building, modes of reception, and coherence (Jenkins 2020) in transmedia storytelling, the individual chapters of this book have repeatedly shown that Lynch's art world aims at association rather than continuity and comprehension. For example, the Georgia Coffee commercials (see Chapter 4) evoke characters and aspects of *Twin Peaks*, but do not expand the story-world of the series. Rather, the characters and the plot points work here as free-floating signifiers that allow for recognition rather than continuation. In this manner, individual elements from 'Lynchtown' allow for semiotic units that relate to or recall Lynch's 'Gesamtkunstwerk' but do not explicitly add to their narratives. Lynch's network allows for separate and distinct working units that branch out of his œuvre horizontally and are only rooted in the source of its composer/director. These units do not need a bigger structure or whole to be understood and processed. As a consequence, the networked Lynch follows the logic of a leitmotif: the whole composition can be taken apart for recall and recognition but is in itself open-ended and allows for infinite variation. In comparison to Richard Wagner's 'Gesamtkunstwerk' one should also bear in mind that in the 1860s, Wagner preferred concert performances of torso-like fragments from *Der Ring des Nibelungen* to full staged performances, which did not meet his standards of the "Festspiel" (festival) idea (Voss 1997: 551–2). As such, different aesthetic units can be traced back to their root, such as recurring metaphors for electricity (Chapter 3), haunted cityscapes (Chapter 9), or archetypes (Chapter 10), but they allow for meaningful compositions or units of their own that sprawl, sustain themselves, and yet are interconnected with each other.

A majority of the contributions collected in this anthology point to the significance of *Twin Peaks: The Return* in Lynch's network. The arrival of *The Return* initiated discussions about whether the series could be considered through the lens of a film or if it would be better understood as a work of television. From the transmedia approach given here one could respond that this is not the right question to ask to begin with. As an approach, transmediality emphasises openness to different discourses, deviating aesthetic strategies, seemingly incompatible media formats and divergent media types. The intertextual clusters, iconographic connections, and audiovisual associations surrounding the transmedia network connect different discourses, forms of mediated knowledge, and aesthetic strategies. In hindsight they also provide a historical perspective on the Lynchian œuvre and postmodernism. Far from being reduced to empty signifiers, the building blocks of the Lynchian network take on different meanings depending on the configurations created by cultural contexts and participatory perspectives.

Whereas film and media scholar Marsha Kinder in 1991 would have described a transmedia approach as something that merely takes into consideration 'multiplatform and multi-modal expansion[s] of media content' (quoted in Freeman and Gambarato 2019: 1), Jenkins sees a trajectory to such a perspective in that it is 'for the purpose of creating a unified and coordinated entertainment experience' (Jenkins 2007). Yet, the discussions of transmedia configurations in this volume elaborated on a more expanded understanding of transmedia, one that takes into consideration academic models from musicology, cultural studies and film studies. As a result, these excursions reject a unified entertainment experience or a common core, and rather look for recurring themes, symbols or motifs that allow for the experience of a common aesthetic. Parts I–IV in this book have repeatedly shown that a search for associations merits a recognition of emergent systems that stray from their preordained nodes within an overall structure. Themes that recur on different levels of these structures allow for new meanings and new associations at every new node of the system that we here call a networked David Lynch. Rather than a mapping of David Lynch's œuvre, this transmedia approach looks for the possibility of connectivity and a branching out across platforms.

Such an expanded transmedia approach is applied in this volume and provides perspectives for further study. An investigation of the transmedia intersections of such directors as Tim Burton, David Fincher or Wes Anderson might give a better insight into their styles and aesthetics. Such studies could also sharpen the theoretical understanding of transmediality (for example, a 'sharp' border between intertextuality and transmediality).

The discussion of a director's output is no longer limited to the internal structure of his or her films but can also integrate extensions and spin-offs in other media like soundtracks, design concepts, key visuals, fine arts and cultural practices (in regard to this tendency also see the edited volume *Transmedia Directors* by Carol Vernallis, Holly Rogers and Lisa Perrott, and the German study on Jim Jarmusch's cartography of popular culture, *Mind the Map* by Sofia Glasl). Within the networked structure, and depending on the configuration of their mise-en-scène, the films can exchange ideas with spaces like the gallery, the concert stage, and interactive arts from new media installations to video games. They also inspire performative fan practices like cosplay, conventions, fan fiction and creative analysis. In contrast to transmedia approaches focused on a narrative perspective, the networked structures of cinematic configurations allow for independent considerations of visuals, sounds, and architecture.

Transmedia aesthetics can serve as a starting point for thinking about film and culture in images and sounds, from intertextual references to critical reflections in video essays. Developing a theoretically valid perspective by the recontextualisation of images and sounds continues the idea of the nouvelle vague that the best criticism of a film could be provided by another film. In contrast to some rather conservative and pessimistic assumptions that reduced postmodernism to pure pastiche, the momentum of images can inspire critical configurations. On a more complex level, there are also structural parallels to the concept of iconology and the 'Pathosformeln' (pathos formula, see Becker 2013). Illustrative examples can be found in the use of the song 'In Dreams' in *Blue Velvet* – the association with sinister and dark threats mesmerising the unconscious has been brought about by David Lynch's interpretation in the film, and it reverberated through popular culture. The echoes of this new contextualisation can be found, for example, in Neil Gaiman's graphic novel *The Sandman* (see Volume 2.3, 'Dream a Little Dream of Me'). New associations resulting from these audiovisual transmedia passages are reminiscent of the iconological meaning of pictures and poses discussed by Aby Warburg and Erwin Panofsky (see Becker 2013). Another recurring example in Lynch's works across media – besides the obvious red curtains and the floor of the Black Lodge – comes from the iconic passage on a deserted highway through the night (see Röttger and Jakobs 2006). The motif not only appears from the joyride in *Blue Velvet* but onwards through *Wild at Heart* and the LA trilogy. In the video clip accompanying Lynch's collaboration with Swedish singer-songwriter Lykke Li 'I'm Waiting', the whole clip consists of a long travelling shot along a deserted highway, including the variation of starting out in broad daylight and driving into the familiar night.

In this light, the transmedia network of David Lynch illustrates how cinema becomes a wide-reaching phenomenon on different platforms and media contexts. This invites an understanding of transmediality in a broader sense, one which takes the operations of TV and cinema beyond their restrictive understandings of media platforms providing content, to one that takes into consideration aesthetic associations, cultural contexts, and heterogenous reading strategies. The transmedial aspects of David Lynch's cinema challenge the limitations of traditional artistic boundaries and schematic theories, even if they operate no longer from the epicentre of popular culture, but from a transient creative space in-between the forms of different media and cultural contexts.

Bibliography

Becker, Colleen. 'Aby Warburg's "Pathosformel" as Methodological Paradigm'. *Journal of Art Historiography*, vol. 9, 2013, pp. 1–25.

Freeman, Matthew and Renira Gambarato. 'Introduction: Transmedia Studies – Where Now?' *The Routledge Companion to Transmedia Studies*, Matthew Freeman and Renira Gambarato (eds). Routledge, 2019, pp. 1–12.

Glasl, Sofia. *Mind the Map – Jim Jarmusch als Kartograph von Popkultur*. Schüren Verlag, 2014.

Jenkins, Henry. 'Why *Twin Peaks*?'. *Mysterium Twin Peaks*, Caroline Frank (ed). Springer, 2020, pp. 29–38.

Kinder, Marsha. *Playing with Power in Movies, Television, and Video Games. From Muppet Babies to Teenage Mutant Ninja Turtles*. University of California Press, 1991.

Mittel, Jason. *Complex TV. The Poetics of Contemporary Television Storytelling*. New York University Press, 2015.

Röttger, Kati and Alexander Jakobs. 'Bilder einer unendlichen Fahrt. David Lynchs *Mulholland Drive* in bildwissenschaftlicher Perspektive'. *Bildtheorie und Film*, Thomas Koebner, Thomas Meder and Fabienne Liptay (eds). Edition Text und Kritik, 2006, pp. 572–83.

Vernallis, Carol, Holly Rogers and Lisa Perrott (eds). *Transmedia Directors. Artistry, Industry and New Audiovisual Aesthetics*. Bloomsbury Academic, 2020.

Voss, Egon. 'Wagner konzertant oder *Der Walkürenritt* im Zirkus als Rettung vor der Oper'. *Festschrift für Walter Wiora zum 90. Geburtstag* (30. December 1996), edited by Christoph-Hellmut Mahling and Ruth Seiberts. Hans Schneider, 1997, pp. 547–54.

Filmography

Blue Velvet. Directed by David Lynch, performances by Kyle MacLachlan, Isabella Rosselini, Dennis Hopper, and Laura Dern, Dino De Laurentiis Entertainment Group, 1986.

Twin Peaks: The Return [on DVD and BluRay *Twin Peaks: A Limited Event Series*]. Directed by David Lynch, performances by Sheryl Lee and Kyle MacLachlan, Showtime, 2017.

Wild at Heart. Directed by David Lynch, performances by Laura Dern and Nicolas Cage, PolyGram Filmed Entertainment and Propaganda Films, 1990.

Other Media and Sources Cited

Jenkins, Henry (2007). *Transmedia Storytelling 101*. http://henryjenkins.org/blog/2007/03/transmedia_storytelling_101.html (last accessed 17 February 2022).

Index